Windows 95

Nuts & Bolts:
For Experienced Programmers

About the Author...

Herbert Schildt is the leading authority on the C and C++ languages, and an expert Windows programmer. His programming books have sold more than one and a half million copies worldwide and have been translated into all major foreign languages. He has written 26 books on C and C++ and several on Windows, including the recent **Schildt's Windows 95 Programming in C and C++**, and is co-author of the three-volume **Osborne Windows Programming Series**. He is president of Universal Computing Laboratories, Inc., and holds a master's degree in computer science from the University of Illinois at Urbana-Champaign.

Windows 95 Programming
Nuts & Bolts:
For Experienced Programmers

Herbert Schildt

Osborne **McGraw-Hill**

Berkeley New York St. Louis San Francisco Auckland Bogotá
Hamburg London Madrid Mexico City Milan Montreal New Delhi
Panama City Paris São Paulo Singapore Sydney Tokyo Toronto

Osborne **McGraw-Hill**
2600 Tenth Street
Berkeley, California 94710
U.S.A.

For information on translations or book distributors outside the U.S.A., or to arrange bulk purchase discounts for sales promotions, premiums, or fundraisers, please contact Osborne **McGraw-Hill** at the above address.

Windows 95 Programming Nuts & Bolts:
For Experienced Programmers

1234567890 DOC 998765

ISBN 0-07-882147-9

Publisher *Lawrence Levitsky*
Acquisitions Editor *Cynthia Brown*
Project Editor *Nancy McLaughlin*
Copy Editor *Janice Jue*
Proofreader *Stefany Otis*

Indexer *Sheryl Schildt*
Computer Designer *Roberta Steele*
Illustrator *Lance Ravella*
Quality Control Specialist *Joe Scuderi*
Cover Design *Ted Mader Associates*

Contents

Preface

This book teaches you how to write programs for Windows 95. Windows 95 will almost certainly become the most important operating system in the world. Here is why.

First, Windows 95 has rendered DOS irrelevant as either a development or target environment. Because Windows 95 no longer requires it, DOS no longer has a reason to exist as a stand-alone operating system. Of course, maintenance releases and minor updates of DOS will probably occur for the next several years because of the current user base. But virtually no new users will choose DOS over Windows 95. With the death of DOS, so dies the text-based interface. Certainly some text-based utility programs will continue to be written, but the overwhelming number of new programs will be designed for the graphical user interface provided by Windows 95.

Second, Windows 95 solves certain fundamental problems that have plagued programmers over the years. For example, Windows 95 finally gets rid of the segmented memory model. Instead, Windows 95 uses flat addressing. Further, it gives each process in the system 4 gigabytes of virtual address space! This is what programmers have been waiting for. Windows 95 also supports thread-based multitasking, independent message queues, and a rich set of new common controls (such as toolbars and status windows). Unlike Windows 3.1, which always seemed to get in the way of programming, Window 95 provides features that will encourage the writing of great programs. We finally have a platform upon which the next generation of software can be built.

The third reason Windows 95 will have such a profound effect on computing is easy to understand: It provides a much better user interface. And it is the user interface that defines any program and to a large extent determines whether users like it or not. The Windows 95 user interface is snappy, visually appealing, and most importantly, easy to work with. The addition of the task bar and the replacement of the old File Manager with the Explorer make Windows 95 a pleasure to use. It is also more stable than Windows 3.1. That is, it crashes far less frequently! Although we, as programmers, can tolerate a crash now and then, software failures are both annoying and even potentially dangerous for end users. (For example, if the software running a heart monitor crashes, so could the patient's vital signs!) The added stability of Windows 95 will make it all the more appealing to users.

By the time you finish this book, you will be able to write programs for this exciting new environment.

Who Is This Book For?

This book is designed specifically for experienced programmers who are moving to Windows 95. It assumes that you have had substantial experience writing programs for other operating systems, such as DOS or Unix. Further, it assumes that you are an accomplished C or C++ programmer. Although this book covers all the necessary Windows 95 programming fundamentals, it does not dwell on the basics of programming. Put directly, there is a lot of material packed into this book, and it moves quickly.

Windows 95 is arguably the most flexible and powerful operating system designed for general purpose use on a PC. It is also very complex. Despite this complexity, it is one of the most thoroughly thought-out operating systems in existence and is logically consistent from one subsystem to the next. Once you have mastered its essentials and created a reserve of reusable code fragments, it is a pleasure to work with. Without question, learning to program for Windows 95 is worth all the time and effort that you expend.

One last point: If you have never written a Windows-style program before, be patient! Windows programs are much different from the type of programs that you have been writing.

Watch for the Boxes

Throughout this book you will find two special types of boxed text. The first is called a *Fast Track Tip*. Fast Track Tips tell you about things that you will want to explore on your own. That is, they contain brief descriptions of special Windows 95 features not described in the text, proper. In essence, Fast Track Tips are pointers to interesting aspects of Windows 95 that you will want to examine in detail, when you have time.

The second type of box is called *Nuts & Bolts*. Typically, a Nuts & Bolts box contains options, enhancements, or alternative methods which can be applied to an example described in the book. For instance, one Nuts & Bolts box describes how to disable a dialog box control. Another, shows how to add a progress bar to an example program. In general, the Nuts & Bolts boxes contain programming tips that you can apply immediately.

The Programming Tools You Will Need

The code in this book was written, compiled, and tested using Microsoft's Visual C++, version 2. You will need either this compiler or another C/C++ compiler that is designed to produce Windows 95-compatible object code.

Diskette Offer

There are many useful and interesting programs contained in this book. If you're like me, you probably would like to try them, but hate typing them into the computer. When I key in routines from a book it always seems that I type something wrong and spend hours trying to get the program to work. This is especially true for Windows 95 programs, which tend to be long. For this reason, I am offering a diskette containing the source code for all the programs contained in this book for $24.95. Just fill in the order blank on the next page and mail it, along with your payment, to the address shown. Or, if you're in a hurry, just call (217) 586-4021 (the number of my consulting office) and place your order by telephone. You can FAX your order to (217) 586-4997. (VISA and MasterCard accepted.)

Please send me _____ copies, at $24.95 each, of the programs in *Windows 95 Programming Nuts & Bolts: For Experienced Programmers* on an IBM-compatible diskette.

(Foreign orders: Checks must be drawn on a U.S. bank. Please add $5.00 shipping and handling.)

_____
Name

_____
Address

_____ _____ _____
City   State   ZIP

_____
Telephone

Diskette size (check one): 5.25"_____   3.5"_____

Method of payment: Check_____   VISA_____   MC___

Credit card number: _____

Expiration date: _____

Signature: _____

Send to:

Herbert Schildt
398 County Rd 2500 N
Mahomet, IL 61853

Phone: (217) 586-4021
FAX: (217) 586-4997

For Further Study

Windows 95 Programming Nuts & Bolts: For Experienced Programmers is just one of the many programming books written by Herbert Schildt. Here are some others that you will find of interest.

✦ To learn more about Windows 95, we recommend the following:

   Schildt's Windows 95 Programming in C and C++

✦ This book provides an in-depth look at Windows 95 programming. You will also want to examine the *Osborne Windows Programming Series,* co-authored by Herbert Schildt. You will find it to be invaluable as you try to understand the complexities of Windows. The series titles are:

   Volume 1: Programming Fundamentals
   Volume 2: General Purpose API Functions
   Volume 3: Special Purpose API Functions

✦ If you want to learn more about the C language then the following titles will be of interest:

   C: The Complete Reference, Third Edition
   The Annotated ANSI C Standard
   Teach Yourself C, Second Edition

✦ To learn more about C++, you will find these books especially helpful:

   C++: The Complete Reference, Second Edition
   Teach Yourself C++, Second Edition
   C++ From the Ground Up

✦ Finally, here are some other books about C and C++ written by Herbert Schildt:

   The Art of C
   The Craft of C
   Turbo C/C++: The Complete Reference

When you need solid answers fast, turn to Herbert Schildt, the recognized authority on programming.

CHAPTER 1

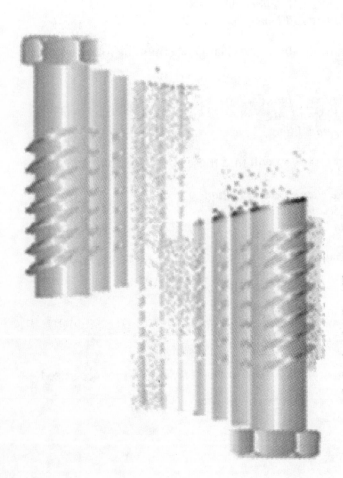

Windows 95 Fundamentals

Before you can begin programming for Windows 95, you must understand, in a general way, how Windows 95 operates, how it interacts with your programs, what constitutes the basic elements of any Windows 95 application, and what rules your programs must follow. It is also important to know how Windows 95 differs from its predecessor, Windows 3.1. Toward these ends, this chapter presents an overview of Windows 95, discusses ways in which it relates to and differs from its forerunners, and concludes with a Windows 95 skeleton program. This skeleton will be used as the foundation for the rest of the programs presented in this book.

Remember that Windows 95 is a very large, complex programming environment. It cannot be fully described in one book. (Indeed, a full description would require several volumes!) This books covers those elements of Windows 95 programming that are common to all programs, that are frequently used, or that are important innovations unique to Windows 95. In essence, this book provides a rapid "jump start" into the world of Windows 95 programming. After you have completed this book, you will have sufficient understanding of Windows 95 to begin writing your own programs and to easily explore any of its subsystems, in detail.

Note: If you have never written a Windows program, then most of the information in this book will be new to you. Just be patient. Even an experienced programmer may find many of the fundamental concepts in Windows 95 strange at first. If you have programmed for Windows 3.1, then you will be able to advance more quickly, but be careful. There are some differences between Windows 95 and Windows 3.1 that will affect the way that you write programs.

What Is Windows 95?

Windows 95 is part of the next generation of operating systems intended to operate PCs well into the next century. As you probably know, Windows 95 features a graphical user interface (GUI) that uses the desktop model. It fully supports the mouse and keyboard as input devices. Windows 95 was designed specifically to overcome several of the limitations imposed by its earlier incarnation, Windows 3.1. It also adds a substantial number of new features and provides a new (and improved) user interface. (These differences and enhancements will be discussed shortly.)

Perhaps the single most important characteristic of Windows 95 is that it is a 32-bit operating system. By moving to a 32-bit implementation, Windows 95 has left behind many of the quirks and problems associated with the older 16-bit systems. Although the move to 32 bits is largely transparent to the user, it makes programming Windows 95 easier.

A primary design goal of Windows 95 was compatibility with both DOS and Windows 3.1—and with the programs designed to run under them. That is, Windows 95 is designed to be upwardly compatible with the large base of existing PC applications. Toward this end, Windows 95 can run three types of programs: those written for DOS, those written for Windows 3.1, and those written specifically for Windows 95. Windows 95 automatically creates the right environment for the type of program you run. For example, when you execute a DOS program, Windows 95 automatically creates a windowed command prompt in which the program runs.

Let's look at a few of the more important features of Windows 95.

Windows 95 Uses Thread-Based Multitasking

As you likely know, Windows 95 is a multitasking operating system. As such, it can run two or more programs concurrently. Of course, the programs share the CPU and do not, technically, run simultaneously, but, because of the computer's speed, they appear to. Windows 95 supports two forms of multitasking: process based and thread based. A *process* is a program that is executing. Because Windows 95 can multitask processes, it can run more than one program at a time. Thus, Windows 95 supports the traditional, process-based multitasking you are probably familiar with.

Windows 95's second form of multitasking is thread based. A *thread* is a dispatchable unit of executable code. The name comes from the concept of a "thread of execution." All processes have at least one thread. However, a Windows 95 process can have several.

Since Windows 95 multitasks threads and each process can have more than one thread, this implies that it is possible for one process to have two or more pieces of itself executing simultaneously. As it turns out, this implication is correct. Therefore, when you are working with Windows 95, it is possible to multitask both programs and pieces of a single program. As you will see later in this book, this makes it possible to write very efficient programs.

The Windows 95 Call-Based Interface

If you come from a DOS background, then you know that a program accesses DOS by using various software interrupts. For example, the standard DOS interrupt is 0x21. While using a software interrupt to access DOS services is perfectly acceptable (given the limited scope of the DOS operating system), it is completely inadequate as a means of interfacing to a full-featured, multitasking operating system like Windows 95. Instead, Windows 95, like Windows 3.1 before it, uses a *call-based interface* to access the operating system.

The Windows 95 call-based interface has a rich set of system-defined functions to access operating system features. Collectively, these functions are called the *application programming interface* (API). The API contains several hundred functions that your application program calls in order to communicate with Windows 95. These functions include all necessary operating system-related activities, such as memory allocation, outputting to the screen, creating windows, and the like.

Dynamic Link Libraries (DLLs)

Because the API consists of several hundred functions, you might think that a large amount of code is linked into every program that is compiled for Windows 95, causing each program to contain much duplicate code. However, this is not the case. Instead, the Windows 95 API functions are contained in *dynamic link libraries* (DLLs), which each program has access to when it is executed. Here is how dynamic linking works.

The Windows 95 API functions are stored in a relocatable format within a DLL. During the compilation phase, when your program calls an API function, the linker does not add the code for that function to the executable version of your program. Instead, it adds loading instructions for that function, such as what DLL it resides in and its name. When your program is executed, the necessary API routines are also loaded by the Windows 95 loader. In this way, each application program does not need to contain the actual API code. The API functions are added only when the application is loaded into memory for execution.

Dynamic linking has some very important benefits. First, since virtually all programs will use the API functions, DLLs prevent disk space from being wasted by the significant amount of duplicated object code that would be created if the API functions were actually added to each program's executable file on disk. Second, updates and enhancements to Windows 95 can be accomplished by changing the dynamic link library routines. Existing application programs do not need to be recompiled.

Windows 95 versus Windows 3.1

Since many readers of this book will already be familiar with Windows 3.1, a brief comparison with Windows 95 is in order. Although Windows 95 is the next step in the Windows product line, which began with Windows' original release in 1985, it also represents a major step forward in operating system design. However, from the point of view of the applications programmer, the approach to programming will be similar.

The good news is that if you are familiar with Windows 3.1, you will have no trouble learning to use or program Windows 95. From the user's point of view, Windows 95 adds an improved interface and has moved toward a document-centered organization. Specifically, such fundamental items as the Program Manager and the File Manager have been replaced by the Start menu and the Explorer. However, if you can run Windows 3.1, you will feel at home with Windows 95. Things still work essentially the same way.

From the programmer's point of view, the more important good news is that you program for Windows 95 in much the same way that you did for

1

Windows 3.1. Windows 95 preserves the name space of the original Windows API functions. When Windows 95 added functionality, it generally did so by adding new functions. While there are some differences between Windows 3.1 and Windows 95, for the most part these differences are easy to accommodate. Also, old Windows 3.1 programs run fine under Windows 95, so you won't have to port all of your applications at once.

The following sections look at the differences between Windows 3.1 and Windows 95 in more detail.

User Differences

From the user's point of view, Windows 95 differs from Windows 3.1 in four major ways:

♦ The desktop interface has changed.

♦ The window style has been altered.

♦ New control elements are available to applications.

♦ DOS is no longer required.

As mentioned, the Program Manager found in Windows 3.1 has been replaced by the Start menu. Further, the desktop now contains the Task Bar. The *Task Bar* displays a list of all active tasks in the system and allows you to switch to a task by clicking on it. Most users will find the Start menu and Task Bar a significant improvement over the Program Manager.

The appearance of windows under Windows 95 has been redesigned. To most users, the new look will seem more stylish and snappy. One of the criticisms of Windows 3.1 was its rather clunky look. Windows 95 has improved this. Also, when you use Windows 95 applications, you will notice that several new control elements, such as toolbars, spin controls, tree views, and status bars, will appear quite frequently. These modern controls give the user a more convenient means of setting the various attributes associated with a program.

Windows 95 does not require DOS. As you probably know, Windows 3.1 was not a completely stand-alone operating system. It ran on top of DOS, which provided support for the file system. Windows 95 is a complete operating system, and DOS is no longer needed. However, Windows 95 still provides support for DOS programs. (In fact, some DOS programs run better under Windows 95 than they do under DOS!) Using Windows 95, you can have multiple "DOS" sessions.

Windows 95 also adds substantial functionality, including the ability to transparently run DOS programs. When you run a DOS program, a windowed command prompt interface is automatically created. This command prompt is fully integrated into the overall Windows 95 graphical interface. For example, you can now execute Windows programs directly from the prompt. (Under Windows 3.1, you had to execute Windows programs from within Windows.)

Another new feature of Windows 95 is its support for long filenames. Both DOS and Windows 3.1 only allowed 8-character filenames followed by a 3-character extension. Windows 95 allows filenames to be up to 255 characters long.

Windows 95 includes a number of accessories and administrative tools not supported by Windows 3.1. For example, there is now support of portable computing, e-mail, pen-based computing, networking, and remote computing. It also supports "plug and play," which allows the easy installation of new hardware components.

Programming Differences

From the programmer's viewpoint there are two main differences between Windows 3.1 and Windows 95. First, Windows 95 supports 32-bit addressing and uses virtual memory. Windows 3.1 uses a 16-bit segmented addressing mode. For many application programs this difference will have little effect. For others, the effect will be substantial. While the transition may not be painless, you will find the Windows 95 32-bit memory model much easier to program for.

The second difference concerns the way that multitasking is accomplished. Windows 3.1 uses a nonpreemptive approach to task switching. This means that a Windows 3.1 task must manually return control to the scheduler in order for another task to run. In other words, a Windows 3.1 program retains control of the CPU until it decides to give it up. Therefore, an ill-behaved program could monopolize the CPU. By contrast, Windows 95 uses preemptive, time-slice based tasking. In this scheme, tasks are automatically preempted by Windows 95, and the CPU is then assigned to the next task (if one exists). Preemptive multitasking is generally the superior method because it allows the operating system to fully control tasking and prevents one task from dominating the system. Most programmers view the move to preemptive multitasking as a step forward.

In addition to the two major changes just described, Windows 95 differs from Windows 3.1 in some other, less dramatic ways, which are described here.

Input Queues

One difference between Windows 3.1 and Windows 95 is found in the *input queue*. (Input queues hold messages such as a keypress or mouse activity until they can be sent to your program.) In Windows 3.1, there is just one input queue for all tasks running in the system. However, Windows 95 supplies each thread with its own input queue. The advantage to each thread having its own queue is that no one process can reduce system performance by responding to its messages slowly.

Although multiple input queues are an important addition, this change has no direct impact on how you program for Windows 95.

Threads and Processes
Windows 3.1 only supports process-based multitasking. That is, the process is Windows 3.1's smallest dispatchable unit. As mentioned earlier, Windows 95 multitasks both threads and processes. While older Windows 3.1 programs will not require changes to run under Windows 95, you may want to enhance them to take advantage of thread-based multitasking.

Consoles
In the past, text-based (that is, nonwindowed) applications were fairly inconvenient to use from Windows. However, Windows 95 supports a special type of window called a *console*. A console window provides a standard text-based interface, command-prompt environment. Yet, aside from being text-based, a console acts and can be manipulated like other windows. The addition of the text-based console not only allows nonwindowed applications to run in a full Windows environment, but also makes it more convenient for you to create short, throwaway utility programs. Perhaps more importantly, the inclusion of consoles in Windows 95 is a final acknowledgment that some text-based applications make sense, and now they can be managed as part of the overall Windows environment. In essence, the addition of console windows completes the Windows application environment.

Flat Addressing and Virtual Memory
Windows 95 applications have available to them 4 gigabytes (Gb) of virtual memory in which to run! Further, this address space is *flat*. Unlike Windows 3.1, DOS, and other 8086-family operating systems which use segmented memory, Windows 95 treats memory as linear. And, because it virtualizes it, each application has as much memory as it could possibly (and reasonably) want. While the change to flat addressing is mostly transparent to the programmer, it does relieve much of the tedium and frustration of dealing with the old, segmented approach.

Because of the move to flat, 32-bit addressing (and other enhancements), each Windows 95 process runs in its own address space and is insulated from other processes. This means that if one process crashes, the other processes are unaffected. (That is, one misbehaved program cannot take down the entire system.)

Changes to Messages and Parameter Types
Because of Windows 95's shift to 32-bit addressing, some messages passed to a Windows 95 program will be organized differently than they are when passed to a Windows 3.1 program. Also, the parameter types used to declare a window function have changed because of 32-bit addressing.

New Common Controls
As mentioned earlier, Windows 95 supports a rich and expanded set of control elements. Like Windows 3.1, Windows 95 still supports the standard controls, such as push buttons, check boxes, radio buttons, edit boxes, and the like. To these standard controls, Windows 95 adds support for several new ones. The new controls added by Windows 95 are called *common controls*. The common controls include such things as toolbars, tooltips, status bars, progress bars, track bars, and tree views (to name a few). Using the new common controls gives your application the modern look and feel that will clearly identify it as a Windows 95 program.

Installable File System
Under DOS and Windows 3.1, the file system was accessed via interrupt 0x21. This file system uses 16-bit code and operates in real mode. However, Windows 95 uses a 32-bit, protected-mode, installable file system. Windows 95 provides an installable file system manager to coordinate accesses to the file system and its devices. Because the new file system operates in protected mode, no time is wasted switching to 16-bit real mode to access the file system. (Windows 3.1 had to switch between the two modes with each file system access.) This achieves greater overall file system performance. Since the file system is generally accessed by using high-level functions provided by Windows 95-compatible C/C++ compilers, this improvement will not alter the way you handle files in your programs. However, it will improve the performance of programs that you write.

The NT Connection
You have probably heard about Windows NT. Perhaps you have even used it. Windows NT is Microsoft's high-end Windows-based operating system. Windows NT has much in common with Windows 95. Both support 32-bit, flat addressing. Both support thread-based multitasking. And, both support the console-based interface. However, Windows 95 is *not* Windows NT. For example, Windows NT uses a special approach to operating system implementation based on the client/server model. Windows 95 does not.

1

Windows NT supports a full security system, Windows 95 does not. While much of the basic technology developed for use in Windows NT eventually found its way into Windows 95, they are not the same.

Windows 95 Programs Are Unique

If you have never written a Windows program before, you may be in for a surprise. Windows programs are structured differently from programs that you are probably used to writing. The unique structure of a Windows-style program is dictated by two constraints. The first is determined by the way your program interacts with Windows. The second is governed by the rules that must be followed to create a standard, Windows-style application interface. (That is, to make a program that "looks like" a Windows program.)

The goal of Windows 95 (and Windows in general) is to enable a person who has basic familiarity with the system to sit down and run virtually any application without prior training. Toward this end, Windows provides a consistent interface to the user. In theory, if you can run one Windows-based program, you can run them all. Actually, most useful programs will still require some training to be used effectively, but at least this instruction can be restricted to *what* the program *does,* not *how* the user must *interact* with it. In fact, much of the code in a Windows application is there just to support the user interface.

Although creating a consistent, Windows-style interface is a crucial part of writing any Windows 95 program, it does not happen automatically. It is possible to write Windows programs that do not take advantage of the Windows interface elements. To create a Windows-style program, you must purposely do so by using the techniques described in this book. Only those programs written to take advantage of Windows will look and feel like Windows programs. While you can override the basic Windows design philosophy, you had better have a good reason to do so, because the users of your programs will, most often, be very disturbed by the differences. In general, if you are writing application programs for Windows 95, they should use the normal Windows interface and conform to the standard Windows design practices.

How Windows 95 and Your Program Interact

When you write a program for many operating systems, it is your program that initiates interaction with the operating system. For example, in a DOS program, it is the program that requests such things as input and output. Put differently, programs written in the "traditional way" call the operating system. The operating system does not call your program. However, in large measure, Windows 95 works in the opposite way. It is Windows 95 that calls your program. The process works like this: a Windows 95 program waits until it is sent a *message* by Windows. The message is passed to your program through a special function that is called by Windows. Once a message is received, your program is expected to take an appropriate action. While your program can call one or more Windows 95 API functions when responding to a message, it is still Windows 95 that initiates the activity. More than anything else, it is the message-based interaction with Windows 95 that dictates the general form of all Windows 95-compatible programs.

There are many types of messages that Windows 95 can send your program. For example, each time the mouse is clicked on a window belonging to your program, a mouse-clicked message will be sent to your program. Another type of message is sent each time a window belonging to your program must be redrawn. Still another message is sent each time the user presses a key when your program is the focus of input. Keep one fact firmly in mind: as far as your program is concerned, messages arrive randomly. This is why Windows 95 programs resemble interrupt-driven programs. You can't know what message will be next.

Win32: The Windows 95 API

As mentioned earlier, the Windows environment is accessed through a call-based interface called the API (application programming interface). The API consists of several hundred functions that your program calls as needed. The API functions provide all the system services performed by Windows 95. A subset to the API called the *graphics device interface* (GDI) is the part of Windows that provides device-independent graphics support. The GDI functions make it possible for a Windows application to run on a variety of hardware.

Windows 95 programs use the Win32 API. For the most part, Win32 is a superset of the older Windows 3.1 API (Win16). Indeed, for the most part the functions are called by the same name and are used in the same way. However, though similar in spirit and purpose, the two APIs differ because Windows 95 supports 32-bit, flat addressing, while Win16 supports only the 16-bit, segmented memory model. This difference has caused several API functions to be widened to accept 32-bit arguments and return 32-bit values. Also, a few API functions were altered to accommodate the 32-bit architecture. API functions have also been added to support the new approach to multitasking, its new interface elements, and the other enhanced Windows 95 features. If you are new to Windows programming in general, then these changes will not affect you significantly. However, if you will be porting code from Windows 3.1 to Windows 95, then you will need to carefully examine the arguments you pass to each API function.

Because Windows 95 supports full 32-bit addressing, it makes sense that integers are also 32 bits long. This means that types **int** and **unsigned** will be 32 bits, not 16 bits long as is the case for Windows 3.1. If you want to use a 16-bit integer, it must be declared as **short**. (Portable **typedef** names are provided by Windows 95 for these types, as you will see shortly.) This means that if you will be porting code from the 16-bit environment, you will need to check your use of integers because they will automatically be expanded from 16 to 32 bits, and side effects may result.

Another result of 32-bit addressing is that pointers no longer need to be declared as **near** or **far**. Any pointer can access any part of memory. In Windows 95, both **far** and **near** are defined as nothing. This means you can leave **far** and **near** in your programs when porting to Windows 95, but they will have no effect.

1

The Components of a Window

Before you consider specific aspects of Windows 95 programming, a few important terms need to be defined. Figure 1-1 shows a standard window with each of its elements pointed out.

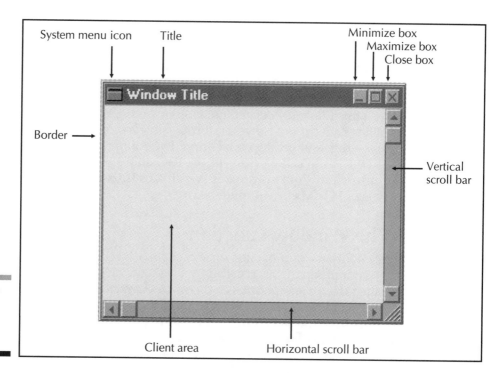

The elements
of a standard
window

Figure 1-1.

All windows have a border that defines the limits of the window and that is used to resize the window. At the top of the window are several items. On the far left is the system menu icon (also called the title bar icon). Clicking on this box displays the system menu. To the right of the system menu icon is the window's title. At the far right are the minimize, maximize, and close icons. (Previous versions of Windows did not include a close icon. This is a Windows 95 innovation.) The *client area* is the part of the window in which your program activity takes place. Most windows also have horizontal and vertical scroll bars that are used to move information through the window.

Some Windows 95 Application Fundamentals

Before the Windows 95 application skeleton is developed, some fundamental concepts common to all Windows 95 programs need to be considered. If you already know how to write programs for Windows 3.1, then this and the next few sections contain material with which you are familiar. (In fact, Windows 3.1 and Windows 95 programs are, on the surface, almost identical.) However, you should at least skim through this material because there are some important differences between Windows 3.1 and Windows 95.

WinMain( )

All Windows 95 programs begin execution with a call to **WinMain( )**. As a general rule, Windows programs do not have a **main( )** function. **WinMain( )** has some special properties that differentiate it from other functions in your application. First, it must be compiled by using the **WINAPI** calling convention. (You will also see **APIENTRY** used. They mean the same thing.) By default, functions in your C or C++ programs use the C calling convention. However, it is possible to compile a function so that it uses a different calling convention. For example, a common alternative is to use the Pascal calling convention. For various technical reasons, the calling convention Windows 95 uses to call **WinMain( )** is **WINAPI**. The return type of **WinMain( )** should be **int**.

The Window Function

All Windows 95 programs must contain a special function that is *not* called by your program, but is called by Windows 95. This function is generally called the *window function* or the *window procedure*. It is through this function that Windows 95 communicates with your program. The window function is called by Windows 95 when it needs to pass a message to your program. The window function receives the message in its parameters. All window functions must be declared as returning type **LRESULT CALLBACK**. The type **LRESULT** is a **typedef** that (at the time of this writing) is another name for a long integer. The **CALLBACK** calling convention is used with those functions that will be called by Windows 95. In Windows terminology, any function that is called by Windows is a *callback* function.

In addition to receiving the messages sent by Windows 95, the window function must initiate any actions indicated by a message. Typically, a window function's body consists of a **switch** statement that links a specific response to each message that the program will respond to. Your program need not respond to every message that Windows 95 will send. For messages that your program doesn't care about, you can let Windows 95 provide default processing of them. Since there are hundreds of different messages that Windows 95 can generate, it is common for most messages to simply be processed by Windows 95 and not your program.

All messages are 32-bit integer values. Further, all messages are linked with any additional information that the messages require.

Window Classes

When your Windows 95 program first begins execution, it will need to define and register a *window class*. (Here, the word *class* is not being used in its C++ sense. Rather, it means *style* or *type*.) When you register a window class, you are telling Windows 95 about the form and function of the window. However, registering the window class does not cause a window to come into existence. To actually create a window requires additional steps.

The Message Loop

As explained earlier, Windows 95 communicates with your program by sending it messages. All Windows 95 applications must establish a *message loop* inside the **WinMain( )** function. This loop reads any pending message from the application's message queue and then dispatches that message back to Windows 95, which then calls your program's window function with that message as a parameter. This may seem to be an overly complex way of passing messages, but it is, nevertheless, the way that all Windows programs must function. (Part of the reason for this is to return control to Windows 95 so that the scheduler can allocate CPU time as it sees fit, rather than waiting for your application's time slice to end.)

Windows Data Types

As you will soon see, Windows 95 programs do not extensively use standard C/C++ data types, such as **int** or **char ***. Instead, all data types used by Windows 95 have been **typdef**ed within the WINDOWS.H file and/or its related files. This file is supplied by Microsoft (and any other company that makes a Windows 95 C/C++ compiler) and must be included in all Windows 95 programs. Some of the most common types are **HANDLE**, **HWND**, **BYTE**, **WORD**, **DWORD**, **UINT**, **LONG**, **BOOL**, **LPSTR**, and **LPCSTR**. **HANDLE** is a 32-bit integer that is used as a handle. As you will see, there are a number of handle types, but they all are the same size as **HANDLE**. A *handle* is simply a value that identifies some resource. For example, **HWND** is a 32-bit integer that is used as a window handle. Also, all handle types begin with an H. **BYTE** is an 8-bit unsigned character. **WORD** is a 16-bit unsigned short integer. **DWORD** is an unsigned long integer. **UINT** is an unsigned 32-bit integer. **LONG** is another name for **long**. **BOOL** is an integer used to indicate values that are either true or false. **LPSTR** is a pointer to a string, and **LPCSTR** is a **const** pointer to a string.

In addition to the basic types just described, Windows 95 defines several structures. The two that are needed by the skeleton program are **MSG** and **WNDCLASSEX**. The **MSG** structure holds a Windows 95 message, and **WNDCLASSEX** is a structure that defines a window class. These structures will be discussed later in this chapter.

A Windows 95 Skeleton

Now that the necessary background information has been covered, it is time to develop a minimal Windows 95 application. As stated, all Windows 95 programs have certain things in common. In this section a Windows 95 skeleton is developed that provides these necessary features. In the world of Windows programming, application skeletons are commonly used because there is a substantial "price of admission" when creating a Windows program. Unlike DOS programs that you may have written, in which a minimal program is about 5 lines long, a minimal Windows program is approximately 50 lines long.

A minimal Windows 95 program contains two functions: **WinMain( )** and the window function. The **WinMain( )** function must perform the following general steps:

1. Define a window class.
2. Register that class with Windows 95.
3. Create a window of that class.
4. Display the window.
5. Begin running the message loop.

The window function must respond to all relevant messages. Since the skeleton program does nothing but display its window, the only message that it must respond to is the one that tells the application that the user has terminated the program.

Before considering the specifics, examine the following program, which is a minimal Windows 95 skeleton. It creates a standard window that includes a title. The window contains the system menu and is, therefore, capable of being minimized, maximized, moved, resized, and closed. It also contains the standard minimize, maximize, and close boxes. This skeleton (and all the other code in this book) is written in standard C/C++. It can be compiled by any standard C/C++ compiler capable of producing Windows 95 programs.

```c
/* A minimal Windows 95 skeleton. */

#include <windows.h>

LRESULT CALLBACK WindowFunc(HWND, UINT, WPARAM, LPARAM);

char szWinName[] = "MyWin"; /* name of window class */

int WINAPI WinMain(HINSTANCE hThisInst, HINSTANCE hPrevInst,
                   LPSTR lpszArgs, int nWinMode)
{
  HWND hwnd;
  MSG msg;
  WNDCLASSEX wcl;

  /* Define a window class. */
  wcl.hInstance = hThisInst; /* handle to this instance */
  wcl.lpszClassName = szWinName; /* window class name */
  wcl.lpfnWndProc = WindowFunc; /* window function */
  wcl.style = 0; /* default style */

  wcl.cbSize = sizeof(WNDCLASSEX); /* set size of WNDCLASSEX */

  wcl.hIcon = LoadIcon(NULL, IDI_APPLICATION); /* large icon */
  wcl.hIconSm = LoadIcon(NULL, IDI_WINLOGO); /* small icon */

  wcl.hCursor = LoadCursor(NULL, IDC_ARROW); /* cursor style */
  wcl.lpszMenuName = NULL; /* no menu */

  wcl.cbClsExtra = 0; /* no extra */
  wcl.cbWndExtra = 0; /* information needed */

  /* Make the window background white. */
  wcl.hbrBackground = (HBRUSH) GetStockObject(WHITE_BRUSH);

  /* Register the window class. */
```

```
if(!RegisterClassEx(&wcl)) return 0;

/* Now that a window class has been registered, a window
   can be created. */
hwnd = CreateWindow(
  szWinName, /* name of window class */
  "Windows 95 Skeleton", /* title */
  WS_OVERLAPPEDWINDOW, /* window style - normal */
  CW_USEDEFAULT, /* X coordinate - let Windows decide */
  CW_USEDEFAULT, /* Y coordinate - let Windows decide */
  CW_USEDEFAULT, /* width - let Windows decide */
  CW_USEDEFAULT, /* height - let Windows decide */
  HWND_DESKTOP, /* no parent window */
  NULL, /* no menu */
  hThisInst, /* handle of this instance of the program */
  NULL /* no additional arguments */
);

/* Display the window. */
ShowWindow(hwnd, nWinMode);
UpdateWindow(hwnd);

/* Create the message loop. */
while(GetMessage(&msg, NULL, 0, 0))
{
  TranslateMessage(&msg); /* allow use of keyboard */
  DispatchMessage(&msg); /* return control to Windows */
}
return msg.wParam;
}


/* This function is called by Windows 95 and is passed
   messages from the message queue.
*/
LRESULT CALLBACK WindowFunc(HWND hwnd, UINT message,
                            WPARAM wParam, LPARAM lParam)
{
  switch(message) {
    case WM_DESTROY: /* terminate the program */
      PostQuitMessage(0);
      break;
    default:
      /* Let Windows 95 process any messages not specified in
         the preceding switch statement. */
      return DefWindowProc(hwnd, message, wParam, lParam);
  }
  return 0;
}
```

When you run this program, you will see a window similar to that shown in Figure 1-2. Let's go through this program step by step.

First, all Windows 95 programs must include the header file WINDOWS.H. As stated, this file (along with its support files) contains the API function prototypes and various types, macros, and definitions used by Windows 95. For example, the data types **HWND** and **WNDCLASSEX** are defined by including WINDOWS.H.

1

The window function used by the program is called **WindowFunc( )**. It is declared as a callback function because this is the function that Windows 95 calls to communicate with the program.

As stated, program execution begins with **WinMain( )**. **WinMain( )** is passed four parameters. **hThisInst** and **hPrevInst** are handles. **hThisInst** refers to the current instance of the program. Remember, Windows 95 is a multitasking system, so it is possible that more than one instance of your program may be running at the same time. **hPrevInst** will always be NULL. (In Windows 3.1 programs, **hPrevInst** would be nonzero if there were other instances of the program currently executing, but this no longer applies to Windows 95.) The **lpszArgs** parameter is a pointer to a string that holds any command line arguments specified when the application was begun. The **nWinMode** parameter contains a value that determines how the window will be displayed when your program begins execution.

Inside the function, three variables are created. The **hwnd** variable will hold the handle to the program's window. The **msg** structure variable will hold window messages, and the **wcl** structure variable will be used to define the window class.

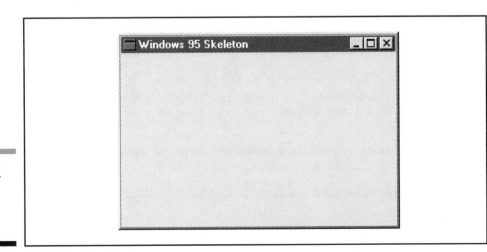

The window produced by the skeleton program

Figure 1-2.

Exploring WINDOWS.H

One of the best ways to get a quick overview of the Windows 95 programming environment is to examine the contents of WINDOWS.H and its support files. In these files are all of the macros, enumerations, structures, unions, type definitions, and function prototypes used by the API. At this point, not a lot of the information in these files will make sense, but it will give you an idea of the magnitude of the application programming interface and a feel for the way things work in Windows 95. Later, as you become more proficient at Windows 95 programming, you will find that the header files can be quite useful in your day-to-day programming. For example, you can refer to the header files to double-check the spelling of a macro name, to confirm the type of the arguments used by an API function, to examine the members of a structure or to see what new options might have become available.

Although not technically necessary, most compiler manufacturers divide the information needed by a Windows 95 program into several header files that are conditionally included by WINDOWS.H. In this way, WINDOWS.H acts as a master header file. For example, here are some subordinate header files commonly found when this approach is taken.

Header File	Contents
WINDEF.H	Various type definitions
WINBASE.H	Basic API definitions and prototypes
WINGDI.H	GDI-related definitions and prototypes
WINUSER.H	General-purpose API definitions and prototypes

To see what subordinate header files are used by your compiler, simply search the contents of WINDOWS.H for **#include** directives.

Caution: Although it is perfectly fine to examine WINDOWS.H and its support files, you must *never* alter these files.

Defining the Window Class

The first two actions that **WinMain( )** takes are to define a window class and to register it. A window class is defined by filling in the fields defined by the **WNDCLASSEX** structure. Its fields are shown here:

```
UINT cbSize; /* size of the WNDCLASSEX structure */
UINT style; /* type of window */
WNDPROC lpfnWndProc; /* address to window func */
int cbClsExtra; /* extra class info */
int cbWndExtra; /* extra window info */
HINSTANCE hInstance; /* handle of this instance */
HICON hIcon; /* handle of large icon */
HICON hIconSm; /* handle of small icon */
HCURSOR hCursor; /* handle of mouse cursor */
HBRUSH hbrBackground; /* background color */
LPCSTR lpszMenuName; /* name of main menu */
LPCSTR lpszClassName; /* name of window class */
```

As you can see from the program, **cbSize** is assigned the size of the **WNDCLASSEX** structure. The **hInstance** field is assigned the current instance handle as specified by **hThisInst**. The name of the window class is pointed to by **lpszClassName**, which points to the string "MyWin" in this case. The address of the window function is assigned to **lpfnWndProc**. No default style is specified. No extra information is needed.

All Windows applications need to define a default shape for the mouse cursor and for the application's icons. An application can define its own custom version of these resources, or it can use one of the built-in styles, as the skeleton does. In either case, handles to these resources must be assigned to the appropriate members of the **WNDCLASSEX** structure. To see how this is done, let's begin with icons.

A Windows 95 application has two icons associated with it: one large and one small. The small icon is used when the application is minimized. It is also the icon that is used for the system menu. The large icon is displayed when you move or copy an application to the desktop. Typically, large icons are 32 × 32 bitmaps, and small icons are 16 × 16 bitmaps. The style of each icon is loaded by the API function **LoadIcon( )**, whose prototype is shown here:

HICON LoadIcon(HINSTANCE *hInst*, LPCSTR *lpszName*);

This function returns a handle to an icon. Here, *hInst* specifies the handle of the module that contains the icon and its name is specified in *lpszName*. However, to use one of the built-in icons, you must use **NULL** for the first parameter and specify one of the following macros for the second.

Icon Macro	Shape
IDI_APPLICATION	Default icon
IDI_ASTERISK	Information icon
IDI_EXCLAMATION	Exclamation point icon
IDI_HAND	Stop sign
IDI_QUESTION	Question mark icon
IDI_WINLOGO	Windows 95 logo

In the skeleton, **IDI_APPLICATION** is used for the large icon. **IDI_WINLOGO** is used for the small icon. Later in this book, you will learn how to define your own icons.

To load the mouse cursor, use the API **LoadCursor( )** function. This function has the following prototype:

HCURSOR LoadCursor(HINSTANCE *hInst*, LPCSTR *lpszName*);

This function returns a handle to a cursor resource. Here, *hInst* specifies the handle of the module that contains the mouse cursor, and its name is specified in *lpszName*. However, to use one of the built-in cursors, you must use **NULL** for the first parameter and specify one of the built-in cursors using its macro for the second parameter. Here is a list of some of the most common built-in cursors:

Cursor Macro	Shape
IDC_ARROW	Default arrow pointer
IDC_CROSS	Cross hairs
IDC_IBEAM	Vertical I-beam
IDC_WAIT	Hourglass

The background color of the window created by the skeleton is specified as white. A handle to this *brush* is obtained by using the API function **GetStockObject( )**. A brush is a resource that paints the screen by using a predetermined size, color, and pattern. The function **GetStockObject( )** is used to obtain a handle to a number of standard display objects, including brushes, pens (which draw lines), and character fonts. It has this prototype:

HGDIOBJ GetStockObject(int *object*);

The function returns a handle to the object specified by *object*. (The type **HGDIOBJ** is a GDI handle.) Some of the built-in brushes available to your program are listed here:

Brush Macro	Background Type
BLACK_BRUSH	Black
DKGRAY_BRUSH	Dark gray
HOLLOW_BRUSH	See-through window
LTGRAY_BRUSH	Light gray
WHITE_BRUSH	White

You can use these macros as parameters to **GetStockObject( )** to obtain a brush.

Once the window class has been fully specified, it is registered with Windows 95 by use of the API function **RegisterClassEx( )**, whose prototype is shown here:

    ATOM RegisterClassEx(CONST WNDCLASSEX *lpWClass);

This function returns a value that identifies the window class. **ATOM** is a **typedef** that means **WORD**. Each window class is given a unique value. *lpWClass* must be the address of a **WNDCLASSEX** structure.

Creating a Window

Once a window class has been defined and registered, your application can actually create a window of that class by using the API function **CreateWindow( )**, whose prototype is shown here:

```
HWND CreateWindow(
  LPCSTR lpClassName, /* name of window class */
  LPCSTR lpWinName, /* title of window */
  DWORD dwStyle, /* type of window */
  int X, int Y, /* upper-left coordinates */
  int Width, int Height, /* dimensions of window */
  HWND hParent, /* handle of parent window */
  HMENU hMenu, /* handle of main menu */
  HINSTANCE hThisInst, /* handle of creator */
  LPVOID lpszAdditional /* pointer to additional info */
);
```

As you can see by looking at the skeleton program, many of the parameters to **CreateWindow( )** can be defaulted or specified as **NULL**. In fact, most often the *X, Y, Width*, and *Height* parameters will simply use the macro **CW_USEDEFAULT**, which tells Windows 95 to select an appropriate size and location for the window. If the window has no parent, which is the case in the skeleton, then *hParent* must be specified as **HWND_DESKTOP**. (You can also use **NULL** for this parameter.) If the window does not contain a main menu, then *hMenu* must be **NULL**. Also, if no additional information is required, as is usually the case, then *lpszAdditional* is **NULL**. (The type **LPVOID** is **typedef**ed as **void ***. Historically, **LPVOID** stands for long pointer to **void**.)

The remaining four parameters must be explicitly set by your program. First, *lpszClassName* must point to the name of the window class. (This is the name you gave the class when it was registered.) The title of the window is a string pointed to by *lpszWinName*. It can be a null string, but usually a window will be given a title. The style (or type) of window actually created is determined by the value of *dwStyle*. The macro **WS_OVERLAPPED-WINDOW** specifies a standard window that has a system menu, a border, and minimize, maximize, and close boxes. While this style of window is the most common, you can construct one to your specifications. To accomplish this, you simply OR together the various style macros that you want. Some other common styles are listed here:

Style Macro	Window Feature
WS_OVERLAPPED	Overlapped window with border
WS_MAXIMIZEBOX	Maximize box
WS_MINIMIZEBOX	Minimize box
WS_SYSMENU	System menu
WS_HSCROLL	Horizontal scroll bar
WS_VSCROLL	Vertical scroll bar

The *hThisInst* parameter must contain the current instance handle of the application.

The **CreateWindow( )** function returns either the handle of the window it creates or **NULL** if the window cannot be created.

Once the window has been created, it is still not displayed on the screen. To cause the window to be displayed, call the **ShowWindow( )** API function. This function has the following prototype:

    BOOL ShowWindow(HWND *hwnd*, int *nHow*);

The handle of the window to display is specified in *hwnd*. The display mode is specified in *nHow*. The first time the window is displayed, you will want to pass **WinMain( )**'s **nWinMode** as the *nHow* parameter. Remember that

Positioning a Window

Although it is common for an application to let Windows 95 choose a position and size for its window when the program begins execution, it is possible to specify these attributes. To do so, simply pass the coordinates of the window's upper-left corner, along with its width and height dimensions, to **CreateWindow( )**. For example, if you substitute the following call to **CreateWindow( )** into the skeleton, the window will be displayed in the upper-left corner of the screen and will be 300 units wide and 100 units tall.

```
hwnd = CreateWindow(
    szWinName, /* name of window class */
    "Windows 95 Skeleton", /* title */
    WS_OVERLAPPEDWINDOW, /* window style - normal */
    0, /* X coordinate */
    0, /* Y coordinate */
    300, /* width */
    100, /* height */
    HWND_DESKTOP, /* no parent window */
    NULL, /* no menu */
    hThisInst, /* handle of this instance of the program */
    NULL /* no additional arguments */
);
```

When determining the location and dimensions of your program's main window, keep in mind that these are specified in *device units,* which are the physical units used by the device (in this case, pixels). This means that the coordinates and dimensions are relative to the screen. As you will see later in this book, output to a window is generally specified in terms of *logical units,* which are mapped to a window according to the current mapping mode. However, since the position of a program's main window is relative to the entire screen, it makes sense that **CreateWindow( )** would require physical units rather than logical ones.

the value of **nWinMode** determines how the window will be displayed when the program begins execution. Subsequent calls can display (or remove) the window as necessary. Some common values for *nHow* are listed in the following table:

Display Macros	Effect
SW_HIDE	Removes window
SW_MINIMIZE	Minimizes window into icon
SW_MAXIMIZE	Maximizes window
SW_RESTORE	Returns window to normal size

The **ShowWindow( )** function returns the previous display status of the window. If the window was displayed, then nonzero is returned. If the window was not displayed, zero is returned.

Although not technically necessary for the skeleton, a call to **Update-Window( )** is included because it is needed by virtually every Windows 95 application that you will create. It essentially tells Windows 95 to send a message to your application that the main window needs to be updated. (This message will be discussed in the next chapter.)

The Message Loop

The final part of the skeletal **WinMain( )** is the *message loop*. The message loop is a part of all Windows applications. Its purpose is to receive and process messages sent by Windows 95. When an application is running, it is continually being sent messages. These messages are stored in the application's message queue until they can be read and processed. Each time your application is ready to read another message, it must call the API function **GetMessage( )**, which has this prototype:

    BOOL GetMessage(LPMSG *msg*, HWND *hwnd*, UINT *min*, UINT *max*);

The message will be received by the structure pointed to by *msg*. All Windows messages are of structure type **MSG**, shown here:

```
/* Message structure */
typedef struct tagMSG
{
  HWND hwnd; /* window that message is for */
  UINT message; /* message */
  WPARAM wParam; /* message-dependent info */
  LPARAM lParam; /* more message-dependent info */
  DWORD time; /* time message posted */
  POINT pt; /* X,Y location of mouse */
} MSG;
```

In **MSG**, the handle of the window for which the message is intended is contained in **hwnd**. Every Windows 95 message is a 32-bit integer. The

1

message itself is contained in **message**, and additional information relating to the message is passed in **wParam** and **lParam**. The type **WPARAM** is a **typedef** for **UINT,** and **LPARAM** is a **typedef** for **LONG**.

The time the message was sent (posted) is specified in milliseconds in the **time** field.

The **pt** member will contain the coordinates of the mouse when the message was sent. The coordinates are held in a **POINT** structure which is defined like this:

```
typedef struct tagPOINT {
  LONG x, y;
} POINT;
```

If there are no messages in the application's message queue, then a call to **GetMessage( )** will pass control back to Windows 95. (We will explore messages in greater detail in the next chapter.)

The *hwnd* parameter to **GetMessage( )** specifies for which window messages will be obtained. It is possible (even likely) that an application will contain several windows, and you may only want to receive messages for a specific window. If you want to receive all messages directed at your application, this parameter must be **NULL**.

The remaining two parameters to **GetMessage( )** specify a range of messages that will be received. Generally, you want your application to receive all messages. To accomplish this, specify both *min* and *max* as 0, as the skeleton does.

GetMessage( ) returns zero when the user terminates the program, causing the message loop to terminate. Otherwise it returns nonzero.

Inside the message loop two functions are called. The first is the API function **TranslateMessage( )**. This function translates virtual key codes generated by Windows 95 into character messages. (Virtual keys are discussed later in this book.) Although it is not necessary for all applications, most call **TranslateMessage( )** because it is needed to allow full integration of the keyboard into your application program.

Once the message has been read and translated, it is dispatched back to Windows 95 by using the **DispatchMessage( )** API function. Windows 95 then holds this message until it can pass it to the program's window function.

Once the message loop terminates, the **WinMain( )** function ends by returning the value of **msg.wParam** to Windows 95. This value contains the return code generated when your program terminates.

The Window Function

The second function in the application skeleton is its window function. In this case the function is called **WindowFunc( )**, but it could have any name you like. The window function is passed the first four members of the **MSG** structure as parameters. For the skeleton, the only parameter that is used is the message itself. However, in the next chapter you will learn more about the parameters to this function.

The skeleton's window function responds to only one message explicitly: **WM_DESTROY**. This message is sent when the user terminates the program. When this message is received, your program must execute a call to the API function **PostQuitMessage( )**. The argument to this function is an exit code that is returned in **msg.wParam** inside **WinMain( )**. Calling **PostQuitMessage( )** causes a **WM_QUIT** message to be sent to your application, which causes **GetMessage( )** to return false and thus stops your program.

Any other messages received by **WindowFunc( )** are passed along to Windows 95, via a call to **DefWindowProc( )**, for default processing. This step is necessary because all messages must be dealt with in one fashion or another.

Naming Conventions

Before this chapter concludes, a short comment on naming functions and variables needs to be made. If you are new to Windows 95 programming, several of the variable and parameter names in the skeleton program and its description probably seemed unusual. The reason is that they follow a set of naming conventions that was invented by Microsoft for Windows programming. For functions, the name consists of a verb followed by a noun. The first character of the verb and noun are capitalized. For the most part, this book will use this convention for function names.

For variable names, Microsoft has chosen to use a rather complex system of embedding the data type into a variable's name. To accomplish this, a lowercase type prefix is added to the start of the variable's name. The name itself begins with an uppercase letter. The type prefixes are shown in Table 1-1. The use of type prefixes is controversial and is not universally supported. Many Windows programmers use this method, many do not. This method will be used by the Windows 95 programs in this book when it seems reasonable to do so. However, you are free to use any naming convention you like.

Prefix	Data Type
b	Boolean (one byte)
c	Character (one byte)
dw	Long unsigned integer
f	16-bit bit-field (flags)
fn	Function
h	Handle
l	Long integer
lp	Long pointer
n	Short integer
p	Pointer
pt	Long integer holding screen coordinates
w	Short unsigned integer
sz	Pointer to null-terminated string
lpsz	Long pointer to null-terminated string
rgb	Long integer holding RGB color values

Variable Type
Prefix
Characters
Table 1-1.

FAST TRACK TIP

Zap the Definition File

If you are familiar with Windows 3.1 programming, then you have used *definition files*. For Windows 3.1, all programs need to have a definition file associated with them. A definition file is simply a text file that specifies certain information and settings needed by your Windows 3.1 program. Definition files use the file extension .DEF. However, because of the 32-bit architecture of Windows 95 (and its other improvements), definition files are not needed for Windows 95 programs. Definition files were always a nuisance, and it is a good thing that they are gone.

Although definition files are not required for Windows 95 programs, there is no harm in supplying one. For example, if you want to include one for the sake of downward compatibility with Windows 3.1, then you are free to do so.

CHAPTER 2

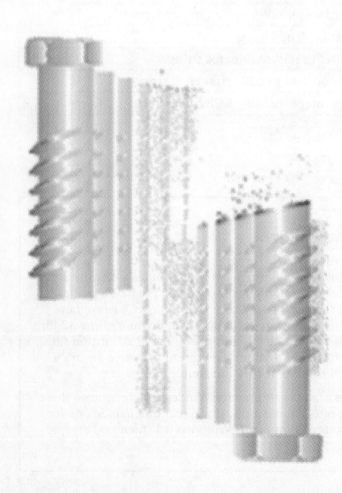

Application Essentials: Messages and Basic I/O

Although the skeleton developed in Chapter 1 forms the framework for a Windows 95 program, by itself it is useless. To be useful, a program must be capable of performing two fundamental operations. First, it must be able to respond to various messages sent by Windows 95. As explained in Chapter 1, Windows 95 communicates with your application by sending it messages. As you will see, the processing of these messages is at the core of all Windows 95 applications. Second, your program must provide some means of outputting information to the user (that is, displaying information on the screen). Unlike programs that you may have written for other operating systems, outputting information to the user is a nontrivial task in Windows 95.

Without the ability to process messages and display information, no useful Windows program can be written. For this reason, message processing and the basic I/O operations are the subject of this chapter.

Let's begin with a discussion of one of Windows' easiest-to-use output mechanisms: the message box.

Message Boxes

Before you can develop useful programs, you will need some way for your program to communicate with you. That is, you will need some mechanism to output information to the screen. Although this was probably a trivial task for the other types of programs that you have written, it is a nontrivial task when you work with Windows. In fact, managing output forms a large part of any Windows 95 application. Fortunately, Windows does provide one fairly easy (but limited) means of displaying information: the message box. As you will see, many of the examples in this book use message boxes.

A message box is a simple window that displays a message to the user and waits for an acknowledgment. Unlike other types of windows that you must explicitly create, a message box is a system-defined window that you can use as-is. In general, the purpose of a message box is to inform the user that some event has taken place. However, it is possible to construct a message box that allows the user to select between a few basic alternatives as a response to the message. For example, one common form of message box allows a user to select either Abort, Retry, or Ignore.

Note: In the term *message box*, the word *message* refers to human-readable text that is displayed on the screen. It does not refer to Windows 95 messages that are sent to your program's window function. Although the terms sound similar, *message boxes* and *messages* are two entirely separate concepts.

To create a message box, use the **MessageBox( )** API function, which has this prototype:

> int MessageBox(HWND *hwnd*, LPCSTR *lpText*, LPCSTR *lpCaption*,
> UINT *wMBType*);

Here, *hwnd* is the handle to the parent window. The *lpText* parameter is a pointer to a string that will appear inside the message box. The string pointed to by *lpCaption* is used as the title for the box. The value of *wMBType* determines the exact nature of the message box, including what type of buttons will be present. Some of its most common values are listed in

2

Value	Effect
MB_ABORTRETRYIGNORE	Displays the Abort, Retry, and Ignore push buttons
MB_ICONEXCLAMATION	Displays the exclamation point icon
MB_ICONHAND	Displays the stop sign icon
MB_ICONINFORMATION	Displays the information icon
MB_ICONQUESTION	Displays the question mark icon
MB_ICONSTOP	Same as MB_ICONHAND
MB_OK	Displays the OK button
MB_OKCANCEL	Displays the OK and Cancel push buttons
MB_RETRYCANCEL	Displays the Retry and Cancel push buttons
MB_YESNO	Displays Yes and No push buttons
MB_YESNOCANCEL	Displays the Yes, No, and Cancel push buttons

Common Values for *wMBType*
Table 2-1.

Table 2-1. These macros are defined by including WINDOWS.H, and you can OR together two or more of these macros, so long as they are not mutually exclusive.

MessageBox( ) returns the user's response to the box. The possible return values are shown here:

Button Pressed	Return Value
Abort	IDABORT
Retry	IDRETRY
Ignore	IDIGNORE
Cancel	IDCANCEL
No	IDNO
Yes	IDYES
OK	IDOK

These macros are defined by including WINDOWS.H. Remember, depending upon the value of *wMBType*, only certain buttons will be present. Quite often message boxes are simply used to display an item of information, and the only response offered to the user is the OK button. In these cases, the return value of a message box is simply ignored by the program.

To display a message box, simply call the **MessageBox( )** function. Windows 95 will display it at its first opportunity. **MessageBox( )** automatically creates a window and displays your message in it. For example, this call to **MessageBox( )**

```
i = MessageBox(hwnd, "This is Caption", "This is Title", MB_OKCANCEL);
```

produces the following message box:

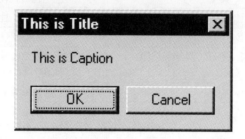

Depending upon which button the user presses, **i** will contain either **IDOK** or **IDCANCEL**.

As stated, message boxes are typically used to notify the user that some event has occurred. However, because message boxes are so easy to use, they also make excellent debugging tools when you need a simple way to output something to the screen. As you will see, examples in this book will use a message box whenever a simple means of displaying information is required.

Now that we have a means of outputting information, we can move on to processing messages.

Understanding Windows 95 Messages

As it relates to Windows 95, a message is a unique 32-bit integer value. Windows 95 communicates with your program by sending it messages. Each message corresponds to some event. For example, there are messages to indicate that the user has pressed a key, that the mouse has moved, or that a window has been resized.

Although you could, in theory, refer to each message by its numeric value, in practice this is seldom done. Instead, there are macro names defined for all Windows 95 messages. Typically, you will use the macro name, not the

2

actual integer value, when referring to a message. The standard names for the messages are defined by including WINDOWS.H in your program. Here are some common Windows 95 message macros:

    WM_CHAR
    WM_PAINT
    WM_MOVE
    WM_CLOSE
    WM_LBUTTONUP
    WM_LBUTTONDOWN
    WM_COMMAND
    WM_HSCROLL

Two other values accompany each message and contain information related to each message. One of these values is of type **WPARAM**, the other is of type **LPARAM**. For Windows 95, both of these types translate into 32-bit integers. These values are commonly called **wParam** and **lParam**, respectively. The contents of **wParam** and **lParam** are determined by which message is received. They typically hold things like mouse coordinates, the value of a keypress, or a system-related value. As each message is discussed, the meaning of the values contained in **wParam** and **lParam** will be described.

As mentioned in Chapter 1, the function that actually processes messages is your program's window function. As you should recall, this function is passed four parameters: the handle of the window that the message is for, the message itself, **wParam**, and **lParam**.

Sometimes two pieces of information are encoded in the two words that comprise the **wParam** and **lParam** parameters. To provide easy access to each half of **wParam** and **lParam,** Windows defines two macros called **LOWORD** and **HIWORD**. They return the low-order and high-order words of a long integer, respectively. They are used like this:

```
x = LOWORD(lParam);
x = HIWORD(lParam);
```

You will see these macros in use shortly.

Although it is not possible to examine every message used by Windows 95, this chapter discusses some of its most common ones. Other messages are described, as needed, throughout the remainder of this book.

Responding to a Keypress

One of the most common Windows 95 messages is generated when a key is pressed. This message is called **WM_CHAR**. It is important to understand that your application never receives, per se, keystrokes directly from the keyboard. Instead, each time a key is pressed, a **WM_CHAR** message is sent to the active window. To see how this process works, this section extends the skeletal application developed in Chapter 1 so that it processes keystroke messages.

Each time **WM_CHAR** is sent, **wParam** contains the ASCII value of the key pressed. **LOWORD(lParam)** contains the number of times the key has been repeated as a result of the key being held down. The bits of **HIWORD(lParam)** are encoded as shown here:

15: Set if the key is being released; cleared if the key is being pressed.

14: Set if the key was pressed before the message sent; cleared if it was not pressed.

13: Set if the Alt key is also being pressed; cleared if Alt is not pressed.

12: Used by Windows 95

11: Used by Windows 95

10: Used by Windows 95

9: Used by Windows 95

8: Set if the key pressed is a function key or an extended key; cleared otherwise.

7 - 0: Manufacturer-dependent key code (i.e., the scan code)

For our purposes, the only value that is important now is **wParam**, since it holds the key that was pressed. However, notice how detailed the information is that Windows 95 supplies about the state of the system. Of course, you are free to use as much or as little of this information as you like.

To process a **WM_CHAR** message, you must add it to the **switch** statement inside your program's window function. For example, here is a program that processes a keystroke by displaying the character on the screen by means of a message box.

```
/* Processing WM_CHAR messages. */

#include <windows.h>
#include <string.h>
#include <stdio.h>

LRESULT CALLBACK WindowFunc(HWND, UINT, WPARAM, LPARAM);

char szWinName[] = "MyWin"; /* name of window class */

char str[255] = ""; /* holds output string */

int WINAPI WinMain(HINSTANCE hThisInst, HINSTANCE hPrevInst,
                   LPSTR lpszArgs, int nWinMode)
{
  HWND hwnd;
  MSG msg;
  WNDCLASSEX wcl;

  /* Define a window class. */
  wcl.hInstance = hThisInst; /* handle to this instance */
  wcl.lpszClassName = szWinName; /* window class name */
  wcl.lpfnWndProc = WindowFunc; /* window function */
  wcl.style = 0; /* default style */

  wcl.cbSize = sizeof(WNDCLASSEX); /* set size of WNDCLASSEX */

  wcl.hIcon = LoadIcon(NULL, IDI_APPLICATION); /* large icon */
  wcl.hIconSm = LoadIcon(NULL, IDI_APPLICATION); /* small icon */

  wcl.hCursor = LoadCursor(NULL, IDC_ARROW); /* cursor style */
  wcl.lpszMenuName = NULL; /* no menu */

  wcl.cbClsExtra = 0; /* no extra */
  wcl.cbWndExtra = 0; /* information needed */

  /* Make the window white. */
  wcl.hbrBackground = GetStockObject(WHITE_BRUSH);

  /* Register the window class. */
  if(!RegisterClassEx(&wcl)) return 0;

  /* Now that a window class has been registered, a window
     can be created. */
  hwnd = CreateWindow(
```

```
    szWinName, /* name of window class */
    "Processing WM_CHAR Messages", /* title */
    WS_OVERLAPPEDWINDOW, /* window style - normal */
    CW_USEDEFAULT, /* X coordinate - let Windows decide */
    CW_USEDEFAULT, /* Y coordinate - let Windows decide */
    CW_USEDEFAULT, /* width - let Windows decide */
    CW_USEDEFAULT, /* height - let Windows decide */
    HWND_DESKTOP, /* no parent window */
    NULL, /* no menu */
    hThisInst, /* handle of this instance of the program */
    NULL /* no additional arguments */
  );

  /* Display the window. */
  ShowWindow(hwnd, nWinMode);
  UpdateWindow(hwnd);

  /* Create the message loop. */
  while(GetMessage(&msg, NULL, 0, 0))
  {
    TranslateMessage(&msg); /* allow use of keyboard */
    DispatchMessage(&msg); /* return control to Windows */
  }
  return msg.wParam;
}

/* This function is called by Windows 95 and is passed
   messages from the message queue.
*/
LRESULT CALLBACK WindowFunc(HWND hwnd, UINT message,
                            WPARAM wParam, LPARAM lParam)
{
  switch(message) {
    case WM_CHAR: /* process keystroke */
      sprintf(str, "Character is %c", (char) wParam);
      MessageBox(hwnd, str, "WM_CHAR Received", MB_OK);
      break;
    case WM_DESTROY: /* terminate the program */
      PostQuitMessage(0);
      break;
    default:
      /* Let Windows 95 process any messages not specified in
         the preceding switch statement. */
      return DefWindowProc(hwnd, message, wParam, lParam);
  }
  return 0;
}
```

Sample output produced by this program is shown in Figure 2-1.

In the program, look carefully at these lines of code from **WindowFunc( )**:

```
case WM_CHAR: /* process keystroke */
      sprintf(str, "Character is %c", (char) wParam);
      MessageBox(hwnd, str, "WM_CHAR Received", MB_OK);
      break;
```

As you can see, the **WM_CHAR** message has been added to the **case** statement. When you run the program, each time you press a key, a **WM_CHAR** message is generated and sent to **WindowFunc( )**. Inside the **WM_CHAR** case, the character received in **wParam** is displayed by use of a message box.

2

Outputting Text to a Window

Although the message box is the easiest means of displaying information, it is obviously not suitable for all situations. Although it is a little more complicated than using a message box, there is another way for your program to output information: it can write directly to the client area of its window. As you probably know, Windows 95 supports both text and graphics output. In this section, you will learn the basics of text output. Graphics output is reserved for later in this book.

The first thing to understand about outputting text to a window is that you cannot use the standard C or C++ I/O system. The reason: the standard C/C++ I/O functions and operators direct their output to standard output. However, in a Windows program, output must be directed to a window. To see how text can be written to a window, let's begin with an example.

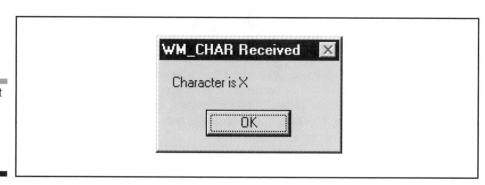

Sample output
from the
WM_CHAR
program
Figure 2-1.

Specifically, let's change the preceding program so that it outputs each character that you type to the program's window, instead of using a message box. To do this, change **WindowFunc( )** so that it looks like this:

```
LRESULT CALLBACK WindowFunc(HWND hwnd, UINT message,
                            WPARAM wParam, LPARAM lParam)
{
  HDC hdc;
  static unsigned j=0;

  switch(message) {
    case WM_CHAR: /* process keystroke */
      hdc = GetDC(hwnd); /* get device context */
      sprintf(str, "%c", (char) wParam); /* stringize character */
      TextOut(hdc, j*10, 0, str, strlen(str)); /* output char */
      j++; /* try commenting-out this line */
      ReleaseDC(hwnd, hdc); /* release device context */
      break;
    case WM_DESTROY: /* terminate the program */
      PostQuitMessage(0);
      break;
    default:
      /* Let Windows 95 process any messages not specified in
         the preceding switch statement. */
      return DefWindowProc(hwnd, message, wParam, lParam);
  }
  return 0;
}
```

Look carefully at the code inside the **WM_CHAR** case. It simply echoes each character that you type to the program's window. Compared to using the standard C/C++ I/O functions or operators, this code probably seems overly complex. The reason for this is that Windows must establish a link between your program and the screen. This is called a *device context* (DC), and it is acquired by a call to **GetDC( )**. For now, don't worry about precisely what a device context is. It will be discussed in the next section. However, once you obtain a device context, you may write to the window. At the end of the process, the device context is released by use of **ReleaseDC( )**. Your program *must* release the device context when it is done with it. There are a finite number of device contexts. If your program doesn't release the DC, eventually the available DCs will be exhausted, and a subsequent call to **GetDC( )** will fail. Both **GetDC( )** and **ReleaseDC( )** are API functions. Their prototypes are shown here:

HDC GetDC(HWND *hwnd*);

int ReleaseDC(HWND *hwnd*, HDC *hdc*);

GetDC( ) returns a device context associated with the window whose handle is specified by *hwnd*. The type **HDC** specifies a handle to a device context. If a device context cannot be obtained, the function returns **NULL**.

ReleaseDC( ) returns true if the device context was released, false otherwise. The *hwnd* parameter is the handle of the window for which the device context is released. The *hdc* parameter is the handle of the device context obtained through the call to **GetDC( )**.

2

The function that actually outputs the character is the API function **TextOut( )**. Its prototype is shown here:

BOOL TextOut(HDC *DC*, int *X*, int *Y*, LPCSTR *lpstr*, int *nlength*);

The **TextOut( )** function outputs the string pointed to by *lpstr* at the window coordinates specified by *X, Y*. (By default, these coordinates are in terms of pixels.) The length of the string is specified in *nlength*. The **TextOut( )** function returns nonzero if successful, zero otherwise.

Inside **WindowFunc( )**, each time a **WM_CHAR** message is received, the character typed by the user is converted (using **sprintf( )**) into a one-character string and then displayed (using **TextOut( )**) in the window. The first character is displayed at location 0, 0. Remember, in a window, the upper-left corner of the client area is location 0, 0. Window coordinates are always relative to the window, not the screen. Therefore, the first character is displayed in the upper-left corner no matter where the window is physically located on the screen. The variable **j** allows each character to be displayed to the right of the preceding character. That is, the second character is displayed at 10, 0, the third at 20, 0, and so on. Windows does not support any concept of a text cursor that is automatically advanced. Instead, you must explicitly specify where each **TextOut( )** string will be written. Also, **TextOut( )** does not advance to the next line when a newline character is encountered, nor does it expand tabs. You must perform all these activities yourself.

Before moving on, you might want to try one simple experiment: comment-out the line of code that increments **j**. This will cause all characters to be displayed at location 0, 0. Next, run the program and try typing several characters. Specifically, try typing a **W** followed by an **i**. Because Windows is a graphics-based system, characters are of different sizes, and the overwriting of one character by another does not necessarily cause all of the previous character to be erased. For example, when you typed a **W** followed by an **i**, part of the **W** was still displayed. The fact that characters are not proportional also explains why the spacing between characters that you type is uneven.

Understand that the method used in this program to output text to a window is quite crude. In fact, no real Windows 95 application would use this approach. Later in this book, you will learn how to manage text output in a more sophisticated fashion.

No Windows 95 API function will allow output beyond the borders of a window. Output will automatically be clipped to prevent the boundaries from being crossed. To confirm this for yourself, try typing characters past the border of the window. As you will see, once the right edge of the window has been reached, no further characters are displayed.

At first you might think that using **TextOut( )** to output a single character is not an efficient application of the function. The fact is that Windows 95 (and Windows, in general) does not contain a function that simply outputs a character. As you will see, Windows 95 performs much of its user interaction through dialog boxes, menus, toolbars, and so on. For this reason it only contains a few functions that output text to the client area. Further, you will generally construct output in advance and then use **TextOut( )** to simply move that output to the screen. (Again, techniques for managing text output are examined in detail, later in this book.)

Here is the entire program that echoes keystrokes to the window. Figure 2-2 shows sample output.

```
/* Displaying text using TextOut(). */

#include <windows.h>
#include <string.h>
#include <stdio.h>

LRESULT CALLBACK WindowFunc(HWND, UINT, WPARAM, LPARAM);

char szWinName[] = "MyWin"; /* name of window class */

char str[255] = ""; /* holds output string */

int WINAPI WinMain(HINSTANCE hThisInst, HINSTANCE hPrevInst,
                   LPSTR lpszArgs, int nWinMode)
{
  HWND hwnd;
  MSG msg;
  WNDCLASSEX wcl;

  /* Define a window class. */
  wcl.hInstance = hThisInst; /* handle to this instance */
  wcl.lpszClassName = szWinName; /* window class name */
  wcl.lpfnWndProc = WindowFunc; /* window function */
```

```
wcl.style = 0; /* default style */

wcl.cbSize = sizeof(WNDCLASSEX); /* set size of WNDCLASSEX */

wcl.hIcon = LoadIcon(NULL, IDI_APPLICATION); /* large icon */
wcl.hIconSm = LoadIcon(NULL, IDI_APPLICATION); /* small icon */

wcl.hCursor = LoadCursor(NULL, IDC_ARROW); /* cursor style */
wcl.lpszMenuName = NULL; /* no menu */

wcl.cbClsExtra = 0; /* no extra */
wcl.cbWndExtra = 0; /* information needed */

/* Make the window white. */
wcl.hbrBackground = GetStockObject(WHITE_BRUSH);

/* Register the window class. */
if(!RegisterClassEx(&wcl)) return 0;

/* Now that a window class has been registered, a window
   can be created. */
hwnd = CreateWindow(
  szWinName, /* name of window class */
  "Display WM_CHAR Messages Using TextOut", /* title */
  WS_OVERLAPPEDWINDOW, /* window style - normal */
  CW_USEDEFAULT, /* X coordinate - let Windows decide */
  CW_USEDEFAULT, /* Y coordinate - let Windows decide */
  CW_USEDEFAULT, /* width - let Windows decide */
  CW_USEDEFAULT, /* height - let Windows decide */
  HWND_DESKTOP, /* no parent window */
  NULL, /* no menu */
  hThisInst, /* handle of this instance of the program */
  NULL /* no additional arguments */
);

/* Display the window. */
ShowWindow(hwnd, nWinMode);
UpdateWindow(hwnd);

/* Create the message loop. */
while(GetMessage(&msg, NULL, 0, 0))
{
  TranslateMessage(&msg); /* allow use of keyboard */
  DispatchMessage(&msg); /* return control to Windows */
}
return msg.wParam;
}
```

```
/* This function is called by Windows 95 and is passed
   messages from the message queue.
*/
LRESULT CALLBACK WindowFunc(HWND hwnd, UINT message,
                           WPARAM wParam, LPARAM lParam)
{
  HDC hdc;
  static unsigned j=0;

  switch(message) {
    case WM_CHAR: /* process keystroke */
      hdc = GetDC(hwnd); /* get device context */
      sprintf(str, "%c", (char) wParam); /* stringize character */
      TextOut(hdc, j*10, 0, str, strlen(str)); /* output char */
      j++; /* try commenting-out this line */
      ReleaseDC(hwnd, hdc); /* release device context */
      break;
    case WM_DESTROY: /* terminate the program */
      PostQuitMessage(0);
      break;
    default:
      /* Let Windows 95 process any messages not specified in
         the preceding switch statement. */
      return DefWindowProc(hwnd, message, wParam, lParam);
  }
  return 0;
}
```

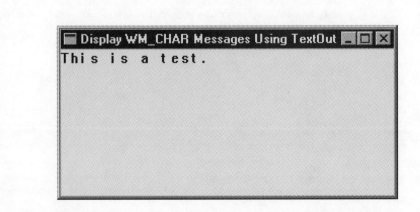

Sample
window
produced with
TextOut( )
Figure 2-2.

Device Contexts

The program in the previous section had to obtain a device context before outputting to the window. Also, that device context had to be released before the termination of that function. It is now time to understand what a device context is. A device context is an output path from your Windows 95 application, through the appropriate device driver, to the client area of your window. The device context also fully defines the state of the device driver.

Before your application can output information to the client area of the window, a device context must be obtained. Until this is done, there is no linkage between your program and the window relative to output. Thus, it is necessary to obtain a device context before performing any output to a window. Since **TextOut( )** and other output functions require a handle to a device context, this is a self-enforcing rule.

2

Getting the User's Attention

Sometimes your program may receive a message that requires action on the part of the user. For example, a clock program may notify a user that a certain time has been reached, a file transfer program may notify the user that an error has occurred, or a numeric analysis program may report a floating-point overflow. Whatever the reason, there can be instances in which you want to get the user's attention. To accomplish this, Windows 95 contains two useful functions: **FlashWindow( )** and **MessageBeep( )**. **FlashWindow( )** flashes a window's title bar (or icon if the window is minimized). **MessageBeep( )** beeps the computer's speaker. Their prototypes are shown here:

BOOL FlashWindow(HWND *hwnd*, BOOL *How*);

BOOL MessageBeep(UINT *Sound*);

For **FlashWindow( )**, the handle of the window to be flashed is specified in *hwnd*. If *How* is nonzero, then the window is flashed. If *How* is zero, the window is returned to its original state before being flashed. Each call to **FlashWindow( )** only flashes the window once, so you will most likely want to call **FlashWindow( )** several times, by use of a loop. **FlashWindow( )** returns nonzero if the title bar was highlighted before the first call and zero if it was not.

For **MessageBeep( )**, *Sound* specifies the type of sound that you want to make. It can be –1, which produces a standard beep, or one of these built-in values:

```
MB_ICONASTERISK
MB_ICONEXCLAMATION
MB_ICONHAND
MB_ICONQUESTION
MB_OK
```

MessageBeep( ) returns nonzero if successful or zero on failure.

To try these two functions, substitute the following **WindowFunc( )** into the skeleton program. Each time a key is pressed, the window flashes and a beep sounds.

```
LRESULT CALLBACK WindowFunc(HWND hwnd, UINT message,
                           WPARAM wParam, LPARAM lParam)
{
  int i;

  switch(message) {
    case WM_CHAR: /* Demo MessageBeep and FlashWindow */
      MessageBeep(MB_ICONQUESTION);
      for(i=0; i<100; i++) FlashWindow(hwnd, 1);
      break;
    case WM_DESTROY: /* terminate the program */
      PostQuitMessage(0);
      break;
    default:
      /* Let Windows 95 process any messages not specified in
          the preceding switch statement. */
      return DefWindowProc(hwnd, message, wParam, lParam);
  }
  return 0;
}
```

Processing the WM_PAINT Message

One of the most important messages that your program will receive is **WM_PAINT**. This message is sent when your program needs to restore the contents of its window. To understand why this is important, run the program from the previous section and enter a few characters. Next, minimize and then restore the window. As you will see, the characters that you typed are not displayed after the window is restored. Also, if the window is overwritten by another window and then redisplayed, the characters are not redisplayed. The reason for this is simple: in general, Windows does not keep a record of what a window contains. Instead, it is your program's job to maintain the contents of a window. To help your program accomplish this, each time the contents of a window must be redisplayed, your program will be sent a **WM_PAINT** message. (This message will also be sent when your window is first displayed.) Each time your program receives this message, it must redisplay the contents of the window.

Before you learn how to respond to a **WM_PAINT** message, it might be useful to learn why Windows does not automatically rewrite your window. The answer is short and to the point. In many situations, it is easier for your program, which has intimate knowledge of the contents of the window, to rewrite it than it would be for Windows to do so. While the merits of this approach have been much debated by programmers, you should simply accept it, because it is unlikely to change.

The first step to processing a **WM_PAINT** message is to add it to the **switch** statement inside the window function. For example, here is one way to add a **WM_PAINT** case to the previous program.

```
case WM_PAINT: /* process a repaint request */
  hdc = BeginPaint(hwnd, &paintstruct); /* get DC */
  TextOut(hdc, 0, 0, str, strlen(str));
  EndPaint(hwnd, &paintstruct); /* release DC */
  break;
```

Let's look at this closely. First, notice that a device context is obtained by use of a call to **BeginPaint( )** instead of **GetDC( )**. For various reasons, when you process a **WM_PAINT** message, you must obtain a device context by using **BeginPaint( )**, which has this prototype:

HDC BeginPaint(HWND *hwnd*, PAINTSTRUCT **lpPS*);

BeginPaint( ) returns a device context if successful or **NULL** on failure. Here, *hwnd* is the handle of the window for which the device context is being obtained. The second parameter is a pointer to a structure of type **PAINTSTRUCT**. The structure pointed to by *lpPS* will contain information that your program can use to repaint the window. **PAINTSTRUCT** is defined like this:

```
typedef struct tagPAINTSTRUCT {
  HDC hdc; /* handle to device context */
```

```
  BOOL fErase; /* true if background must be erased */
  RECT rcPaint; /* coordinates of region to redraw */
  BOOL fRestore;  /* reserved */
  BOOL fIncUpdate; /* reserved */
  BYTE rgbReserved[32]; /* reserved */
} PAINTSTRUCT;
```

Here, **hdc** will contain the device context of the window that needs to be repainted. This DC is also returned by the call to **BeginPaint( )**. **fErase** will be nonzero if the background of the window needs to be erased. However, as long as you specified a background brush when you created the window, you can ignore the **fErase** member. Windows 95 will erase the window for you.

The type **RECT** is a structure that specifies the upper-left and lower-right coordinates of a rectangular region. This structure is shown here:

```
typedef tagRECT {
  LONG left, top; /* upper left */
  LONG right, bottom; /* lower right */
} RECT;
```

In **PAINTSTRUCT**, the **rcPaint** element contains the coordinates of the region of the window that needs to be repainted. For now, you will not need to use the contents of **rcPaint** because you can assume that the entire window must be repainted. However, real programs that you write will probably need to utilize this information.

Once the device context has been obtained, output can be written to the window. Once the window has been repainted, you must release the device context by using a call to **EndPaint( )**, which has this prototype:

BOOL EndPaint(HWND *hwnd*, CONST PAINTSTRUCT **lpPS*);

EndPaint( ) returns nonzero. (It cannot fail.) Here, *hwnd* is the handle of the window that was repainted. The second parameter is a pointer to the **PAINTSTRUCT** structure used in the call to **BeginPaint( )**.

Remember: It is critical to understand that a device context obtained by use of **BeginPaint( )** must be released only through a call to **EndPaint( )**. Further, **BeginPaint( )** must only be used when a **WM_PAINT** message is being processed.

Here is the full program, which now processes **WM_PAINT** messages.

```c
/* Process WM_PAINT Messages */

#include <windows.h>
#include <string.h>
#include <stdio.h>

LRESULT CALLBACK WindowFunc(HWND, UINT, WPARAM, LPARAM);

char szWinName[] = "MyWin"; /* name of window class */

char str[255] = "Sample Output"; /* holds output string */

int WINAPI WinMain(HINSTANCE hThisInst, HINSTANCE hPrevInst,
                   LPSTR lpszArgs, int nWinMode)
{
  HWND hwnd;
  MSG msg;
  WNDCLASSEX wcl;

  /* Define a window class. */
  wcl.hInstance = hThisInst; /* handle to this instance */
  wcl.lpszClassName = szWinName; /* window class name */
  wcl.lpfnWndProc = WindowFunc; /* window function */
  wcl.style = 0; /* default style */

  wcl.cbSize = sizeof(WNDCLASSEX); /* set size of WNDCLASSEX */

  wcl.hIcon = LoadIcon(NULL, IDI_APPLICATION); /* large icon */
  wcl.hIconSm = LoadIcon(NULL, IDI_APPLICATION); /* small icon */

  wcl.hCursor = LoadCursor(NULL, IDC_ARROW); /* cursor style */
  wcl.lpszMenuName = NULL; /* no menu */

  wcl.cbClsExtra = 0; /* no extra */
  wcl.cbWndExtra = 0; /* information needed */

  /* Make the window white. */
  wcl.hbrBackground = GetStockObject(WHITE_BRUSH);

  /* Register the window class. */
  if(!RegisterClassEx(&wcl)) return 0;

  /* Now that a window class has been registered, a window
     can be created. */
```

2

```
hwnd = CreateWindow(
  szWinName, /* name of window class */
  "Process WM_PAINT Messages", /* title */
  WS_OVERLAPPEDWINDOW, /* window style - normal */
  CW_USEDEFAULT, /* X coordinate - let Windows decide */
  CW_USEDEFAULT, /* Y coordinate - let Windows decide */
  CW_USEDEFAULT, /* width - let Windows decide */
  CW_USEDEFAULT, /* height - let Windows decide */
  HWND_DESKTOP, /* no parent window */
  NULL, /* no menu */
  hThisInst, /* handle of this instance of the program */
  NULL /* no additional arguments */
);

/* Display the window. */
ShowWindow(hwnd, nWinMode);
UpdateWindow(hwnd);

/* Create the message loop. */
while(GetMessage(&msg, NULL, 0, 0))
{
  TranslateMessage(&msg); /* allow use of keyboard */
  DispatchMessage(&msg); /* return control to Windows */
}
return msg.wParam;
}

/* This function is called by Windows 95 and is passed
   messages from the message queue.
*/
LRESULT CALLBACK WindowFunc(HWND hwnd, UINT message,
                            WPARAM wParam, LPARAM lParam)
{
  HDC hdc;
  static unsigned j=0;
  PAINTSTRUCT paintstruct;

  switch(message) {
    case WM_CHAR: /* process keystroke */
      hdc = GetDC(hwnd); /* get device context */
      sprintf(str, "%c", (char) wParam); /* stringize character */
      TextOut(hdc, j*10, 0, str, strlen(str)); /* output char */
      j++; /* try commenting-out this line */
      ReleaseDC(hwnd, hdc); /* release device context */
      break;
    case WM_PAINT: /* process a repaint request */
```

```
      hdc = BeginPaint(hwnd, &paintstruct); /* get DC */
      TextOut(hdc, 0, 0, str, strlen(str));
      EndPaint(hwnd, &paintstruct); /* release DC */
      break;
    case WM_DESTROY: /* terminate the program */
      PostQuitMessage(0);
      break;
    default:
      /* Let Windows 95 process any messages not specified in
         the preceding switch statement. */
      return DefWindowProc(hwnd, message, wParam, lParam);
  }
  return 0;
}
```

2

Before you continue: enter, compile, and run this program. Try typing a few characters and then minimizing and restoring the window. As you will see, each time the window is redisplayed, the last character you typed is automatically redrawn. Only the last character is redisplayed because **str** only contains the last character that you typed. You might find it fun to alter the program so that it adds each character to a string, and then redisplay that string each time a **WM_PAINT** message is displayed. (You will see one way to do this in the next example.) Notice that the global array **str** is initialized to **Sample Output** and that this is displayed when the program begins execution. The reason is that when a window is created, a **WM_PAINT** message is automatically generated.

While the handling of the **WM_PAINT** message in this program is quite simple, it must be emphasized that most real-world applications will be more complex because most windows contain considerably more output. Since it is your program's responsibility to restore the window if it is resized or overwritten, you must always provide some mechanism to accomplish this. In real-world programs, this is usually done one of three ways: First, your program can simply regenerate the output by computational means. This is most feasible when no user input is used. Second, in some instances, you can keep a record of events and replay the events when the window needs to be redrawn. Finally, your program can maintain a virtual window that you simply copy to the window each time it must be redrawn. This is the most general method. (The implementation of this approach is described later in this book.) Which approach is best depends completely upon the application. Most of the examples in this book won't bother to redraw the window because doing so typically involves substantial additional code, which often just muddies the point of an example. However, your programs will need to restore their windows to be conforming Windows 95 applications.

Generating a WM_PAINT Message

It is possible for your program to cause a **WM_PAINT** message to be generated. At first, you might wonder why your program would need to generate a **WM_PAINT** message, since it seems that it can repaint its window whenever it wants. However, this can be a false assumption. Keep in mind that updating a window is time-consuming. Because Windows is a multitasking system that might be running other programs which are also demanding CPU time, there may be situations when your program should simply tell Windows that it wants to output information—but let Windows decide when it is best to actually perform that output. This allows Windows to better manage the system and efficiently allocate CPU time to all the tasks in the system. Using this approach, your program simply holds all output until a **WM_PAINT** message is received.

In the previous example, the **WM_PAINT** message was only received when the window was resized or uncovered. However, if all output is held until a **WM_PAINT** message is received, then to achieve interactive I/O, there must be some way to tell Windows that it needs to send a **WM_PAINT** message to your window whenever output is pending. As expected, Windows 95 includes such a feature. Thus, when your program has information to output, it simply requests that a **WM_PAINT** message be sent when Windows is ready to do so.

To cause Windows to send a **WM_PAINT** message, your program will call the **InvalidateRect( )** API function. Its prototype is shown here:

BOOL InvalidateRect(HWND *hwnd*, CONST RECT **lpRect*, BOOL *bErase*);

Here, *hwnd* is the handle of the window that you want to send the **WM_PAINT** message to. The **RECT** structure pointed to by *lpRect* specifies the coordinates within the window that must be redrawn. If this value is **NULL**, then the entire window will be specified. If *bErase* is true, then the background will be erased. If it is 0, then the background is left unchanged. The function returns nonzero if successful, zero otherwise. (In general, this function will always succeed.)

When **InvalidateRect( )** is called, it tells Windows that the window is invalid and must be redrawn. This, in turn, causes Windows to send a **WM_PAINT** message to the program's window function.

Here is a reworked version of the previous program that routes all output through the **WM_PAINT** message. The code that responds to a **WM_CHAR** message simply stores each character and then calls **InvalidateRect( )**. In this version of the program, notice that inside the **WM_CHAR** case, each character you type is added to the string **str**. Thus, each time the window is repainted, the entire string containing all the characters you typed is output, not just the last character, as was the case with the preceding program.

```
/* A Windows skeleton that routes output through
   the WM_PAINT message. */

#include <windows.h>
#include <string.h>
#include <stdio.h>

LRESULT CALLBACK WindowFunc(HWND, UINT, WPARAM, LPARAM);

char szWinName[] = "MyWin"; /* name of window class */

char str[255] = ""; /* holds output string */

int WINAPI WinMain(HINSTANCE hThisInst, HINSTANCE hPrevInst,
                   LPSTR lpszArgs, int nWinMode)
{
  HWND hwnd;
  MSG msg;
  WNDCLASSEX wcl;

  /* Define a window class. */
  wcl.hInstance = hThisInst; /* handle to this instance */
  wcl.lpszClassName = szWinName; /* window class name */
  wcl.lpfnWndProc = WindowFunc; /* window function */
  wcl.style = 0; /* default style */

  wcl.cbSize = sizeof(WNDCLASSEX); /* set size of WNDCLASSEX */

  wcl.hIcon = LoadIcon(NULL, IDI_APPLICATION); /* large icon */
  wcl.hIconSm = LoadIcon(NULL, IDI_APPLICATION); /* small icon */

  wcl.hCursor = LoadCursor(NULL, IDC_ARROW); /* cursor style */
  wcl.lpszMenuName = NULL; /* no menu */

  wcl.cbClsExtra = 0; /* no extra */
  wcl.cbWndExtra = 0; /* information needed */

  /* Make the window white. */
  wcl.hbrBackground = GetStockObject(WHITE_BRUSH);

  /* Register the window class. */
  if(!RegisterClassEx(&wcl)) return 0;

  /* Now that a window class has been registered, a window
     can be created. */
  hwnd = CreateWindow(
    szWinName, /* name of window class */
    "Routing Output Through WM_PAINT", /* title */
```

```
      WS_OVERLAPPEDWINDOW, /* window style - normal */
      CW_USEDEFAULT, /* X coordinate - let Windows decide */
      CW_USEDEFAULT, /* Y coordinate - let Windows decide */
      CW_USEDEFAULT, /* width - let Windows decide */
      CW_USEDEFAULT, /* height - let Windows decide */
      HWND_DESKTOP, /* no parent window */
      NULL, /* no menu */
      hThisInst, /* handle of this instance of the program */
      NULL /* no additional arguments */
    );

    /* Display the window. */
    ShowWindow(hwnd, nWinMode);
    UpdateWindow(hwnd);

    /* Create the message loop. */
    while(GetMessage(&msg, NULL, 0, 0))
    {
      TranslateMessage(&msg); /* allow use of keyboard */
      DispatchMessage(&msg); /* return control to Windows */
    }
    return msg.wParam;
}

/* This function is called by Windows 95 and is passed
   messages from the message queue.
*/
LRESULT CALLBACK WindowFunc(HWND hwnd, UINT message, WPARAM wParam,
                            LPARAM lParam)
{
  HDC hdc;
  PAINTSTRUCT paintstruct;
  char temp[2];

  switch(message) {
    case WM_CHAR: /* process keystroke */
      hdc = GetDC(hwnd); /* get device context */
      sprintf(temp, "%c", (char) wParam); /* stringize character */
      strcat(str, temp); /* add character to string */
      InvalidateRect(hwnd, NULL, 1); /* paint the screen */
      break;
    case WM_PAINT: /* process a repaint request */
      hdc = BeginPaint(hwnd, &paintstruct); /* get DC */
      TextOut(hdc, 0, 0, str, strlen(str)); /* output char */
      EndPaint(hwnd, &paintstruct); /* release DC */
      break;
    case WM_DESTROY: /* terminate the program */
      PostQuitMessage(0);
```

```
      break;
   default:
      /* Let Windows 95 process any messages not specified in
         the preceding switch statement. */
      return DefWindowProc(hwnd, message, wParam, lParam);
   }
   return 0;
}
```

Many Windows applications route all (or most) output to the client area through **WM_PAINT**, for the reasons already stated. However, there is nothing wrong with outputting text or graphics directly to the window as needed. Which method you use will depend on each situation.

Generating a Message

As you know, **InvalidateRect( )** is used to generate a **WM_PAINT** message. However, this raises a larger question: How does a program generate a message, in general? You will be happy to learn that the answer is quite easy. Simply use another API function: **SendMessage( )**. Using **SendMessage( )**, you can send a message to any window you want. Its prototype is shown here:

LRESULT SendMessage(HWND *hwnd*, UINT *message*, WPARAM *wParam*, LPARAM *lParam*);

Here, *hwnd* is the handle of the window to which the message will be sent. The message to send is specified in *message*. Any additional information associated with the message is passed in *wParam* and *lParam*. **SendMessage( )** returns a response related to the message.

SendMessage( ) is used frequently when working with Windows's control elements—especially its new common controls. You will see examples of this use later in this book. However, it can be used any time you want to send a message to a window. For example, the following version of **WindowFunc( )** uses **SendMessage( )** to generate a stream of **WM_CHAR** messages whenever the user presses CTRL-A.

```
LRESULT CALLBACK WindowFunc(HWND hwnd, UINT message,
                            WPARAM wParam, LPARAM lParam)
{
  HDC hdc;
  unsigned i;
```

```
static unsigned j=0;
char s[] = "Hello There";

switch(message) {
  case WM_CHAR: /* process keystroke */
    hdc = GetDC(hwnd); /* get device context */

    /* print Hello There if user presses Ctrl-A */
    if((char)wParam == (char) 1) for(i=0; s[i]; i++)
      SendMessage(hwnd, WM_CHAR, (WPARAM) s[i], (LPARAM) 0);
    else {
      sprintf(str, "%c", (char) wParam); /* stringize
                                            character */
      TextOut(hdc, j*10, 0, str, strlen(str)); /* output
                                                   char */

      j++;
    }

    ReleaseDC(hwnd, hdc); /* release device context */
    break;
  case WM_DESTROY: /* terminate the program */
    PostQuitMessage(0);
    break;
  default:
    /* Let Windows 95 process any messages not specified in
       the preceding switch statement. */
    return DefWindowProc(hwnd, message, wParam, lParam);
  }
  return 0;
}
```

If you substitute this version of **WindowFunc( )** into one of the preceding programs, then each time you press CTRL-A, the string "Hello There" will be sent as a series of **WM_CHAR** messages to your program. You could use this basic concept to provide a keyboard macro capability in programs that you write.

One other point: since the information contained in **lParam** is not used by the program when a **WM_CHAR** message is processed, this parameter was simply specified as zero inside the call to **SendMessage( )**. However, in other contexts you may need to generate the appropriate values for this information.

Responding to Mouse Messages

Since Windows is, to a great extent, a mouse-based operating system, all Windows 95 programs should respond to mouse input. Because the mouse is so important, there are several types of mouse messages. This section examines the two most common. These are **WM_LBUTTONDOWN** and **WM_RBUTTONDOWN**, which are generated when the left and right buttons, respectively, are pressed.

When either a **WM_LBUTTONDOWN** or a **WM_RBUTTONDOWN** message is received, the mouse's current *x, y* location is specified in **LOWORD(lParam)** and **HIWORD(lParam)**, respectively. The following program uses this fact when it responds to the mouse messages. Each time you press a mouse button, a message will be displayed at the current location of the mouse pointer.

2

Here is the complete program that responds to the mouse messages. Figure 2-3 shows sample output.

```
/* Process Mouse Messages. */

#include <windows.h>
#include <string.h>
#include <stdio.h>

LRESULT CALLBACK WindowFunc(HWND, UINT, WPARAM, LPARAM);

char szWinName[] = "MyWin"; /* name of window class */

char str[255] = ""; /* holds output string */

int WINAPI WinMain(HINSTANCE hThisInst, HINSTANCE hPrevInst,
                   LPSTR lpszArgs, int nWinMode)
{
  HWND hwnd;
  MSG msg;
  WNDCLASSEX wcl;

  /* Define a window class. */
  wcl.hInstance = hThisInst; /* handle to this instance */
  wcl.lpszClassName = szWinName; /* window class name */
  wcl.lpfnWndProc = WindowFunc; /* window function */
  wcl.style = 0; /* default style */

  wcl.cbSize = sizeof(WNDCLASSEX); /* set size of WNDCLASSEX */

  wcl.hIcon = LoadIcon(NULL, IDI_APPLICATION); /* large icon */
  wcl.hIconSm = LoadIcon(NULL, IDI_APPLICATION); /* small icon */
```

```
wcl.hCursor = LoadCursor(NULL, IDC_ARROW); /* cursor style */
wcl.lpszMenuName = NULL; /* no menu */

wcl.cbClsExtra = 0; /* no extra */
wcl.cbWndExtra = 0; /* information needed */

/* Make the window white. */
wcl.hbrBackground = GetStockObject(WHITE_BRUSH);

/* Register the window class. */
if(!RegisterClassEx(&wcl)) return 0;

/* Now that a window class has been registered, a window
   can be created. */
hwnd = CreateWindow(
  szWinName, /* name of window class */
  "Processing Mouse Messages", /* title */
  WS_OVERLAPPEDWINDOW, /* window style - normal */
  CW_USEDEFAULT, /* X coordinate - let Windows decide */
  CW_USEDEFAULT, /* Y coordinate - let Windows decide */
  CW_USEDEFAULT, /* width - let Windows decide */
  CW_USEDEFAULT, /* height - let Windows decide */
  HWND_DESKTOP, /* no parent window */
  NULL, /* no menu */
  hThisInst, /* handle of this instance of the program */
  NULL /* no additional arguments */
);

/* Display the window. */
ShowWindow(hwnd, nWinMode);
UpdateWindow(hwnd);

/* Create the message loop. */
while(GetMessage(&msg, NULL, 0, 0))
{
  TranslateMessage(&msg); /* allow use of keyboard */
  DispatchMessage(&msg); /* return control to Windows */
}
return msg.wParam;
}

/* This function is called by Windows 95 and is passed
   messages from the message queue.
*/
LRESULT CALLBACK WindowFunc(HWND hwnd, UINT message,
                            WPARAM wParam, LPARAM lParam)
{
  HDC hdc;
```

```
switch(message) {
  case WM_RBUTTONDOWN: /* process right button */
    hdc = GetDC(hwnd); /* get DC */
    sprintf(str, "Right button is down at %d, %d",
            LOWORD(lParam), HIWORD(lParam));
    TextOut(hdc, LOWORD(lParam), HIWORD(lParam),
            str, strlen(str));
    ReleaseDC(hwnd, hdc); /* Release DC */
    break;
  case WM_LBUTTONDOWN: /* process left button */
    hdc = GetDC(hwnd); /* get DC */
    sprintf(str, "Left button is down at %d, %d",
            LOWORD(lParam), HIWORD(lParam));
    TextOut(hdc, LOWORD(lParam), HIWORD(lParam),
            str, strlen(str));
    ReleaseDC(hwnd, hdc); /* Release DC */
    break;
  case WM_DESTROY: /* terminate the program */
    PostQuitMessage(0);
    break;
  default:
    /* Let Windows 95 process any messages not specified in
       the preceding switch statement. */
    return DefWindowProc(hwnd, message, wParam, lParam);
}
return 0;
}
```

2

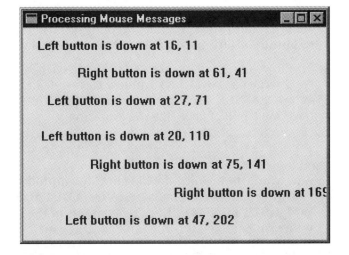

Sample output from the Mouse Messages program

Figure 2-3.

More About Mouse Messages

Each time a **WM_LBUTTONDOWN** or a **WM_RBUTTONDOWN** message is generated, several pieces of information are also supplied in the **wParam** parameter. It can contain any combination of the following values:

MK_CONTROL
MK_SHIFT
MK_MBUTTON
MK_RBUTTON
MK_LBUTTON

If CTRL is pressed when a mouse button is pressed, then **wParam** will contain **MK_CONTROL**. If SHIFT is pressed when a mouse button is pressed, then **WParam** will contain **MK_SHIFT**. If the right button is down when the left button is pressed, then **wParam** will contain **MK_RBUTTON**. If the left button is down when the right button is pressed, then **wParam** will contain **MK_LBUTTON**. If the middle button (assuming there is one) is down when one of the other buttons is pressed, then **wParam** will contain **MK_MBUTTON**. Before moving on, you might want to try experimenting with these messages.

FAST TRACK TIP

Responding to a Double-Click

If your program needs to know when a mouse button has been double-clicked, then you must take two steps. First, you must enable your program to receive double-click messages. By default, double-click messages are not sent to your program. Second, you will need to add message response code for the double-click message you want to respond to.

To allow your program to receive double-click messages, you will need to specify the **CS_DBLCLKS** window class style in the **style** member of the **WNDCLASSEX** structure before registering the window class. That is, you must use a line of code like the following:

```
wcl.style = CS_DBLCLKS; /* allow double-clicks */
```

After you have enabled double-clicks, your program can receive the following double-click messages: **WM_LBUTTONDBLCLK** and **WM_RBUTTONDBLCLK**. The contents of the **lParam** and **wParam** parameters is the same for these messages as for the

WM_LBUTTONDOWN and **WM_RBUTTONDOWN** messages, discussed earlier.

As you know, a double-click is two presses of a mouse button in quick succession. You can obtain and/or set the time interval in which two presses of a mouse button must occur in order for a double-click message to be generated. To obtain the double-click interval, use the API function **GetDoubleClickTime( )**, whose prototype is shown here:

    UINT GetDoubleClickTime(void);

This function returns the interval of time (specified in milliseconds) in which a double-click must occur. To set the double-click interval, use **SetDoubleClickTime( )**. Its prototype is shown here:

    BOOL SetDoubleClickTime(UINT *interval*);

Here, *interval* specifies the number of milliseconds in which two presses of a mouse button must occur in order for a double-click to be generated. If you specify zero, then the default double-click time is used. (The default interval is approximately half a second.) The function returns nonzero if successful and zero on failure.

The following version of **WindowFunc( )** responds to double-click messages and reports the current double-click interval. Try substituting it into the mouse program. (Remember to set the **style** member of the **WNDCLASSEX** to **CS_DBLCLKS**.)

```
LRESULT CALLBACK WindowFunc(HWND hwnd, UINT message,
                            WPARAM wParam, LPARAM lParam)
{
  HDC hdc;
  UINT interval;

  switch(message) {
    case WM_RBUTTONDOWN: /* process right button */
      hdc = GetDC(hwnd); /* get DC */
      sprintf(str, "Right button is down at %d, %d",
              LOWORD(lParam), HIWORD(lParam));
      TextOut(hdc, LOWORD(lParam), HIWORD(lParam),
              str, strlen(str));
      ReleaseDC(hwnd, hdc); /* Release DC */
      break;
    case WM_LBUTTONDOWN: /* process left button */
      hdc = GetDC(hwnd); /* get DC */
```

```
            sprintf(str, "Left button is down at %d, %d",
                    LOWORD(lParam), HIWORD(lParam));
            TextOut(hdc, LOWORD(lParam), HIWORD(lParam),
                    str, strlen(str));
            ReleaseDC(hwnd, hdc); /* Release DC */
            break;
        case WM_LBUTTONDBLCLK: /* process left button double-click */
            interval = GetDoubleClickTime();
            sprintf(str, "Left Button\nInterval is %u milliseconds",
                        interval);
            MessageBox(hwnd, str, "Double Click", MB_OK);
            break;
        case WM_RBUTTONDBLCLK: /* process right double-click */
            interval = GetDoubleClickTime();
            sprintf(str, "Right Button\nInterval is %u milliseconds",
                        interval);
            MessageBox(hwnd, str, "Double Click", MB_OK);
            break;
        case WM_DESTROY: /* terminate the program */
            PostQuitMessage(0);
            break;
        default:
            /* Let Windows 95 process any messages not specified in
                the preceding switch statement. */
            return DefWindowProc(hwnd, message, wParam, lParam);
    }
    return 0;
}
```

For fun, you might want to try setting the double-click interval. One interesting way to do this is to increase its value by 10 milliseconds each time you press the left button and decrease it by 10 milliseconds each time you press the right button.

Note: The double-click interval is a systemwide setting. Therefore, if your program changes it, it will affect all other programs in the system.

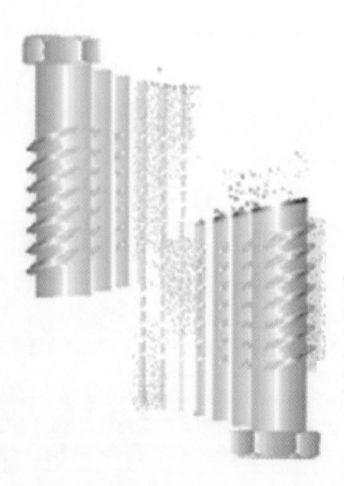

CHAPTER 3

Using Menus

Now that you know the basic constituents of a Windows 95 application, it is time to begin exploring Windows' user interface components. If you are learning to program Windows for the first time, it is important to understand that your application will most often communicate with the user through one or more predefined interface components. There are several types of interface elements supported by Windows 95. This chapter discusses its most fundamental: the menu. Virtually any program you write will use one. As you will see, the basic style of the menu is predefined. You need only supply the specific information that relates to your application.

This chapter also introduces the *resource.* A resource is, essentially, an object defined outside your program but used by your program. Icons, cursors, menus, and bitmaps are common resources. Resources are a crucial part of nearly all Windows applications.

Introducing Menus

In Windows the most common element of control is the menu. Virtually all main windows have some type of menu associated with them. Because menus are so common and important in Windows applications, Windows provides substantial built-in support for them. As you will see, adding a menu to a window involves these relatively few steps:

1. Define the form of the menu in a resource file.
2. Load the menu when your program creates its main window.
3. Process menu selections.

In a Windows application, the main (top level) menu is displayed across the top of the window. Submenus are displayed as pop-up menus. (You should be accustomed to this approach because it is used by virtually all Windows programs.)

Before you begin, it is necessary that you understand what resources and resource files are.

Using Resources

Windows defines several common types of objects as *resources.* As mentioned at the beginning of this chapter, resources are, essentially, objects that are used by your program, but that are defined outside your program. They include objects such as menus, icons, dialog boxes, and bitmapped graphics. Since a menu is a resource, you need to understand resources before you can add a menu to your program.

A resource is created separately from your program, but is added to the .EXE file when your program is linked. Resources are contained in *resource files,* which have the extension .RC. In general, the resource filename should be the same as that of your program's .EXE file. For example, if your program is called PROG.EXE, then its resource file should be called PROG.RC.

Depending upon the resource, some are text files that you create by use of a standard text editor. Text resources are typically defined within the resource file. Others, such as icons, are most easily generated by use of a resource editor, but they still must be referred to in the .RC file that is associated with your application. The example resource files in this chapter are simply text files because menus are text-based resources.

Resource files do not contain C or C++ statements. Instead, resource files consist of special resource statements. In the course of this chapter, the resource commands needed to support menus are discussed.

Compiling .RC Files

Resource files are not used directly by your program. Instead, they must be converted into a linkable format, which is stored in an .RES file. Once you have created an .RC file, you compile it into an .RES file by using the *resource compiler*. (Often, the resource compiler is called RC.EXE, but this varies.) Exactly how you compile a resource file will depend upon what compiler you are using. Also, some integrated development environments automatically handle this phase for you. In any event, the output of the resource compiler will be an .RES file. It is this file that you will link with your program to build the final Windows 95 application.

3

Creating a Simple Menu

Before a menu can be included, you must define its content in a resource file. All menu definitions have this general form:

```
MenuName MENU [options]
{
  menu items
}
```

Here, *MenuName* is the name of the menu. (It can also be an integer value identifying the menu, but all examples in this book will use the name when referring to the menu.) The keyword **MENU** tells the resource compiler that a menu is being created. There are several options which can be specified when you create the menu. They are shown in Table 3-1. (These macros are defined by including WINDOWS.H.) The examples in this book simply use the default settings and specify no options.

There are two types of items that can be used to define the menu: **MENUITEM**s and **POPUP**s. A **MENUITEM** specifies a final selection. A **POPUP** specifies a pop-up submenu, which may, in itself, contain other **MENUITEM**s or **POPUP**s. The general forms of these two statements are shown here:

MENUITEM "*ItemName*", *MenuID* [,*Options*]

POPUP "*PopupName*" [,*Options*]

Option	Meaning
DISCARDABLE	Menu can be removed from memory when no longer needed.
FIXED	Menu is fixed in memory.
LOADONCALL	Menu is loaded when used.
MOVEABLE	Menu can be moved in memory.
PRELOAD	Menu is loaded when your program begins execution.

The **MENU**
Options
Table 3-1.

ItemName is the name of a menu selection, such as "Help" or "File." *MenuID* is a unique integer associated with a menu item that will be sent to your application when a selection is made. Typically, these values are defined as macros inside a header file that is included in both your application code and its resource file. *PopupName* is the name of the pop-up menu. For both cases, the values for *Options* (defined by including WINDOWS.H) are shown in Table 3-2.

Option	Meaning
CHECKED	A check mark is displayed next to the name. (Not applicable to top-level menus.)
GRAYED	The name is shown in gray and cannot be selected.
HELP	May be associated with a help selection. This applies to MENUITEMs only.
INACTIVE	The option cannot be selected.
MENUBARBREAK	For menu bar, causes the item to be put on a new line. For pop-up menus, causes the item to be put in a different column. In this case, the item is separated by use of a bar.
MENUBREAK	Same as MENUBARBREAK, except that no separator bar is used.

The
MENUITEM
and **POPUP**
Options
Table 3-2.

Here is a simple menu that will be used by subsequent example programs. You should enter it at this time. Call the file MENU.RC.

```
; Sample menu resource file.
#include "menu.h"

MYMENU MENU
{
  POPUP "&File"
  {
    MENUITEM "&Open", IDM_OPEN
    MENUITEM "&Close", IDM_CLOSE
    MENUITEM "&Exit", IDM_EXIT
  }
  POPUP "&Options"
  {
    MENUITEM "&Colors", IDM_COLORS
    POPUP "&Response Time"
    {
      MENUITEM "&Slow", IDM_SLOW
      MENUITEM "&Fast", IDM_FAST
    }
    MENUITEM "&Sound", IDM_SOUND
    MENUITEM "&Video", IDM_VIDEO
  }
  MENUITEM "&Help", IDM_HELP
}
```

3

This menu, called **MYMENU**, contains three top-level menu bar options: File, Options, and Help. The File and Options entries contain pop-up submenus. The Response Time option activates a pop-up submenu of its own. Notice that options that activate submenus do not have menu ID values associated with them. Only actual menu items have ID numbers. In this menu, all menu ID values are specified as macros beginning with **IDM**. (These macros are defined in the header file MENU.H.) What names you give these values is arbitrary.

An **&** in an item's name causes the letter that it precedes to become the shortcut key associated with that option. That is, once that menu is active, pressing that key causes that menu item to be selected. It doesn't have to be the first letter in the name, but it should be unless a conflict with another name exists.

Note: You can embed comments into a resource file on a line-by-line basis by beginning them with a semicolon, as the first line of the resource file shows. You can also use C-style and C++-style comments.

The MENU.H header file, which is included in MENU.RC, contains the macro definitions of the menu ID values. It is shown here. Enter it at this time.

```
#define IDM_OPEN     100
#define IDM_CLOSE    101
#define IDM_EXIT     102
#define IDM_COLORS   103
#define IDM_SLOW     104
#define IDM_FAST     105
#define IDM_SOUND    106
#define IDM_VIDEO    107
#define IDM_HELP     108
```

This file defines the menu ID values that will be returned when the various menu items are selected. This file will also be included in the program that uses the menu. Remember, the actual names and values you give the menu items are arbitrary. But each value must be unique. Also, the valid range for ID values is 0 through 65,565.

Including a Menu in Your Program

Once you have created a menu, you include that menu in a program by specifying its name when you create the window's class. Specifically, you assign **lpszMenuName** a pointer to a string that contains the name of the menu. For example, to load the menu **MYMENU**, you would use the following line when defining the window's class.

```
wcl.lpszMenuName = "MYMENU"; /* main menu */
```

Responding to Menu Selections

Each time the user makes a menu selection, your program's window function is sent a **WM_COMMAND** command message. When that message is received, the value of **LOWORD(wParam)** contains the menu item's ID value. (That is, **LOWORD(wParam)** contains the value you associated with the item when you defined the menu in its .RC file.) Since **WM_COMMAND** is sent whenever a menu item is selected and the value associated with that item is contained in **LOWORD(wParam)**, you will need to use a nested **switch** statement to determine which item was selected. For example, this fragment responds to a selection made from MYMENU.

```
switch(message) {
    case WM_COMMAND:
      switch(LOWORD(wParam)) {
        case IDM_OPEN: MessageBox(hwnd, "Open File", "Open",
                                  MB_OK);
          break;
        case IDM_CLOSE: MessageBox(hwnd, "Close File", "Close",
                                  MB_OK);
          break;
        case IDM_EXIT:
          response = MessageBox(hwnd, "Quit the Program?",
                                  "Exit", MB_YESNO);
          if(response == IDYES) PostQuitMessage(0);
          break;
        case IDM_COLORS: MessageBox(hwnd, "Set Colors", "COLORS",
                                  MB_OK);
          break;
        case IDM_SLOW: MessageBox(hwnd, "Slow Speed", "Slow",
                                  MB_OK);
          break;
        case IDM_FAST: MessageBox(hwnd, "Fast Speed", "Fast",
                                  MB_OK);
          break;
        case IDM_SOUND: MessageBox(hwnd, "Sound Options",
                                  "Sound", MB_OK);
          break;
        case IDM_VIDEO: MessageBox(hwnd, "Video Options",
                                  "Video", MB_OK);
          break;
        case IDM_HELP: MessageBox(hwnd, "No Help", "Help", MB_OK);
          break;
      }
      break;
```

For the sake of illustration, the response to each selection simply displays an acknowledgment of that selection on the screen. Of course, in a real application, the response to menu selections will perform the specified operations.

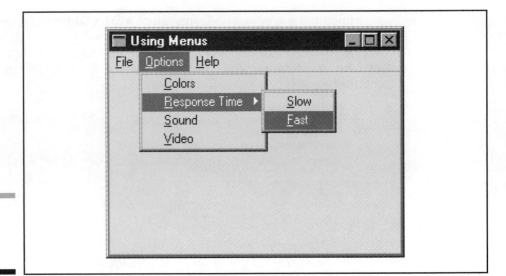

Output from
the menu
example

Figure 3-1.

A Sample Menu Program

Here is a program that demonstrates the previously defined menu. Enter it at
this time, calling it MENU.C. Sample output from the program is shown in
Figure 3-1.

```
/* Demonstrate menus. */

#include <windows.h>
#include <string.h>
#include <stdio.h>
#include "menu.h"

LRESULT CALLBACK WindowFunc(HWND, UINT, WPARAM, LPARAM);

char szWinName[] = "MyWin"; /* name of window class */

int WINAPI WinMain(HINSTANCE hThisInst, HINSTANCE hPrevInst,
                   LPSTR lpszArgs, int nWinMode)
{
  HWND hwnd;
  MSG msg;
  WNDCLASSEX wcl;

  /* Define a window class. */
  wcl.hInstance = hThisInst; /* handle to this instance */
  wcl.lpszClassName = szWinName; /* window class name */
  wcl.lpfnWndProc = WindowFunc; /* window function */
```

```
wcl.style = 0; /* default style */

wcl.cbSize = sizeof(WNDCLASSEX); /* set size of WNDCLASSEX */

wcl.hIcon = LoadIcon(NULL, IDI_APPLICATION); /* large icon */
wcl.hIconSm = LoadIcon(NULL, IDI_APPLICATION); /* small icon */

wcl.hCursor = LoadCursor(NULL, IDC_ARROW); /* cursor style */

/* specify name of menu resource */
wcl.lpszMenuName = "MYMENU"; /* main menu */

wcl.cbClsExtra = 0; /* no extra */
wcl.cbWndExtra = 0; /* information needed */

/* Make the window white. */
wcl.hbrBackground = GetStockObject(WHITE_BRUSH);

/* Register the window class. */
if(!RegisterClassEx(&wcl)) return 0;

/* Now that a window class has been registered, a window
   can be created. */
hwnd = CreateWindow(
  szWinName, /* name of window class */
  "Using Menus", /* title */
  WS_OVERLAPPEDWINDOW, /* window style - normal */
  CW_USEDEFAULT, /* X coordinate - let Windows decide */
  CW_USEDEFAULT, /* Y coordinate - let Windows decide */
  CW_USEDEFAULT, /* width - let Windows decide */
  CW_USEDEFAULT, /* height - let Windows decide */
  HWND_DESKTOP, /* no parent window */
  NULL, /* no menu */
  hThisInst, /* handle of this instance of the program */
  NULL /* no additional arguments */
);

/* Display the window. */
ShowWindow(hwnd, nWinMode);
UpdateWindow(hwnd);

/* Create the message loop. */
while(GetMessage(&msg, NULL, 0, 0))
{
  TranslateMessage(&msg); /* allow use of keyboard */
  DispatchMessage(&msg); /* return control to Windows */
}
return msg.wParam;
```

3

```
}

/* This function is called by Windows 95 and is passed
   messages from the message queue.
*/
LRESULT CALLBACK WindowFunc(HWND hwnd, UINT message,
                            WPARAM wParam, LPARAM lParam)
{
  int response;

  switch(message) {
    case WM_COMMAND:
      switch(LOWORD(wParam)) {
        case IDM_OPEN: MessageBox(hwnd, "Open File", "Open",
                                  MB_OK);
          break;
        case IDM_CLOSE: MessageBox(hwnd, "Close File", "Close",
                                   MB_OK);
          break;
        case IDM_EXIT:
          response = MessageBox(hwnd, "Quit the Program?",
                                "Exit", MB_YESNO);
          if(response == IDYES) PostQuitMessage(0);
          break;
        case IDM_COLORS: MessageBox(hwnd, "Set Colors", "COLORS",
                                    MB_OK);
          break;
        case IDM_SLOW: MessageBox(hwnd, "Slow Speed", "Slow",
                                  MB_OK);
          break;
        case IDM_FAST: MessageBox(hwnd, "Fast Speed", "Fast",
                                  MB_OK);
          break;
        case IDM_SOUND: MessageBox(hwnd, "Sound Options",
                                   "Sound", MB_OK);
          break;
        case IDM_VIDEO: MessageBox(hwnd, "Video Options",
                                   "Video", MB_OK);
          break;
        case IDM_HELP: MessageBox(hwnd, "No Help", "Help", MB_OK);
          break;
      }
      break;
    case WM_DESTROY: /* terminate the program */
      PostQuitMessage(0);
      break;
    default:
      /* Let Windows 95 process any messages not specified in
```

```
      the preceding switch statement. */
    return DefWindowProc(hwnd, message, wParam, lParam);
  }
  return 0;
}
```

Using MessageBox( ) Responses

In the sample menu program, when the user selects Exit, the following code sequence is executed.

```
case IDM_EXIT:
  response = MessageBox(hwnd, "Quit the Program?",
                        "Exit", MB_YESNO);
  if(response == IDYES) PostQuitMessage(0);
  break;
```

The message box displayed by this fragment is shown here:

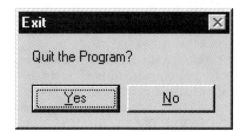

As you can see, the box contains two buttons: Yes and No. As discussed in Chapter 2, a message box will return the user's response. In this case, it means that **MessageBox( )** will return either **IDYES** or **IDNO**. If the user's response is **IDYES**, then the program terminates. Otherwise, it continues execution.

This is an example of using a message box to allow the user to select between two actions. As you begin to write your Windows 95 programs, keep in mind that the message box is useful whenever the user must choose among a few options.

3

Adding Menu Accelerator Keys

There is a one feature of Windows that is commonly used in conjunction with a menu. This feature is the accelerator key. *Accelerator keys* are special keystrokes that you define which, when pressed, automatically select a menu option, even though the menu in which that option resides is not displayed. Put differently, you can select an item directly by pressing an accelerator key, bypassing the menu entirely. The term *accelerator keys* is an accurate description because it is generally faster to press one to select a menu item than to first activate its menu and then select the item.

To define accelerator keys relative to a menu, you must add an accelerator key table to your resource file. All accelerator table definitions have this general form:

```
TableName ACCELERATORS
{
  Key1, MenuID1 [,type] [option]
  Key2, MenuID2 [,type] [option]
  Key3, MenuID3 [,type] [option]
    .
    .
    .
  Keyn, MenuIDn [,type] [option]
}
```

Here, *TableName* is the name of the accelerator table. *Key* is the keystroke that selects the item, and *MenuID* is the ID value associated with the desired item. The *type* specifies whether the key is a standard key (the default) or a virtual key (discussed shortly). The options can be one of the following macros: **NOINVERT**, **ALT**, **SHIFT**, and **CONTROL**. **NOINVERT** prevents the selected menu item from being highlighted when its accelerator key is pressed. **ALT** specifies an ALT key. **SHIFT** specifies a SHIFT key. **CONTROL** specifies a CTRL key.

The value of *Key* will be either a quoted character, an ASCII integer value corresponding to a key, or a virtual key code. If a quoted character is used, then it is assumed to be an ASCII character. If it is an integer value, then you must tell the resource compiler explicitly that this is an ASCII character by specifying *type* as **ASCII**. If it is a virtual key, then *type* must be **VIRTKEY**.

If the key is an uppercase quoted character, then its corresponding menu item will be selected if it is pressed while SHIFT is held down. If it is a lowercase character, then its menu item will be selected if the key is pressed by itself. If the key is specified as a lowercase character and **ALT** is specified as an option, then pressing ALT and the character will select the item. (If the key is uppercase and **ALT** is specified, then you must press SHIFT and ALT to select the item.) Finally, if you want the user to press CTRL and the character to select an item, precede the key with a ^.

A *virtual key* is a system-independent code for a variety of keys. Virtual keys include the function keys F1 through F12, the arrow keys, and various non-ASCII keys. They are defined by macros in the header file WINDOWS.H (or one of its derivatives). All virtual key macros begin with **VK_**. The function keys are **VK_F1** through **VK_F12**, for example. You should refer to WINDOWS.H for the other virtual key code macros. To use a virtual key as an accelerator, simply specify its macro for the *Key* and specify **VIRTKEY** for its *type*. You can also specify **ALT**, **SHIFT**, or **CONTROL** to achieve the desired key combination.

Here are some examples:

```
"A", IDM_x              ; select by pressing Shift-A
"a", IDM_x              ; select by pressing a
"^A", IDM_x             ; select by pressing Ctrl-A
"a", IDM_x, ALT         ; select by pressing Alt-a
VK_F2, IDM_x            ; select by pressing F2
VK_F2, IDM_x, SHIFT     ; select by pressing Shift-F2
```

Here is the MENU.RC resource file that also contains accelerator key definitions for the menu specified in the previous section.

```
; Sample menu resource file
#include <windows.h>
#include "menu.h"

MYMENU MENU
{
  POPUP "&File"
  {
    MENUITEM "&Open\tF2", IDM_OPEN
    MENUITEM "&Close\tF3", IDM_CLOSE
    MENUITEM "&Exit\tCtrl-X", IDM_EXIT
  }
  POPUP "&Options"
  {
    MENUITEM "&Colors\tCtrl-C", IDM_COLORS
    POPUP "&Response Time"
    {
      MENUITEM "&Slow\tF4", IDM_SLOW
      MENUITEM "&Fast\tCtrl-F4", IDM_FAST
    }
    MENUITEM "&Sound\tCtrl-S", IDM_SOUND
```

```
      MENUITEM "&Video\tCtrl-V", IDM_VIDEO
    }
    MENUITEM "&Help", IDM_HELP
  }

  ; Define menu accelerators
  MYMENU ACCELERATORS
  {
    VK_F2, IDM_OPEN, VIRTKEY
    VK_F3, IDM_CLOSE, VIRTKEY
    "^X", IDM_EXIT
    "^C", IDM_COLORS
    VK_F4, IDM_FAST, VIRTKEY, CONTROL
    VK_F4, IDM_SLOW, VIRTKEY
    "^S", IDM_SOUND
    "^V", IDM_VIDEO
    VK_F1, IDM_HELP, VIRTKEY
  }
```

Notice that the menu definition has been enhanced to display which accelerator key selects which option. Each item is separated from its accelerator key by use of a tab. The header file WINDOWS.H is included because it defines the virtual key macros.

Loading the Accelerator Table

Even though the accelerators are contained in the same resource file as the menu, they must be loaded separately by use of another API function called **LoadAccelerators( ).** It has the following prototype:

HACCEL LoadAccelerators(HINSTANCE *ThisInst*, LPCSTR *Name*);

Here, *ThisInst* is the handle of the application and *Name* is the name of the accelerator table. The function returns a handle to the accelerator table or **NULL** if the table cannot be loaded.

You must call **LoadAccelerators( )** soon after the window is created. For example, this shows how to load the **MYMENU** accelerator table:

```
HACCEL hAccel;

hAccel = LoadAccelerators(hThisInst, "MYMENU");
```

The value of **hAccel** will be used later to help process accelerator keys.

Although the **LoadAccelerators( )** function loads the accelerator table, your program still cannot process them until you add another API function to the message loop. This function is called **TranslateAccelerator( )**, and it has the following prototype:

int TranslateAccelerator(HWND *hwnd*, HACCEL *hAccel*, LPMSG *lpMess*);

Here, *hwnd* is the handle of the window for which accelerator keys will be translated. *hAccel* is the handle to the accelerator table that will be used. This is the handle returned by **LoadAccelerator( )**. Finally, *lpMess* is a pointer to the message. The **TranslateAccelerator( )** function returns true if an accelerator key was pressed and false otherwise. It translates accelerator keystrokes into the proper **WM_COMMAND** message and sends that message to the window.

When you use **TranslateAccelerator( )**, your message loop should look like this:

3

```
while(GetMessage(&msg, NULL, 0, 0))
{
  if(!TranslateAccelerator(hwnd, hAccel, &msg)) {
    TranslateMessage(&msg); /* allow use of keyboard */
    DispatchMessage(&msg); /* return control to Windows */
  }
}
```

To try using accelerators, substitute the following version of **WinMain( )** into the preceding application and add the accelerator table to your resource file.

```
/* Process accelerator keys. */

#include <windows.h>
#include <string.h>
#include <stdio.h>
#include "menu.h"

LRESULT CALLBACK WindowFunc(HWND, UINT, WPARAM, LPARAM);

char szWinName[] = "MyWin"; /* name of window class */

int WINAPI WinMain(HINSTANCE hThisInst, HINSTANCE hPrevInst,
                   LPSTR lpszArgs, int nWinMode)
{
  HWND hwnd;
  MSG msg;
  WNDCLASSEX wcl;
  HACCEL hAccel;
```

```
/* Define a window class. */
wcl.hInstance = hThisInst; /* handle to this instance */
wcl.lpszClassName = szWinName; /* window class name */
wcl.lpfnWndProc = WindowFunc; /* window function */
wcl.style = 0; /* default style */

wcl.cbSize = sizeof(WNDCLASSEX); /* set size of WNDCLASSEX */

wcl.hIcon = LoadIcon(NULL, IDI_APPLICATION); /* large icon */
wcl.hIconSm = LoadIcon(NULL, IDI_APPLICATION); /* small icon */

wcl.hCursor = LoadCursor(NULL, IDC_ARROW); /* cursor style */

/* specify name of menu resource */
wcl.lpszMenuName = "MYMENU"; /* main menu */

wcl.cbClsExtra = 0; /* no extra */
wcl.cbWndExtra = 0; /* information needed */

/* Make the window white. */
wcl.hbrBackground = GetStockObject(WHITE_BRUSH);

/* Register the window class. */
if(!RegisterClassEx(&wcl)) return 0;

/* Now that a window class has been registered, a window
   can be created. */
hwnd = CreateWindow(
  szWinName, /* name of window class */
  "Using Menus", /* title */
  WS_OVERLAPPEDWINDOW, /* window style - normal */
  CW_USEDEFAULT, /* X coordinate - let Windows decide */
  CW_USEDEFAULT, /* Y coordinate - let Windows decide */
  CW_USEDEFAULT, /* width - let Windows decide */
  CW_USEDEFAULT, /* height - let Windows decide */
  HWND_DESKTOP, /* no parent window */
  NULL, /* no menu */
  hThisInst, /* handle of this instance of the program */
  NULL /* no additional arguments */
);

/* load the keyboard accelerators */
hAccel = LoadAccelerators(hThisInst, "MYMENU");

/* Display the window. */
ShowWindow(hwnd, nWinMode);
UpdateWindow(hwnd);
```

```
/* Create the message loop. */
while(GetMessage(&msg, NULL, 0, 0))
{
  if(!TranslateAccelerator(hwnd, hAccel, &msg)) {
    TranslateMessage(&msg); /* allow use of keyboard */
    DispatchMessage(&msg); /* return control to Windows */
  }
}
return msg.wParam;
}
```

Creating a Hot Key

3

Although keyboard accelerators are most commonly used to provide a fast means of selecting menu items, they are not limited to this role. For example, you can define an accelerator key for which there is no corresponding menu item. This type of accelerator is sometimes called a *hot key*. A hot key is used to directly activate a feature. For example, you might use a hot key to activate a keyboard macro, to initiate some frequently used option, or to act as an "emergency stop" signal. To define a nonmenu accelerator key, simply add it to the accelerator table, assigning it a unique ID value.

As an example, let's add a hot key to the sample menu program. The hot key will be CTRL-T, and each time it is pressed, the current time and date are displayed in a message box. To begin, change the key table so that it looks like this:

```
MYMENU ACCELERATORS
{
  VK_F2, IDM_OPEN, VIRTKEY
  VK_F3, IDM_CLOSE, VIRTKEY
  "^X", IDM_EXIT
  "^C", IDM_COLORS
  VK_F4, IDM_FAST, VIRTKEY, CONTROL
  VK_F4, IDM_SLOW, VIRTKEY
  "^S", IDM_SOUND
  "^V", IDM_VIDEO
  VK_F1, IDM_HELP, VIRTKEY
  "^T", IDM_TIME
}
```

Next, add the following line to MENU.H.

```
#define IDM_TIME  500
```

Finally, substitute the following version of **WindowFunc( )** into the menu program. You will also need to include the TIME.H header file.

```
LRESULT CALLBACK WindowFunc(HWND hwnd, UINT message,
                           WPARAM wParam, LPARAM lParam)
{
  int response;
  struct tm *tod;
  time_t t;
  char str[80];

  switch(message) {
    case WM_COMMAND:
      switch(LOWORD(wParam)) {
        case IDM_OPEN: MessageBox(hwnd, "Open File", "Open",
                                  MB_OK);
          break;
        case IDM_CLOSE: MessageBox(hwnd, "Close File", "Close",
                                   MB_OK);
          break;
        case IDM_EXIT:
          response = MessageBox(hwnd, "Quit the Program?",
                                "Exit", MB_YESNO);
          if(response == IDYES) PostQuitMessage(0);
          break;
        case IDM_COLORS: MessageBox(hwnd, "Set Colors",
                                    "COLORS", MB_OK);
          break;
        case IDM_SLOW: MessageBox(hwnd, "Slow Speed", "Slow",
                                  MB_OK);
          break;
        case IDM_FAST: MessageBox(hwnd, "Fast Speed", "Fast",
                                  MB_OK);
          break;
        case IDM_SOUND: MessageBox(hwnd, "Sound Options",
                                   "Sound", MB_OK);
          break;
        case IDM_VIDEO: MessageBox(hwnd, "Video Options",
                                   "Video", MB_OK);
          break;
```

```
                    case IDM_TIME: /* process a hot key */
                      t = time(NULL);
                      tod = localtime(&t);
                      strcpy(str, asctime(tod));
                      str[strlen(str)-1] = '\0'; /* remove /r/n */
                      MessageBox(hwnd, str, "Time and Date", MB_OK);
                      break;
                    case IDM_HELP: MessageBox(hwnd, "No Help", "Help",
                                              MB_OK);
                      break;
                  }
                  break;
                case WM_DESTROY: /* terminate the program */
                  PostQuitMessage(0);
                  break;
                default:
                  /* Let Windows 95 process any messages not specified in
                     the preceding switch statement. */
                  return DefWindowProc(hwnd, message, wParam, lParam);
              }
              return 0;
            }
```

When you run this program, each time you press CTRL-T, you will see a
message box similar to the following:

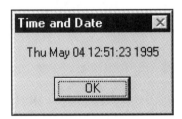

Dynamically Managing a Menu

Although most simple Windows 95 applications fully define their menus in
their resource file, more sophisticated applications frequently need to add or
delete menu items dynamically, during run time, in response to changing
program conditions. For example, an accounting program may add a Purge

option to its File menu when year-end reports are generated. Or, a computer-aided design program might add or delete certain drawing tools depending upon what type of object is being designed. Whatever the reason, it is easy to add or delete menu items during the execution of a program.

Windows 95 includes several menu-management API functions that allow you to manipulate the contents of menus during the execution of your program. The ones used in this chapter are **AppendMenu( )**, **EnableMenuItem( )**, **DeleteMenu( )**, **GetMenu( )**, and **GetSubMenu( )**. These functions are described next.

Adding an Item to a Menu

To add an item to a menu, use **AppendMenu( )**, shown here:

        BOOL AppendMenu(HMENU *hMenu*, UINT *flags*,
                        UINT *ItemID*, LPCSTR *lpContent*);

AppendMenu( ) adds an item to the menu whose handle is specified by *hMenu*. The ID value associated with the new item is passed in *ItemID*. The description of the new item that will be displayed in the menu is pointed to by *lpContent*. The value of *flags* specifies various attributes associated with the new menu item. It can be one or more of the values shown in Table 3-3. **AppendMenu( )** returns nonzero if successful and zero on failure.

Deleting a Menu Item

To remove a menu item, use the **DeleteMenu( )** function, which has this prototype:

        BOOL DeleteMenu(HMENU *hMenu*, UINT *ItemID*, UINT *How*);

Here, *hMenu* specifies the handle of the menu to be affected. The item to be removed is specified in *ItemID*. The value of *How* determines how *ItemID* is interpreted. If *How* is **MF_BYPOSITION**, then the value in *ItemID* must be the index of the item to be deleted. This index is the position of the item within the menu, with the first menu item being zero. If *How* is **MF_BYCOMMAND**, then *ItemID* is the command ID associated with the menu item. **DeleteMenu( )** returns nonzero if successful and zero on failure.

Obtaining a Handle to a Menu

As you have just seen, to add or delete a menu item requires a handle to the menu. To obtain the handle of the main menu, use **GetMenu( )**, shown here:

HMENU GetMenu(HWND *hwnd*);

GetMenu( ) returns the handle of the menu associated with the window specified by *hwnd*. It returns **NULL** on failure.

Given a handle to a window's main menu, you can easily obtain the handles of the pop-up submenus contained in the main menu by using **GetSubMenu( )**. It has this prototype:

HMENU GetSubMenu(HMENU *hMenu*, int *ItemPos*);

Here, *hMenu* is the handle of the parent menu, and *ItemPos* is the position of the desired pop-up menu within the parent window. (The first position is zero.) The function returns the handle of the specified pop-up menu or **NULL** on failure.

Value	Meaning
MF_BITMAP	*lpContent* specifies a bitmap handle.
MF_CHECKED	Checks the new menu item.
MF_DISABLED	Disables the new menu item.
MF_ENABLED	Enables the new menu item.
MF_GRAYED	Disables the menu item and turns it gray.
MF_MENUBARBREAK	For menu bar, causes the item to be put on a new line. For pop-up menus, causes the item to be put in a different column. In this case, the item is separated by a bar.
MF_MENUBREAK	Same as MF_MENUBARBREAK, except that no separator bar is used.
MF_OWNERDRAW	Owner-drawn item.
MF_POPUP	New item is a pop-up menu. In this case, *ItemID* must contain a handle to a pop-up menu.
MF_SEPARATOR	Places a horizontal dividing line between menu items. The values in *ItemID* and *lpContent* are ignored.
MF_STRING	*lpContent* is a pointer to a string that describes the menu item. (This is the default if neither MF_BITMAP nor MF_OWNERDRAW is specified.)
MF_UNCHECKED	Does not check the new menu item.

Valid Values
for the *flags*
Parameter of
AppendMenu( )
Table 3-3.

Obtaining the Size of a Menu

Frequently, when working with menus dynamically, you will need to know how many items are in a menu. To obtain the number of menu items, use **GetMenuItemCount( )**, which has this prototype:

    int GetMenuItemCount(HMENU *hMenu*);

Here, *hMenu* is the handle of the menu in question. The function returns the number of items in the menu, or –1 on failure.

Enabling and Disabling a Menu Item

Sometimes a menu item will only apply to certain situations, not to others. In such cases, you may wish to temporarily disable an item and enable it later. To accomplish this, use the **EnableMenuItem( )** function, shown here:

    BOOL EnableMenuItem(HMENU *hMenu*, UINT *ItemID*, UINT *How*);

The handle of the menu is passed in *hMenu*. The item to be enabled or disabled is specified in *ItemID*. The value of *How* determines two things. First, it specifies how *ItemID* is interpreted. If *How* contains **MF_BYPOSITION**, then the value in *ItemID* must be the index of the item to be deleted. This index is the position of the item within the menu, with the first menu item being zero. If *How* contains **MF_BYCOMMAND**, then *ItemID* is the command ID associated with the menu item. The value in *How* also determines whether the item will be enabled or disabled, based upon the following values.

MF_DISABLED	Disables the menu item
MF_ENABLED	Enables the menu item
MF_GRAYED	Disables the menu item and turns it gray

To construct the desired value of *How*, OR together the appropriate values. **EnableMenuItem( )** returns the previous state of the item, or –1 on failure.

Demonstrating Dynamic Menu Management

The following program demonstrates how an item can be added to or deleted from a menu. In the process it utilizes the menu management functions just described. This program allows a new menu option to be added to or deleted from the File menu of the previous example. Pay special attention to the **IDM_ADDITEM** and **IDM_DELITEM** cases inside **WindowFunc( )**. This is the code that adds or deletes a menu item:

```
/* Dynamically managing menus. */

#include <windows.h>
#include <string.h>
#include <stdio.h>
#include "menu.h"

LRESULT CALLBACK WindowFunc(HWND, UINT, WPARAM, LPARAM);

char szWinName[] = "MyWin"; /* name of window class */

int WINAPI WinMain(HINSTANCE hThisInst, HINSTANCE hPrevInst,
                   LPSTR lpszArgs, int nWinMode)
{
  HWND hwnd;
  MSG msg;
  WNDCLASSEX wcl;
  HACCEL hAccel;

  /* Define a window class. */
  wcl.hInstance = hThisInst; /* handle to this instance */
  wcl.lpszClassName = szWinName; /* window class name */
  wcl.lpfnWndProc = WindowFunc; /* window function */
  wcl.style = 0; /* default style */

  wcl.cbSize = sizeof(WNDCLASSEX); /* set size of WNDCLASSEX */

  wcl.hIcon = LoadIcon(NULL, IDI_APPLICATION); /* large icon */
  wcl.hIconSm = LoadIcon(NULL, IDI_APPLICATION); /* small icon */

  wcl.hCursor = LoadCursor(NULL, IDC_ARROW); /* cursor style */

  /* specify name of menu resource */
  wcl.lpszMenuName = "MYMENU"; /* main menu */

  wcl.cbClsExtra = 0; /* no extra */
  wcl.cbWndExtra = 0; /* information needed */

  /* Make the window white. */
  wcl.hbrBackground = GetStockObject(WHITE_BRUSH);

  /* Register the window class. */
  if(!RegisterClassEx(&wcl)) return 0;

  /* Now that a window class has been registered, a window
     can be created. */
  hwnd = CreateWindow(
    szWinName, /* name of window class */
```

```
    "Dynamically Managing Menus", /* title */
    WS_OVERLAPPEDWINDOW, /* window style - normal */
    CW_USEDEFAULT, /* X coordinate - let Windows decide */
    CW_USEDEFAULT, /* Y coordinate - let Windows decide */
    CW_USEDEFAULT, /* width - let Windows decide */
    CW_USEDEFAULT, /* height - let Windows decide */
    HWND_DESKTOP, /* no parent window */
    NULL, /* no menu */
    hThisInst, /* handle of this instance of the program */
    NULL /* no additional arguments */
  );

  /* load the keyboard accelerators */
  hAccel = LoadAccelerators(hThisInst, "MYMENU");

  /* Display the window. */
  ShowWindow(hwnd, nWinMode);
  UpdateWindow(hwnd);

  /* Create the message loop. */
  while(GetMessage(&msg, NULL, 0, 0))
  {
    if(!TranslateAccelerator(hwnd, hAccel, &msg)) {
      TranslateMessage(&msg); /* allow use of keyboard */
      DispatchMessage(&msg); /* return control to Windows */
    }
  }
  return msg.wParam;
}

/* This function is called by Windows 95 and is passed
   messages from the message queue.
*/
LRESULT CALLBACK WindowFunc(HWND hwnd, UINT message,
                            WPARAM wParam, LPARAM lParam)
{
  int response;
  HMENU hmenu, hsubmenu;
  int count;

  switch(message) {
    case WM_COMMAND:
      switch(LOWORD(wParam)) {
        case IDM_OPEN: MessageBox(hwnd, "Open File", "Open",
                                  MB_OK);
          break;
        case IDM_CLOSE: MessageBox(hwnd, "Close File", "Close",
                                   MB_OK);
```

```
    break;
case IDM_ADDITEM: /* dynamically add menu item */
  /* get handle of main menu */
  hmenu = GetMenu(hwnd);

  /* get handle of 1st popup menu */
  hsubmenu = GetSubMenu(hmenu, 0);

  /* append a separator and a new menu item */
  AppendMenu(hsubmenu, MF_SEPARATOR, 0, "");
  AppendMenu(hsubmenu, MF_ENABLED, IDM_NEW, "&New Item");

  /* deactivate the Add Item option */
  EnableMenuItem(hsubmenu, IDM_ADDITEM,
              MF_BYCOMMAND | MF_GRAYED);

  /* activate the Delete Item option */
  EnableMenuItem(hsubmenu, IDM_DELITEM,
              MF_BYCOMMAND | MF_ENABLED);
  break;
case IDM_DELITEM: /* dynamically delete menu item */
  /* get handle of main menu */
  hmenu = GetMenu(hwnd);

  /* get handle of 1st popup menu */
  hsubmenu = GetSubMenu(hmenu, 0);

  /* delete the new item and the separator */
  count = GetMenuItemCount(hsubmenu);
  DeleteMenu(hsubmenu, count-1, MF_BYPOSITION |
          MF_GRAYED);
  DeleteMenu(hsubmenu, count-2, MF_BYPOSITION |
          MF_GRAYED);

  /* reactivate the Add Item option */
  EnableMenuItem(hsubmenu, IDM_ADDITEM,
              MF_BYCOMMAND | MF_ENABLED);

  /* deactivate the Delete Item option */
  EnableMenuItem(hsubmenu, IDM_DELITEM,
              MF_BYCOMMAND | MF_GRAYED);
  break;
case IDM_EXIT:
  response = MessageBox(hwnd, "Quit the Program?",
                    "Exit", MB_YESNO);
  if(response == IDYES) PostQuitMessage(0);
  break;
case IDM_NEW: MessageBox(hwnd, "New Item", "New Item",
```

3

```
                                      MB_OK);
        break;
      case IDM_COLORS: MessageBox(hwnd, "Set Colors", "COLORS",
                                  MB_OK);
        break;
      case IDM_SLOW: MessageBox(hwnd, "Slow Speed", "Slow",
                                MB_OK);
        break;
      case IDM_FAST: MessageBox(hwnd, "Fast Speed", "Fast",
                                MB_OK);
        break;
      case IDM_SOUND: MessageBox(hwnd, "Sound Options",
                                 "Sound", MB_OK);
        break;
      case IDM_VIDEO: MessageBox(hwnd, "Video Options",
                                 "Video", MB_OK);
        break;
      case IDM_HELP: MessageBox(hwnd, "No Help", "Help", MB_OK);
        break;
    }
    break;
  case WM_DESTROY: /* terminate the program */
    PostQuitMessage(0);
    break;
  default:
    /* Let Windows 95 process any messages not specified in
       the preceding switch statement. */
    return DefWindowProc(hwnd, message, wParam, lParam);
  }
  return 0;
}
```

The resource file required by the program is shown here:

```
; Sample menu resource file
#include <windows.h>
#include "menu.h"

MYMENU MENU
{
  POPUP "&File"
  {
    MENUITEM "&Open\tF2", IDM_OPEN
    MENUITEM "&Close\tF3", IDM_CLOSE
    MENUITEM "&Add Item\tCtrl-A", IDM_ADDITEM
    MENUITEM "&Delete Item\tCtrl-D", IDM_DELITEM, GRAYED
    MENUITEM "&Exit\tCtrl-X", IDM_EXIT
  }
```

```
  POPUP "&Options"
  {
    MENUITEM "&Colors\tCtrl-C", IDM_COLORS
    POPUP "&Response Time"
    {
      MENUITEM "&Slow\tF4", IDM_SLOW
      MENUITEM "&Fast\tCtrl-F4", IDM_FAST
    }
    MENUITEM "&Sound\tCtrl-S", IDM_SOUND
    MENUITEM "&Video Ctrl-V", IDM_VIDEO
  }
  MENUITEM "&Help", IDM_HELP
}

; Define menu accelerators
MYMENU ACCELERATORS
{
  VK_F2, IDM_OPEN, VIRTKEY
  VK_F3, IDM_CLOSE, VIRTKEY
  "^A", IDM_ADDITEM
  "^D", IDM_DELITEM
  "^X", IDM_EXIT
  "^C", IDM_COLORS
  VK_F4, IDM_FAST, VIRTKEY, CONTROL
  VK_F4, IDM_SLOW, VIRTKEY
  "^S", IDM_SOUND
  "^V", IDM_VIDEO
  VK_F1, IDM_HELP, VIRTKEY
}
```

3

As you can see, the File menu now contains two new options: Add Item and Delete Item. These options are used to dynamically add or delete a menu item.

The modified MENU.H header file is shown here:

```
#define IDM_OPEN      100
#define IDM_CLOSE     101
#define IDM_EXIT      102
#define IDM_COLORS    103
#define IDM_SLOW      104
#define IDM_FAST      105
#define IDM_SOUND     106
#define IDM_VIDEO     107
#define IDM_HELP      108

#define IDM_ADDITEM   200
#define IDM_DELITEM   201

#define IDM_NEW       300
```

Sample output from this program is shown in Figure 3-2. Initially, Delete Item is grayed and, therefore, cannot be selected. After the new item has been dynamically added to the menu, the Delete Item option is activated and the Add Item option is grayed. When Delete Item is selected, the new item is deleted, Add Item is reactivated, and Delete Item is once again grayed. This procedure prevents the new menu item from being added or deleted more than once.

Creating Dynamic Menus

In addition to adding new items to an existing menu, you can dynamically create an entire pop-up menu. (That is, you can create a pop-up menu at run time.) Once you have created the menu, it can then be added to an existing menu. To dynamically create a pop-up menu, you first need to create one by using the API function **CreatePopupMenu( )**, shown here:

HMENU CreatePopupMenu(void);

This function creates an empty menu and returns a handle to it. After you have created a menu, you add items to it by using **AppendMenu( )**. Once the menu is fully constructed, you can add it to an existing menu, also by using **AppendMenu( )**.

Menus created by use of **CreatePopupMenu( )** must be destroyed. If the menu is attached to a window, then it will be destroyed automatically when the window is destroyed. A menu is also automatically destroyed when it is

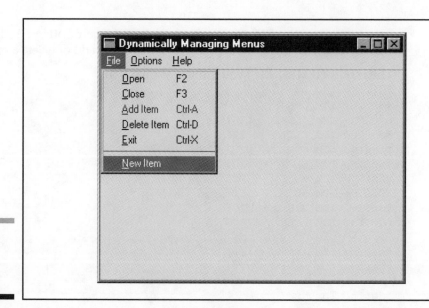

Adding
menu items
dynamically

Figure 3-2.

removed from a parent menu by a call to **DeleteMenu( )**. Dynamic menus can be destroyed explicitly by a call to **DestroyMenu( )**.

More Menu-Management Functions

Because menus are the most fundamental element of its user interface, Windows 95 supplies a rich set of functions that manage them. In addition to the menu-management functions described in this chapter, the API contains several more. While it is not possible to discuss these functions in detail, the following table briefly describes each.

Function	Description
CheckMenuItem( )	Checks or unchecks a menu item.
CreateMenu( )	Creates a menu.
DestroyMenu( )	Destroys a menu.
DrawMenuBar( )	Redraws the menu bar.
GetMenuCheckMark-Dimensions( )	Obtains the dimensions of the check mark.
GetMenuItemID( )	Obtains the ID of the specified menu item.
GetMenuState( )	Obtains the state of a menu item.
GetMenuString( )	Obtains the description of a menu item.
GetSystemMenu( )	Returns the handle of a copy of the system menu.
HiliteMenuItem( )	Highlights a menu item.
InsertMenu( )	Inserts an item into the menu.
LoadMenu( )	Loads a menu resource.
LoadMenuIndirect( )	Loads a menu template.
ModifyMenu( )	Changes a menu item.
RemoveMenu( )	Removes a menu item. (If the item is a pop-up menu, it is not destroyed.)
SetMenu( )	Changes the main menu associated with a window.
SetMenuItemBitmaps( )	Links a bitmap with a menu item.
TrackPopupMenu( )	Activates a floating pop-up menu.

As you experiment with these menu-management functions, you will find that they give you precise and detailed control over the menus used by your application.

3

The following **WindowFunc( )** dynamically creates a pop-up menu. To see its effect, substitute it into the preceding program.

```c
/* This function is called by Windows 95 and is passed
   messages from the message queue.
*/
LRESULT CALLBACK WindowFunc(HWND hwnd, UINT message,
                           WPARAM wParam, LPARAM lParam)
{
  int response;
  HMENU hmenu, hsubmenu;
  static HMENU hpopup;
  int count;

  switch(message) {
    case WM_COMMAND:
      switch(LOWORD(wParam)) {
        case IDM_OPEN: MessageBox(hwnd, "Open File", "Open",
                                  MB_OK);
          break;
        case IDM_CLOSE: MessageBox(hwnd, "Close File", "Close",
                                   MB_OK);
          break;
        case IDM_ADDITEM: /* dynamically add menu */
          /* get handle of main menu */
          hmenu = GetMenu(hwnd);

          /* get handle of 1st popup menu */
          hsubmenu = GetSubMenu(hmenu, 0);

          /* create new popup menu */
          hpopup = CreatePopupMenu();

          /* add items to dynamic popup menu */
          AppendMenu(hpopup, MF_ENABLED, IDM_NEW,
                     "&First New Item");
          AppendMenu(hpopup, MF_ENABLED, IDM_NEW,
                     "&Second New Item");

          /* add new menu to File menu */
          AppendMenu(hsubmenu, MF_SEPARATOR, 0, "");
          AppendMenu(hsubmenu, MF_POPUP, (UINT) hpopup, "&New
                     Popup");

          /* deactivate the Add Menu option */
          EnableMenuItem(hsubmenu, IDM_ADDITEM,
                         MF_BYCOMMAND | MF_GRAYED);
```

```
  /* activate the Delete Menu option */
  EnableMenuItem(hsubmenu, IDM_DELITEM,
                 MF_BYCOMMAND | MF_ENABLED);
  break;
case IDM_DELITEM: /* dynamically delete menu */
  /* get handle of main menu */
  hmenu = GetMenu(hwnd);

  /* get handle of 1st popup menu */
  hsubmenu = GetSubMenu(hmenu, 0);

  /* delete the new menu and the separator */
  count = GetMenuItemCount(hsubmenu);
  DeleteMenu(hsubmenu, count-1, MF_BYPOSITION |
             MF_GRAYED);
  DeleteMenu(hsubmenu, count-2, MF_BYPOSITION |
             MF_GRAYED);

  /* reactivate the Add Menu option */
  EnableMenuItem(hsubmenu, IDM_ADDITEM,
                 MF_BYCOMMAND | MF_ENABLED);

  /* deactivate the Delete Menu option */
  EnableMenuItem(hsubmenu, IDM_DELITEM,
                 MF_BYCOMMAND | MF_GRAYED);
  break;
case IDM_EXIT:
  response = MessageBox(hwnd, "Quit the Program?",
                        "Exit", MB_YESNO);
  if(response == IDYES) PostQuitMessage(0);
  break;
case IDM_NEW: MessageBox(hwnd, "New Item", "New Item",
                         MB_OK);
  break;
case IDM_COLORS: MessageBox(hwnd, "Set Colors", "COLORS",
                            MB_OK);
  break;
case IDM_SLOW: MessageBox(hwnd, "Slow Speed", "Slow",
                          MB_OK);
  break;
case IDM_FAST: MessageBox(hwnd, "Fast Speed", "Fast",
                          MB_OK);
  break;
case IDM_SOUND: MessageBox(hwnd, "Sound Options",
                           "Sound", MB_OK);
  break;
case IDM_VIDEO: MessageBox(hwnd, "Video Options",
                           "Video", MB_OK);
```

3

```
        break;
      case IDM_HELP: MessageBox(hwnd, "No Help", "Help", MB_OK);
        break;
    }
    break;
  case WM_DESTROY: /* terminate the program */
    PostQuitMessage(0);
    break;
  default:
    /* Let Windows 95 process any messages not specified in
       the preceding switch statement. */
    return DefWindowProc(hwnd, message, wParam, lParam);
  }
  return 0;
}
```

This program uses the same MENU.H as the preceding program, but requires the following resource file:

```
; Sample menu resource file
#include <windows.h>
#include "menu1.h"

MYMENU MENU
{
  POPUP "&File"
  {
    MENUITEM "&Open\tF2", IDM_OPEN
    MENUITEM "&Close\tF3", IDM_CLOSE
    MENUITEM "&Add Menu\tCtrl-A", IDM_ADDITEM
    MENUITEM "&Delete Menu\tCtrl-D", IDM_DELITEM, GRAYED
    MENUITEM "&Exit\tCtrl-X", IDM_EXIT
  }
  POPUP "&Options"
  {
    MENUITEM "&Colors\tCtrl-C", IDM_COLORS
    POPUP "&Response Time"
    {
      MENUITEM "&Slow\tF4", IDM_SLOW
      MENUITEM "&Fast\tCtrl-F4", IDM_FAST
    }
    MENUITEM "&Sound\tCtrl-S", IDM_SOUND
    MENUITEM "&Video Ctrl-V", IDM_VIDEO
  }
  MENUITEM "&Help", IDM_HELP
}

; Define menu accelerators
```

```
MYMENU ACCELERATORS
{
  VK_F2, IDM_OPEN, VIRTKEY
  VK_F3, IDM_CLOSE, VIRTKEY
  "^A", IDM_ADDITEM
  "^D", IDM_DELITEM
  "^X", IDM_EXIT
  "^C", IDM_COLORS
  VK_F4, IDM_FAST, VIRTKEY, CONTROL
  VK_F4, IDM_SLOW, VIRTKEY
  "^S", IDM_SOUND
  "^V", IDM_VIDEO
  VK_F1, IDM_HELP, VIRTKEY
}
```

Sample output from this program is shown in Figure 3-3.

One final thought: Since menus are the gateway to your application, their design and implementation deserve significant care and attention to detail. A well-thought-out set of menus will make your program easier to use and more appealing.

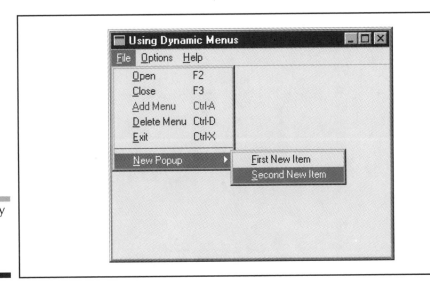

A dynamically created pop-up menu

Figure 3-3.

CHAPTER 4

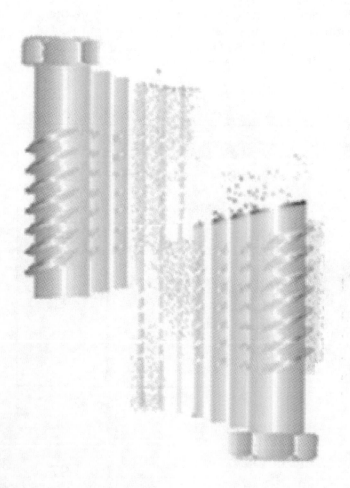

Dialog Boxes

Although menus are an important part of nearly every Windows 95 application, they cannot be used to handle all types of user responses. For example, it would be difficult to use a menu to input the time or date. To handle all types of input, Windows provides the *dialog box*. A dialog box is a special type of window that provides a flexible means by which the user can interact with your application. In general, dialog boxes allow the user to select or enter information that would be difficult or impossible to enter by using a menu. In this chapter, you will learn how to create and manage a dialog box.

Also discussed in this chapter are three of Windows's standard controls. Within a dialog box, interaction with the user is performed through a control. In a sense, a dialog box is simply a container that holds various control elements.

As a means of illustrating the dialog box and several of its control elements, a very simple database application will be developed. The database contains a list of several American cities along with their population, state, and time zone. The dialog box created in this chapter will allow you to select a city and obtain its information. While the database example is, necessarily, quite simple, it will give you the flavor of how a real application can effectively use a dialog box.

Dialog Boxes Use Controls

By itself, a dialog box does nothing. Instead, it is the controls within the dialog box that interact with the user. Technically, the dialog box is simply a management device. Formally stated, a *control* is a special type of input or output window. A control is owned by its parent window, which, for the examples presented in this chapter, is the dialog box. Windows 95 supports several standard controls, including: push buttons, check boxes, radio buttons, list boxes, edit boxes, combination boxes, scroll bars, and static controls. (Windows 95 also supports several enhanced controls, called common controls, which are discussed in Chapter 7 of this book.) In the course of explaining how to use dialog boxes, the examples in this chapter illustrate three of these controls: push buttons, the list box, and the edit box. In the next chapter, other controls will be examined.

A *push button* is a control that the user "pushes on" to activate some response. You have already been using push buttons in message boxes. For example, the OK button that we have been using in most message boxes is a push button.

A *list box* displays a list of items from which the user selects one (or more). List boxes are commonly used to display things such as filenames.

An *edit box* allows the user to enter a string. Edit boxes provide all necessary text editing features required by the user. Therefore, to input a string, your program simply displays an edit box and waits until the user has finished typing in the string. A *combination box* is a combination of a list box and an edit box.

It is important to understand that controls both generate messages (when accessed by the user) and receive messages (from your application). A message generated by a control indicates what type of interaction the user has had with the control. A message sent to the control is essentially an instruction to which the control must respond. You will see examples of this type of message passing later in this chapter.

Modal versus Modeless Dialog Boxes

There are two types of dialog boxes: *modal* and *modeless.* The most common dialog boxes are modal. A modal dialog box demands a response before the parent program will continue. That is, a modal dialog box will not allow the user to refocus input to another part of the parent application without first responding to the dialog box.

A modeless dialog box does not prevent the parent program from running. That is, it does not demand a response before input can be refocused to another part of the program.

We will examine modal dialog boxes first, since they are the most common. A modeless dialog box example concludes this chapter.

Receiving Dialog Box Messages

A dialog box is a type of window. Events that occur within it are sent to your program by use of the same message-passing mechanism that the main window uses. However, dialog box messages are not sent to your program's main window function. Instead, each dialog box that you define will need its own window function, which is generally called a *dialog function*. This function must have the following prototype (of course, the name of the function can be anything that you like):

> BOOL CALLBACK DFunc(HWND *hdwnd*, UINT *message*,
> WPARAM *wParam*, LPARAM *lParam*);

As you can see, a dialog function receives the same parameters as your program's main window function. However, it differs from the main window function in that it returns a true or false result. Like your program's main window function, the dialog box window function will receive many messages. If it processes a message, then it must return true. If it does not respond to a message, it must return false.

In general, each control within a dialog box will be given its own resource ID. Each time that control is accessed by the user, a **WM_COMMAND** message will be sent to the dialog function, indicating the ID of the control and the type of action the user has taken. That function will then decode the message and take appropriate actions. This process parallels the way messages are decoded by your program's main window function.

4

Activating a Dialog Box

To activate a modal dialog box (that is, to cause it to be displayed), you must call the **DialogBox( )** API function. It has the following prototype:

> int DialogBox(HINSTANCE *hThisInst*, LPCSTR *lpName*,
>   HWND *hwnd*, DLGPROC *lpDFunc*);

Here, *hThisInst* is the handle to the application that is passed to your program in the instance parameter to **WinMain( )**. The name of the dialog box as defined in the resource file is pointed to by *lpName*. The handle to the parent window that activates the dialog box is passed in *hwnd*. The *lpDFunc* parameter contains a pointer to the dialog function described in the preceding section. If **DialogBox( )** fails, then it returns –1. Otherwise, the return value is that specified by **EndDialog( )**, discussed next.

Deactivating a Dialog Box

To *deactivate* (that is, destroy and remove from the screen) a modal dialog box, use **EndDialog( )**. It has this prototype:

> BOOL EndDialog(HWND *hdwnd*, int *nStatus*);

Here, *hdwnd* is the handle to the dialog box, and *nStatus* is a status code returned by the **DialogBox( )** function. (The value of *nStatus* can be ignored if it is not relevant to your program.) This function returns nonzero if successful and zero otherwise. (In normal situations, the function is successful.)

Creating a Simple Dialog Box

To illustrate the basic dialog box concepts, we will begin with a simple dialog box. This dialog box will contain four push buttons called Size, State, Zone, and Cancel. When either the Size, State, or Zone button is pressed, it will activate a message box indicating the choice selected. (Later these push buttons will be used to obtain information from the database. For now, the message boxes are simply placeholders.) The dialog box will be removed from the screen when the Cancel button is pressed.

The Dialog Box Resource File

A dialog box is another resource that is contained in your program's resource file. Before developing a program that uses a dialog box, you will need a resource file that specifies one. Although it is possible to specify the contents of a dialog box by using a text editor, entering its specifications as you do when creating a menu, this is seldom done. Instead, most programmers use a dialog editor. The main reason for this is that dialog box definitions involve the positioning of the various controls inside the dialog box, which is best done interactively. However, since the complete .RC files for the examples in this chapter are supplied in their text form, you should simply enter them as text. Just remember that when creating your own dialog boxes, you will want to use a dialog editor.

Since, in practice, most dialog boxes are created by using a dialog editor, only a brief explanation of the dialog box definition in the resource file is given for the examples in this chapter.

Dialog boxes are defined within your program's resource file by use of the **DIALOG** statement. Its general form is shown here:

Dialog-name DIALOG [DISCARDABLE] *X, Y, Width, Height*
Features
{
  Dialog-items
}

4

The *Dialog-name* is the name of the dialog box. The box's upper-left corner will be at *X, Y,* and the box will have the dimensions specified by *Width* × *Height.* If the box can be removed from memory when not in use, then specify it as **DISCARDABLE**. One or more *Features* of the dialog box can be specified. As you will see, two of these are the caption and the style of the box. The *Dialog-items* are the controls that comprise the dialog box.

The following resource file defines the dialog box that will be used by the first sample program. It includes a menu that is used to activate the dialog box, the menu accelerator keys, and then the dialog box, itself. You should enter it into your computer at this time, calling it DIALOG.RC.

```
; Sample dialog box resource file.
#include <windows.h>
#include "dialog.h"

MYMENU MENU
{
  POPUP "&Dialog"
  {
    MENUITEM "&Dialog", IDM_DIALOG
    MENUITEM "&Exit", IDM_EXIT
  }
  MENUITEM "&Help", IDM_HELP
}
```

```
MYMENU ACCELERATORS
{
  VK_F2, IDM_DIALOG, VIRTKEY
  VK_F3, IDM_EXIT, VIRTKEY
  VK_F1, IDM_HELP, VIRTKEY
}

MYDB DIALOG 10, 10, 140, 110
CAPTION "Cities Dialog Box"
STYLE DS_MODALFRAME | WS_POPUP | WS_CAPTION | WS_SYSMENU
{
  DEFPUSHBUTTON "Size", IDD_SIZE, 11, 10, 32, 14,
            WS_CHILD | WS_VISIBLE | WS_TABSTOP
  PUSHBUTTON "State", IDD_STATE, 11, 34, 32, 14,
            WS_CHILD | WS_VISIBLE | WS_TABSTOP
  PUSHBUTTON "Zone", IDD_ZONE, 11, 58, 32, 14,
            WS_CHILD | WS_VISIBLE | WS_TABSTOP
  PUSHBUTTON "Cancel", IDCANCEL, 8, 82, 38, 16,
            WS_CHILD | WS_VISIBLE | WS_TABSTOP
}
```

This resource file defines a dialog box called **MYDB** that has its upper-left corner at location 10, 10. Its width is 140 and its height is 110. The string after **CAPTION** becomes the title of the dialog box. The **STYLE** statement determines what type of dialog box is created. Some common style values, including those used in this chapter, are shown in Table 4-1. You can OR together the values that are appropriate for the style of dialog box that you desire. These style values may also be used by other controls.

Four push buttons are defined in the **MYDB** definition. The first is the default push button. This button is automatically highlighted when the

Some Common Dialog Box Style Options

Table 4-1.

Value	Meaning
DS_MODALFRAME	Dialog box has modal frame. This style can be used with either modal or modeless dialog boxes.
WS_BORDER	Include border.
WS_CAPTION	Include title bar.
WS_CHILD	Create as child window.
WS_POPUP	Create as pop-up window.
WS_MAXIMIZEBOX	Include maximize box.
WS_MINIMIZEBOX	Include minimize box.
WS_SYSMENU	Include system menu.
WS_TABSTOP	Control can be tabbed to.
WS_VISIBLE	Box is visible when activated.

dialog box is first displayed. This is the general form of a push button declaration:

PUSHBUTTON "*string*", *PBID*, *X*, *Y*, *Width*, *Height* [, *Style*]

Here, *string* is the text that will be shown inside the push button. *PBID* is the value associated with the push button. It is this value that is returned to your program when the button is pushed. The button's upper-left corner will be at *X, Y,* and the button will have the dimensions specified by *Width* × *Height.* *Style* determines the exact nature of the push button. To define a default push button, use the **DEFPUSHBUTTON** statement. It has the same parameters as the regular push buttons.

The header file DIALOG.H, which is also used by the example program, is shown here:

```
#define IDM_DIALOG    100
#define IDM_EXIT      101
#define IDM_HELP      102

#define IDD_SIZE      200
#define IDD_STATE     201
#define IDD_ZONE      202
```

Enter this file now.

The Dialog Box Window Function

As stated earlier, events that occur with a dialog box are passed to the window function associated with that dialog box and not to your program's main window function. The following dialog box window function responds to the events that occur within the **MYDB** dialog box.

```
/* A simple dialog function. */
BOOL CALLBACK DialogFunc(HWND hdwnd, UINT message,
                         WPARAM wParam, LPARAM lParam)
{
  switch(message) {
    case WM_COMMAND:
      switch(LOWORD(wParam)) {
        case IDCANCEL:
          EndDialog(hdwnd, 0);
          return 1;
        case IDD_SIZE:
          MessageBox(hdwnd, "Size", "Size", MB_OK);
          return 1;
```

4

```
      case IDD_STATE:
        MessageBox(hdwnd, "State", "State", MB_OK);
        return 1;
      case IDD_ZONE:
        MessageBox(hdwnd, "Zone", "Zone", MB_OK);
        return 1;
    }
  }
  return 0;
}
```

Each time a control within the dialog box is accessed, a **WM_COMMAND** message is sent to **DialogFunc( )**, and **LOWORD(wParam)** contains the ID of the control affected.

DialogFunc( ) processes the four messages that can be generated by the box. If the user presses **Cancel**, then **IDCANCEL** is sent, which causes the dialog box to be closed by use of a call to the API function **EndDialog( )**. (**IDCANCEL** is a standard ID defined by including WINDOWS.H.) Pressing either of the other three buttons causes a message box to be displayed that confirms the selection. As mentioned, these buttons will be used by later examples to display information from the database.

A First Dialog Box Sample Program

Here is the entire dialog box example. When the program begins execution, only the top-level menu is displayed on the menu bar. By selecting Dialog, the user causes the dialog box to be displayed. Once the dialog box is displayed, selecting a push button causes the appropriate response. A sample screen is shown in Figure 4-1. Notice that the cities database is included in

Sample output
from the first
dialog box
program
Figure 4-1.

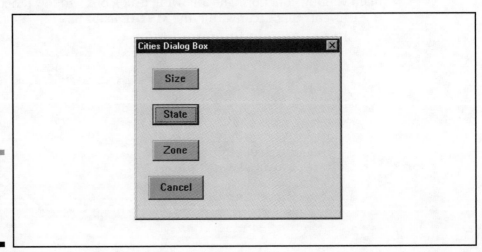

this program, but is not used. It will be used by subsequent examples, however.

```c
/* Demonstrate a Modal Dialog box. */

#include <windows.h>
#include <string.h>
#include <stdio.h>
#include <time.h>
#include "dialog.h"

#define NUMCITIES 6

LRESULT CALLBACK WindowFunc(HWND, UINT, WPARAM, LPARAM);
BOOL CALLBACK DialogFunc(HWND, UINT, WPARAM, LPARAM);

char szWinName[] = "MyWin"; /* name of window class */

HINSTANCE hInst;

/* cities database -- this will be used by later examples */
struct citiesTag {
  char name[30];
  unsigned long size;
  char state[3];
  char timezone[30];
} cities[NUMCITIES] = {
  "New York", 7322564, "NY", "Eastern",
  "Atlanta", 394017, "GA", "Eastern",
  "Chicago", 2783726, "IL", "Central",
  "Houston", 1630553, "TX", "Central",
  "Denver", 467610, "CO", "Mountain",
  "Los Angeles", 3485398, "CA", "Pacific"
};

int WINAPI WinMain(HINSTANCE hThisInst, HINSTANCE hPrevInst,
                   LPSTR lpszArgs, int nWinMode)
{
  HWND hwnd;
  MSG msg;
  WNDCLASSEX wcl;
  HANDLE hAccel;

  /* Define a window class. */
  wcl.hInstance = hThisInst; /* handle to this instance */
  wcl.lpszClassName = szWinName; /* window class name */
  wcl.lpfnWndProc = WindowFunc; /* window function */
  wcl.style = 0; /* default style */
```

4

```
wcl.cbSize = sizeof(WNDCLASSEX); /* set size of WNDCLASSEX */

wcl.hIcon = LoadIcon(NULL, IDI_APPLICATION); /* Large icon */
wcl.hIconSm = LoadIcon(NULL, IDI_APPLICATION); /* Small icon */

wcl.hCursor = LoadCursor(NULL, IDC_ARROW); /* cursor style */

/* specify name of menu resource */
wcl.lpszMenuName = "MYMENU"; /* main menu */

wcl.cbClsExtra = 0; /* no extra */
wcl.cbWndExtra = 0; /* information needed */

/* Make the window white. */
wcl.hbrBackground = GetStockObject(WHITE_BRUSH);

/* Register the window class. */
if(!RegisterClassEx(&wcl)) return 0;

/* Now that a window class has been registered, a window
   can be created. */
hwnd = CreateWindow(
  szWinName, /* name of window class */
  "Demonstrate Dialog Boxes", /* title */
  WS_OVERLAPPEDWINDOW, /* window style - normal */
  CW_USEDEFAULT, /* X coordinate - let Windows decide */
  CW_USEDEFAULT, /* Y coordinate - let Windows decide */
  CW_USEDEFAULT, /* width - let Windows decide */
  CW_USEDEFAULT, /* height - let Windows decide */
  HWND_DESKTOP, /* no parent window */
  NULL, /* no menu */
  hThisInst, /* handle of this instance of the program */
  NULL /* no additional arguments */
);

hInst = hThisInst; /* save the current instance handle */

/* load accelerators */
hAccel = LoadAccelerators(hThisInst, "MYMENU");

/* Display the window. */
ShowWindow(hwnd, nWinMode);
UpdateWindow(hwnd);

/* Create the message loop. */
while(GetMessage(&msg, NULL, 0, 0))
{
```

```
        if(!TranslateAccelerator(hwnd, hAccel, &msg)) {
          TranslateMessage(&msg); /* allow use of keyboard */
          DispatchMessage(&msg); /* return control to Windows */
        }
      }
      return msg.wParam;
}

/* This function is called by Windows 95 and is passed
   messages from the message queue.
*/
LRESULT CALLBACK WindowFunc(HWND hwnd, UINT message,
                                WPARAM wParam, LPARAM lParam)
{
  int response;

  switch(message) {
    case WM_COMMAND:
      switch(LOWORD(wParam)) {
        case IDM_DIALOG:
          DialogBox(hInst, "MYDB", hwnd, DialogFunc);
          break;
        case IDM_EXIT:
          response = MessageBox(hwnd, "Quit the Program?",
                                "Exit", MB_YESNO);
          if(response == IDYES) PostQuitMessage(0);
          break;

          break;
        case IDM_HELP:
          MessageBox(hwnd, "No Help", "Help", MB_OK);
          break;
      }
      break;
    case WM_DESTROY: /* terminate the program */
      PostQuitMessage(0);
      break;
    default:
      /* Let Windows 95 process any messages not specified in
         the preceding switch statement. */
      return DefWindowProc(hwnd, message, wParam, lParam);
  }
  return 0;
}

/* A simple dialog function. */
BOOL CALLBACK DialogFunc(HWND hdwnd, UINT message,
                                WPARAM wParam, LPARAM lParam)
```

```
{
  switch(message) {
    case WM_COMMAND:
      switch(LOWORD(wParam)) {
        case IDCANCEL:
          EndDialog(hdwnd, 0);
          return 1;
        case IDD_SIZE:
          MessageBox(hdwnd, "Size", "Size", MB_OK);
          return 1;
        case IDD_STATE:
          MessageBox(hdwnd, "State", "State", MB_OK);
          return 1;
        case IDD_ZONE:
          MessageBox(hdwnd, "Zone", "Zone", MB_OK);
          return 1;
      }
  }
  return 0;
}
```

Notice the global variable **hInst**. This variable is assigned a copy of the current instance handle passed to **WinMain( )**. The reason for this variable is that the dialog box needs access to the current instance handle. However, the dialog box is not created in **WinMain( )**. Instead, it is created in **WindowFunc( )**. Therefore, a copy of the instance parameter must be made so that it can be accessible outside of **WinMain( )**.

Adding a List Box

To continue exploring dialog boxes, let's add another control to the dialog box defined in the previous program. One of the most common controls after the push button is the list box. We will use the list box to display a list of the cities in the database and allow the user to select the one he/she is interested in. The **LISTBOX** statement has this general form:

LISTBOX *LBID, X, Y, Width, Height* [,*Style*]

Here, *LBID* is the value that identifies the list box. The box's upper-left corner will be at *X, Y,* and the box will have the dimensions specified by *Width* × *Height. Style* determines the exact nature of the list box. (The *Style* values are described in Table 4-1.)

Disabling a Control

Sometimes you will have a control that is not applicable to all situations. When a control is not applicable, it can (and should) be disabled. A control that is disabled is displayed in gray and cannot be selected. To disable a control, use the **EnableWindow( )** API function, shown here:

    BOOL EnableWindow(HWND *hCntl*, BOOL *How*);

In this function, *hCntl* specifies the handle of the control to be affected. (Remember, controls are simply specialized windows.) If *How* is nonzero, then the control is enabled (activated). If *How* is zero, the control is disabled. The function returns nonzero if the control was already disabled. It returns zero if the control was previously enabled.

To obtain the handle of a control, use the **GetDlgItem( )** API function. This is its general form:

    HWND GetDlgItem(HWND *hDwnd*, int *ID*);

Here, *hDwnd* is the handle of the dialog box that owns the control. The control ID is passed in *ID*. This is the value that you associate with the control in its resource file. The function returns the handle of the specified control or **NULL** on failure.

To show you how these functions can be used to disable a control, the following code fragment disables the Zone push button. In this example **hwpb** is a handle of type **HWND**.

```
hwpb = GetDlgItem(hdwnd, IDD_ZONE); /* get handle of button */
EnableWindow(hwpb, 0); /* disable it */
```

On your own, you might want to try disabling and enabling other controls used by the examples in this and later chapters.

4

To add a list box, you must change the dialog box definition in DIALOG.RC. First, add this list box description to the dialog box definition.

```
LISTBOX IDD_LB1, 66, 5, 63, 33, LBS_NOTIFY |
            WS_VISIBLE | WS_BORDER | WS_VSCROLL | WS_TABSTOP
```

Second, add the following push button to the dialog box definition.

```
PUSHBUTTON "Select City", IDD_SELECT, 72, 41, 54, 14,
           WS_CHILD | WS_VISIBLE | WS_TABSTOP
```

After these changes, your dialog box definition should look like this:

```
MYDB DIALOG 10, 10, 140, 110
CAPTION "Cities Dialog Box"
STYLE DS_MODALFRAME | WS_POPUP | WS_CAPTION | WS_SYSMENU
{
  DEFPUSHBUTTON "Size", IDD_SIZE, 11, 10, 32, 14,
           WS_CHILD | WS_VISIBLE | WS_TABSTOP
  PUSHBUTTON "State", IDD_STATE, 11, 34, 32, 14,
           WS_CHILD | WS_VISIBLE | WS_TABSTOP
  PUSHBUTTON "Zone", IDD_ZONE, 11, 58, 32, 14,
           WS_CHILD | WS_VISIBLE | WS_TABSTOP
  PUSHBUTTON "Cancel", IDCANCEL, 8, 82, 38, 16,
           WS_CHILD | WS_VISIBLE | WS_TABSTOP
  LISTBOX IDD_LB1, 66, 5, 63, 33, LBS_NOTIFY |
           WS_VISIBLE | WS_BORDER | WS_VSCROLL | WS_TABSTOP
  PUSHBUTTON "Select City", IDD_SELECT, 72, 41, 54, 14,
           WS_CHILD | WS_VISIBLE | WS_TABSTOP
}
```

You will also need to add these macros to DIALOG.H:

```
#define IDD_LB1      203
#define IDD_SELECT   204
```

IDD_LB1 identifies the list box, and **IDD_SELECT** is the ID value of the Select City push button.

List Box Basics

When using a list box, you must perform two basic operations. First, you must initialize the list box when the dialog box is first displayed. This consists of sending the list box the list that it will display. (By default, the list box will be empty.) Second, once the list box has been initialized, your program will need to respond to the user selecting an item from the list.

List boxes generate various types of messages. The only one we will use is **LBN_DBLCLK**. This message is sent when the user has double-clicked on an entry in the list. This message is contained in **HIWORD(wParam)** each time a **WM_COMMAND** is generated for the list box. (The list box must have the **LBS_NOTIFY** style flag included in its definition in order to generate **LBN_DBLCLK** messages.) Once a selection has been made, you will need to query the list box to find out which item has been selected.

Unlike a push button, a list box is a control that receives messages as well as generating them. You can send a list box several different messages. To send a message to the list box (or to any other control), use the **SendDlg-ItemMessage( )** API function. Its prototype is shown here:

LONG SendDlgItemMessage(HWND *hdwnd*, int *ID*,
                        UINT *IDMsg*, WPARAM *wParam*,
                        LPARAM *lParam*);

SendDlgItemMessage( ) sends to the control (within the dialog box) whose ID is specified by *ID* the message specified by *IDMsg*. The handle of the dialog box is specified in *hdwnd*. Any additional information required by the message is specified in *wParam* and *lParam*. The additional information, if any, varies from message to message. If there is no additional information to pass to a control, the *WParam* and the *LParam* arguments should be 0. The value returned by **SendDlgItemMessage( )** contains the information requested by *IDMsg*.

Here are a few of the most common messages that you can send to a list box:

Macro	Purpose
LB_ADDSTRING	Adds a string (selection) to the list box
LB_GETCURSEL	Requests the index of the selected item
LB_SETCURSEL	Selects an item
LB_FINDSTRING	Finds a matching entry
LB_SELECTSTRING	Finds a matching entry and selects it
LB_GETTEXT	Obtains the text associated with an item

Let's take a closer look at these messages now.

LB_ADDSTRING adds a string to the list box. That is, the specified string becomes another selection within the box. The string must be pointed to by *lParam*. (*wParam* is unused by this message.) The value returned by the list box is the index of the string in the list. If an error occurs, **LB_ERR** is returned.

The **LB_GETCURSEL** message causes the list box to return the index of the currently selected item. All list box indexes begin with 0. Both *lParam* and *wParam* are unused. If an error occurs, **LB_ERR** is returned. If no item is currently selected, then an error results.

4

You can set the current selection inside a list box by using the **LB_SET-CURSEL** command. For this message, *wParam* specifies the index of the item to select. *lParam* is not used. On error, **LB_ERR** is returned.

You can find an item in the list that matches a specified prefix by using **LB_FINDSTRING**. That is, **LB_FINDSTRING** attempts to match a partial string with an entry in the list box. *wParam* specifies the index where the search begins, and *lParam* points to the string that will be matched. If a match is found, the index of the matching item is returned. Otherwise, **LB_ERR** is returned. **LB_FINDSTRING** does not select the item within the list box.

If you want to find a matching item and select it, use **LB_SELECTSTRING**. It takes the same parameters as **LB_FINDSTRING**, but also selects the matching item.

You can obtain the text associated with an item in a list box by using **LB_GETTEXT**. In this case, *wParam* specifies the index of the item, and *lParam* points to the character array that will receive the null-terminated string associated with that index. The length of the string is returned if successful, or **LB_ERR** is returned on failure.

Initializing the List Box

As mentioned, when a list box is created, it is empty. This means that you will need to initialize it each time its dialog box is displayed. This is easy to accomplish because each time a dialog box is activated, its window function is sent a **WM_INITDIALOG** message. Therefore, you will need to add the following case to the outer **switch** statement in **DialogFunc( )**.

```
case WM_INITDIALOG: /* initialize list box */
  /* initialize list box */
  for(i=0; i<NUMCITIES; i++)
    SendDlgItemMessage(hdwnd, IDD_LB1,
            LB_ADDSTRING, 0, (LPARAM)cities[i].name);

  /* select first item */
  SendDlgItemMessage(hdwnd, IDD_LB1, LB_SETCURSEL, 0, 0);
  return 1;
```

This code loads the list box with the names of cities as defined in the **cities** array. Each string is added to the list box by calling **SendDlgItemMessage( )** with the **LB_ADDSTRING** message. The string to add is pointed to by the *lParam* parameter. (The type cast to **LPARAM** is necessary in this case to convert a pointer into an unsigned integer.) In this example, each string is added to the list box in the order it is sent. (However, depending upon how you construct the list box, it is possible to have the items displayed in alphabetical order.) If the number of items you send to a list box exceeds what it can display in its window, a vertical scroll bar will be added automatically.

This code also selects the first item in the list box. When a list box is first created, no item is selected. While this might be desirable under certain circumstances, it is not in this case. Most often, you will want to automatically select the first item in a list box as a convenience to the user.

Remember: **WM_INITDIALOG** is sent to a dialog box each time it is activated. You should perform all initializations required by the dialog box when this message is received.

Processing a Selection

After the list box has been initialized, it is ready for use. There are essentially two ways a user makes a selection from a list box. First, the user may double-click on an item in the list box. This causes a **WM_COMMAND** message to be passed to the dialog box's window function. In this case, **LOWORD(wParam)** contains the ID associated with the list box, and **HIWORD(wParam)** contains the **LBN_DBLCLK** message. Double-clicking causes your program to be immediately aware of the user's selection. The other way to use a list box is to simply highlight a selection (either by single-clicking or by using the arrow keys to move the highlight). This does *not* cause a message to be sent to your program, but the list box remembers the selection and waits until your program requests the selection. Both methods are demonstrated in the example program.

Once an item has been selected in a list box, you determine which item was chosen by sending the **LB_GETCURSEL** message to the list box. The list box then returns the index of the selected item. Remember, if this message is sent before an item has been selected, the list box returns **LB_ERR**. (This is one reason that it is a good idea to select a list box item when the list box is initialized.)

To demonstrate how to process a list box selection, add the following cases to the inner switch inside **DialogFunc( )**.

```
case IDD_LB1: /* process a list box LBN_DBLCLK */
  /* see if user made a selection */
  if(HIWORD(wParam)==LBN_DBLCLK) {
    i = SendDlgItemMessage(hdwnd, IDD_LB1,
          LB_GETCURSEL, 0, 0);  /* get index */
```

4

```
      sprintf(str, "%s, %s\n%s Time Zone\nPop.:%lu",
              cities[i].name, cities[i].state,
              cities[i].timezone, cities[i].size);

    MessageBox(hdwnd, str, "Selection Made", MB_OK);
  }
  return 1;
case IDD_SELECT: /* Select City button has been pressed */
  i = SendDlgItemMessage(hdwnd, IDD_LB1,
          LB_GETCURSEL, 0, 0);  /* get index */
  sprintf(str, "%s, %s\n%s Time Zone\nPop.:%lu",
          cities[i].name, cities[i].state,
          cities[i].timezone, cities[i].size);

  MessageBox(hdwnd, str, "Selection Made", MB_OK);
  return 1;
```

After adding the list box, run the dialog program. Each time you make a selection, either by double-clicking or by pressing the Select City push button, the currently selected city has its information displayed. Sample output is shown in Figure 4-2.

Notice the code under the **IDD_LB1** case. Since the list box can generate several types of notification messages, it is necessary to examine the high-order word of **wParam** to determine if the user double-clicked on an item. That is, just because the control generates a notification message does not mean that it is a double-click message.

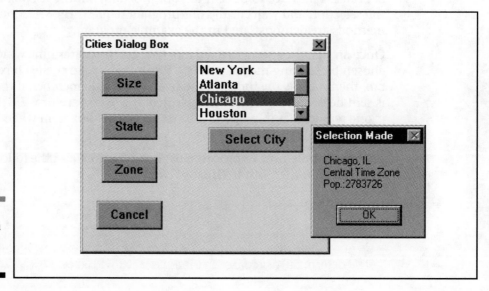

A dialog box that contains a list box

Figure 4-2.

Adding an Edit Box

In this section, we will add an edit control to the dialog box. Edit boxes are particularly useful because they allow users to enter a string of their own choosing. The edit box in this example will be used to allow the user to enter the name of a city. If the city is in the list, then that city will be selected and information about the city can be obtained. Although the addition of an edit box enhances this simple database application, it also serves another purpose. It will illustrate how two controls can work together.

Before you can use an edit box, you must define one in your resource file. For this example, change **MYDB** so that it looks like this:

```
MYDB DIALOG 10, 10, 140, 110
CAPTION "Cities Dialog Box"
STYLE DS_MODALFRAME | WS_POPUP | WS_CAPTION | WS_SYSMENU
{
  DEFPUSHBUTTON "Size", IDD_SIZE, 11, 10, 32, 14,
            WS_CHILD | WS_VISIBLE | WS_TABSTOP
  PUSHBUTTON "State", IDD_STATE, 11, 34, 32, 14,
            WS_CHILD | WS_VISIBLE | WS_TABSTOP
  PUSHBUTTON "Zone", IDD_ZONE, 11, 58, 32, 14,
            WS_CHILD | WS_VISIBLE | WS_TABSTOP
  PUSHBUTTON "Cancel", IDCANCEL, 8, 82, 38, 16,
            WS_CHILD | WS_VISIBLE | WS_TABSTOP
  LISTBOX IDD_LB1, 66, 5, 63, 33, LBS_NOTIFY |
            WS_VISIBLE | WS_BORDER | WS_VSCROLL | WS_TABSTOP
  PUSHBUTTON "Select City", IDD_SELECT, 72, 41, 54, 14,
            WS_CHILD | WS_VISIBLE | WS_TABSTOP
  EDITTEXT IDD_EB1, 65, 73, 63, 12, ES_LEFT | WS_VISIBLE |
            WS_BORDER | ES_AUTOHSCROLL | WS_TABSTOP
  PUSHBUTTON "Enter City", IDD_DONE, 73, 91, 46, 14,
            WS_CHILD | WS_VISIBLE | WS_TABSTOP
}
```

This version adds a push button called Enter City, which will be used to tell the program that you entered the name of a city into the edit box. It also adds the edit box itself. The ID for the edit box is **IDD_EB1**. This definition causes a standard edit box to be created.

The **EDITTEXT** statement has this general form:

   EDITTEXT *EDID, X, Y, Width, Height* [*,Style*]

Here, *EDID* is the value that identifies the edit box. The box's upper-left corner will be at *X, Y*, and its dimensions are specified in *Width × Height*. *Style* determines the exact nature of the list box. (The *Style* values are described in Table 4-1.)

Next, add the following macro definitions to DIALOG.H.

```
#define IDD_EB1    205
#define IDD_DONE   206
```

Edit boxes recognize many messages and generate several of their own. However, for the purposes of this example, there is no need for the program to respond to any messages. As you will see, edit boxes perform the editing function on their own. There is no reason for program interaction when text is edited. Your program simply decides when it wants to obtain the current contents of the edit box.

To obtain the current contents of the edit box, use the API function **GetDlgItemText( )**. It has this prototype:

UINT GetDlgItemText(HWND *hdwnd*, int *nID*, LPSTR *lpstr*, int *nMax*);

This function causes the edit box to copy the current contents of the box to the string pointed to by *lpstr*. The handle of the dialog box is specified by *hdwnd*. The ID of the edit box is specified by *nID*. The maximum number of characters to copy is specified by *nMax*. The function returns the length of the string.

Although not required by all applications, it is possible to initialize the contents of an edit box by using the **SetDlgItemText( )** function. Its prototype is shown here:

BOOL SetDlgItemText(HWND *hdwnd*, int *nID*, LPSTR *lpstr*);

This function sets the contents of the edit box to the string pointed to by *lpstr*. The handle of the dialog box is specified by *hdwnd*. The ID of the edit box is specified by *nID*. The function returns nonzero if successful or zero on failure.

To add an edit box to the sample program, add the following case statement to the inner **switch** of the **DialogFunc( )** function. Each time the Enter City button is pressed, the list box is searched for a city that matches the string that is currently in the edit box. If a match is found, then that city is selected in the list box. Remember that you only need to enter the first few characters of the city. The list box will automatically attempt to match them with a city.

```
case IDD_DONE: /* Enter City button pressed */
  /* get current contents of edit box */
  GetDlgItemText(hdwnd, IDD_EB1, str, 80);
```

```
/* find a matching string in the list box */
i = SendDlgItemMessage(hdwnd, IDD_LB1, LB_FINDSTRING,
        0, (LPARAM) str);

if(i != LB_ERR) { /* if match is found */
  /* select the matching city in list box */
  SendDlgItemMessage(hdwnd, IDD_LB1, LB_SETCURSEL, i, 0);

  /* get string associated with that index */
  SendDlgItemMessage(hdwnd, IDD_LB1, LB_GETTEXT,
      i, (LPARAM) str);

  /* update text in edit box */
  SetDlgItemText(hdwnd, IDD_EB1, str);
}
else MessageBox(hdwnd, str, "No Match With", MB_OK);
return 1;
```

This code first obtains the current contents of the edit box and then looks for a match with the strings inside the list box. If it finds one, it selects the matching item in the list box and then copies the string from the list box back into the edit box. In this way, the two controls work together, complementing each other. As you become a more experienced Windows 95 programmer, you will find that there are often instances in which two or more controls can work together.

You will also need to add the following line of code to the **INITDIALOG** case. It causes the edit box to be initialized each time the dialog box is activated.

```
/* initialize the edit box */
SetDlgItemText(hdwnd, IDD_EB1, "New York");
```

In addition to the changes just shown, the code that processes the list box will be enhanced so that it automatically copies the name of the city selected in the list box into the edit box. These changes are reflected in the full program listing that follows. You should have no trouble understanding them.

The Entire Modal Dialog Box Program

The entire modal dialog box sample program, which includes push buttons, a list box, and an edit box, is shown next. Notice that the code associated

FAST TRACK TIP

Exploring Edit and List Box Messages

Both list boxes and edit boxes respond to a wide range of messages. While none of the examples in this book require the use of any messages not already described in this chapter, you will still want to explore these two controls more thoroughly on your own. To show you why, here is a list of just a few of the messages to which these controls can respond.

EM_GETLIMITTEXT	Gets the current text limit in an edit box
EM_GETLINE	Obtains a line of text from the edit box
EM_GETLINECOUNT	Obtains the number of lines of text currently in a multiline edit control
EM_GETMODIFY	Determines if the text in an edit box has been modified
EM_LIMITTEXT	Limits the number of characters that the user can enter into an edit box
EM_LINELENGTH	Obtains the number of characters currently in the edit box
EM_SETLIMITTEXT	Limits the number of characters that an edit box can hold
EM_UNDO	Undoes the last edit operation
LB_DELETESTRING	Removes a string from the list box
LB_DIR	Adds filenames to the list box
LB_FINDSTRINGEXACT	Finds a string in the list box that exactly matches the one specified
LB_GETCOUNT	Obtains the number of items in a list box
LB_GETTEXTLEN	Obtains the length of the specified string in a list box
LB_INSERTSTRING	Inserts a string into a list box

with the push buttons now displays information about the city currently selected in the list box.

```
/* A modal dialog box example. */

#include <windows.h>
#include <string.h>
#include <stdio.h>
```

```
#include "dialog.h"

#define NUMCITIES 6

LRESULT CALLBACK WindowFunc(HWND, UINT, WPARAM, LPARAM);
BOOL CALLBACK DialogFunc(HWND, UINT, WPARAM, LPARAM);

char szWinName[] = "MyWin"; /* name of window class */

HINSTANCE hInst;

/* cities database */
struct citiesTag {
  char name[30];
  unsigned long size;
  char state[3];
  char timezone[30];
} cities[NUMCITIES] = {
  "New York", 7322564, "NY", "Eastern",
  "Atlanta", 394017, "GA", "Eastern",
  "Chicago", 2783726, "IL", "Central",
  "Houston", 1630553, "TX", "Central",
  "Denver", 467610, "CO", "Mountain",
  "Los Angeles", 3485398, "CA", "Pacific"
};


int WINAPI WinMain(HINSTANCE hThisInst, HINSTANCE hPrevInst,
                   LPSTR lpszArgs, int nWinMode)
{
  HWND hwnd;
  MSG msg;
  WNDCLASSEX wcl;
  HANDLE hAccel;

  /* Define a window class. */
  wcl.hInstance = hThisInst; /* handle to this instance */
  wcl.lpszClassName = szWinName; /* window class name */
  wcl.lpfnWndProc = WindowFunc; /* window function */
  wcl.style = 0; /* default style */

  wcl.cbSize = sizeof(WNDCLASSEX); /* set size of WNDCLASSEX */

  wcl.hIcon = LoadIcon(NULL, IDI_APPLICATION); /* Large icon */
  wcl.hIconSm = LoadIcon(NULL, IDI_APPLICATION); /* Small icon */

  wcl.hCursor = LoadCursor(NULL, IDC_ARROW); /* cursor style */
```

4

```
/* specify name of menu resource */
wcl.lpszMenuName = "MYMENU"; /* main menu */

wcl.cbClsExtra = 0; /* no extra */
wcl.cbWndExtra = 0; /* information needed */

/* Make the window white. */
wcl.hbrBackground = GetStockObject(WHITE_BRUSH);

/* Register the window class. */
if(!RegisterClassEx(&wcl)) return 0;

/* Now that a window class has been registered, a window
   can be created. */
hwnd = CreateWindow(
  szWinName, /* name of window class */
  "Demonstrate Dialog Boxes", /* title */
  WS_OVERLAPPEDWINDOW, /* window style - normal */
  CW_USEDEFAULT, /* X coordinate - let Windows decide */
  CW_USEDEFAULT, /* Y coordinate - let Windows decide */
  CW_USEDEFAULT, /* width - let Windows decide */
  CW_USEDEFAULT, /* height - let Windows decide */
  HWND_DESKTOP, /* no parent window */
  NULL, /* no menu */
  hThisInst, /* handle of this instance of the program */
  NULL /* no additional arguments */
);

hInst = hThisInst; /* save the current instance handle */

/* load accelerators */
hAccel = LoadAccelerators(hThisInst, "MYMENU");

/* Display the window. */
ShowWindow(hwnd, nWinMode);
UpdateWindow(hwnd);

/* Create the message loop. */
while(GetMessage(&msg, NULL, 0, 0))
{
  if(!TranslateAccelerator(hwnd, hAccel, &msg)) {
    TranslateMessage(&msg); /* allow use of keyboard */
    DispatchMessage(&msg); /* return control to Windows */
  }
}
return msg.wParam;
}
```

```
/* This function is called by Windows 95 and is passed
   messages from the message queue.
*/
LRESULT CALLBACK WindowFunc(HWND hwnd, UINT message,
                                WPARAM wParam, LPARAM lParam)
{
  int response;

  switch(message) {
    case WM_COMMAND:
      switch(LOWORD(wParam)) {
        case IDM_DIALOG:
          DialogBox(hInst, "MYDB", hwnd, DialogFunc);
          break;
        case IDM_EXIT:
          response = MessageBox(hwnd, "Quit the Program?",
                                "Exit", MB_YESNO);
          if(response == IDYES) PostQuitMessage(0);
          break;
        case IDM_HELP:
          MessageBox(hwnd, "No Help", "Help", MB_OK);
          break;
      }
      break;
    case WM_DESTROY: /* terminate the program */
      PostQuitMessage(0);
      break;
    default:
      /* Let Windows 95 process any messages not specified in
         the preceding switch statement. */
      return DefWindowProc(hwnd, message, wParam, lParam);
  }
  return 0;
}

/* A simple dialog function. */
BOOL CALLBACK DialogFunc(HWND hdwnd, UINT message,
                         WPARAM wParam, LPARAM lParam)
{
  long i;
  char str[80];

  switch(message) {
    case WM_COMMAND:
      switch(LOWORD(wParam)) {
        case IDCANCEL:
          EndDialog(hdwnd, 0);
          return 1;
```

4

```
case IDD_SIZE:
  i = SendDlgItemMessage(hdwnd, IDD_LB1,
        LB_GETCURSEL, 0, 0);  /* get index */
  sprintf(str, "%lu", cities[i].size);
  MessageBox(hdwnd, str, "Size", MB_OK);
  return 1;
case IDD_STATE:
  i = SendDlgItemMessage(hdwnd, IDD_LB1,
        LB_GETCURSEL, 0, 0);  /* get index */
  sprintf(str, "%s", cities[i].state);
  MessageBox(hdwnd, str, "State", MB_OK);
  return 1;
case IDD_ZONE:
  i = SendDlgItemMessage(hdwnd, IDD_LB1,
        LB_GETCURSEL, 0, 0);  /* get index */
  sprintf(str, "%s", cities[i].timezone);
  MessageBox(hdwnd, str, "Zone", MB_OK);
  return 1;
case IDD_DONE: /* Enter City button pressed */
  /* get current contents of edit box */
  GetDlgItemText(hdwnd, IDD_EB1, str, 80);

  /* find a matching string in the list box */
  i = SendDlgItemMessage(hdwnd, IDD_LB1, LB_FINDSTRING,
        0, (LPARAM) str);

  if(i != LB_ERR) { /* if match is found */
    /* select the matching city in list box */
    SendDlgItemMessage(hdwnd, IDD_LB1, LB_SETCURSEL, i, 0);

    /* get string associated with that index */
    SendDlgItemMessage(hdwnd, IDD_LB1, LB_GETTEXT,
        i, (LPARAM) str);

    /* update text in edit box */
    SetDlgItemText(hdwnd, IDD_EB1, str);
  }
  else MessageBox(hdwnd, str, "No Match With", MB_OK);
  return 1;
case IDD_LB1: /* process a list box LBN_DBLCLK */
  /* see if user made a selection */
  if(HIWORD(wParam)==LBN_DBLCLK) {
    i = SendDlgItemMessage(hdwnd, IDD_LB1,
          LB_GETCURSEL, 0, 0);  /* get index */
    sprintf(str, "%s, %s\n%s Time Zone\nPop.:%lu",
          cities[i].name, cities[i].state,
          cities[i].timezone, cities[i].size);
```

```
                MessageBox(hdwnd, str, "Selection Made", MB_OK);

                /* get string associated with that index */
                SendDlgItemMessage(hdwnd, IDD_LB1, LB_GETTEXT,
                    i, (LPARAM) str);

                /* update edit box */
                SetDlgItemText(hdwnd, IDD_EB1, str);
              }
              return 1;
            case IDD_SELECT: /* Select City button has been pressed */
              i = SendDlgItemMessage(hdwnd, IDD_LB1,
                      LB_GETCURSEL, 0, 0);  /* get index */
              sprintf(str, "%s, %s\n%s Time Zone\nPop.:%lu",
                      cities[i].name, cities[i].state,
                      cities[i].timezone, cities[i].size);

              MessageBox(hdwnd, str, "Selection Made", MB_OK);

              /* get string associated with that index */
              SendDlgItemMessage(hdwnd, IDD_LB1, LB_GETTEXT,
                  i, (LPARAM) str);

              /* update edit box */
              SetDlgItemText(hdwnd, IDD_EB1, str);
              return 1;
          }
          break;
        case WM_INITDIALOG: /* initialize list box */
          for(i=0; i<NUMCITIES; i++)
            SendDlgItemMessage(hdwnd, IDD_LB1,
                    LB_ADDSTRING, 0, (LPARAM)cities[i].name);

          /* select first item */
          SendDlgItemMessage(hdwnd, IDD_LB1, LB_SETCURSEL, 0, 0);

          /* initialize the edit box */
          SetDlgItemText(hdwnd, IDD_EB1, "New York");

          return 1;
      }
      return 0;
    }
```

4

Figure 4-3 shows sample output created by the complete modal dialog box program.

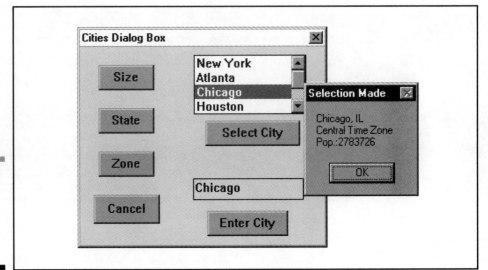

Sample output
produced by
the complete
modal dialog
box program
Figure 4-3.

Using a Modeless Dialog Box

To conclude this chapter, the modal dialog box used by the preceding
program will be converted into a modeless dialog box. As you will see, using
a modeless dialog box requires a little more work than does using a modal
one. The main reason for this is that a modeless dialog box is a more
independent window than is a modal dialog box. Specifically, the rest of
your program is still active when a modeless dialog box is displayed. Also,
both it and your application's window function continue to receive
messages. Thus, as you will see, some additional overhead is required in your
application's message loop to accommodate the modeless dialog box.

To create a modeless dialog box, you do not use **DialogBox( )**. Instead, you
must use the **CreateDialog( )** API function, which has this prototype:

> HWND CreateDialog(HINSTANCE *hThisInst*, LPCSTR *lpName*,
> HWND *hwnd*, DLGPROC *lpDFunc*)

Here, *hThisInst* is the handle to the application that is passed to your
program in the instance parameter to **WinMain( )**. The name of the dialog
box as defined in the resource file is pointed to by *lpName*. The handle to the
parent window that activates the dialog box is passed in *hwnd*. The *lpDFunc*
parameter contains a pointer to the dialog function. The dialog function is
of the same type as that used for a modal dialog box. **CreateDialog( )**
returns a handle to the dialog box. If the dialog box cannot be created,
NULL is returned.

Unlike a modal dialog box, a modeless dialog box is not automatically visible, so you may need to call **ShowWindow( )** to display it after it has been created. However, if you add **WS_VISIBLE** to the dialog box's definition in its resource file, then it will be automatically displayed.

To close a modeless dialog box, your program must call **DestroyWindow( )** rather than **EndDialog( )**. This is the prototype for **DestroyWindow( )**:

BOOL DestroyWindow(HWND *hwnd*);

Here, *hwnd* is the handle to the window (in this case, dialog box) being closed. The function returns nonzero if successful and zero on failure.

Since your application's main window function will continue receiving messages while a modeless dialog box is active, you must make a change to your program's message loop. Specifically, you must add a call to **IsDialogMessage( )**. This function routes dialog box messages to your modeless dialog box. It has this prototype:

BOOL IsDialogMessage(HWND *hdwnd*, LPMSG *msg*);

Here, *hdwnd* is the handle of the modeless dialog box, and **msg** is the message obtained from **GetMessage( )** within your program's message loop. The function returns nonzero if the message is for the dialog box. It returns false otherwise. If the message is for the dialog box, then it is automatically passed to the dialog box function. Therefore, to process modeless dialog box messages, your program's message loop must look something like this:

```
while(GetMessage(&msg, NULL, 0, 0))
  {
    if(!IsDialogMessage(hDlg, &msg)) {
      /* not dialog box message */
      if(!TranslateAccelerator(hwnd, hAccel, &msg)) {
        TranslateMessage(&msg); /* allow use of keyboard */
        DispatchMessage(&msg); /* return control to Windows */
      }
    }
  }
```

As you can see, the message is only processed by the rest of the message loop if it is not a dialog box message.

Creating a Modeless Dialog Box

To convert the modal dialog box shown in the preceding example into a modeless one, surprisingly few changes are needed. The first change that you need to make is to the dialog box definition in the DIALOG.RC resource file. Since a modeless dialog box is not automatically visible, add **WS_VISIBLE** to the dialog box definition. Also, although not technically necessary, you can remove the **DS_MODALFRAME** style, if you like. After making these adjustments, your dialog box definition should look like this one:

```
MYDB DIALOG 10, 10, 140, 110
CAPTION "Cities Dialog Box"
STYLE WS_POPUP | WS_CAPTION | WS_SYSMENU | WS_VISIBLE
{
  DEFPUSHBUTTON "Size", IDD_SIZE, 11, 10, 32, 14,
             WS_CHILD | WS_VISIBLE | WS_TABSTOP
  PUSHBUTTON "State", IDD_STATE, 11, 34, 32, 14,
             WS_CHILD | WS_VISIBLE | WS_TABSTOP
  PUSHBUTTON "Zone", IDD_ZONE, 11, 58, 32, 14,
             WS_CHILD | WS_VISIBLE | WS_TABSTOP
  PUSHBUTTON "Cancel", IDCANCEL, 8, 82, 38, 16,
             WS_CHILD | WS_VISIBLE | WS_TABSTOP
  LISTBOX IDD_LB1, 66, 5, 63, 33, LBS_NOTIFY |
             WS_VISIBLE | WS_BORDER | WS_VSCROLL | WS_TABSTOP
  PUSHBUTTON "Select City", IDD_SELECT, 72, 41, 54, 14,
             WS_CHILD | WS_VISIBLE | WS_TABSTOP
  EDITTEXT IDD_EB1, 65, 73, 63, 12, ES_LEFT | WS_VISIBLE |
             WS_BORDER | ES_AUTOHSCROLL | WS_TABSTOP
  PUSHBUTTON "Enter City", IDD_DONE, 73, 91, 46, 14,
             WS_CHILD | WS_VISIBLE | WS_TABSTOP
}
```

Next, you must make the following changes to the program:

1. Create a global handle called **hDlg**.
2. Add **IsDialogMessage( )** to the message loop.
3. Create the dialog box by using **CreateDialog( )** rather than **DialogBox( )**.
4. Close the dialog box by using **DestroyWindow( )** instead of **EndDialog( )**.

The entire listing (which incorporates these changes) for the modeless dialog box example is shown next. (You should try this program on your own to fully understand the difference between modal and modeless dialog boxes.)

```
/* Demonstrate a Modeless Dialog Box */

#include <windows.h>
#include <string.h>
```

```c
#include <stdio.h>
#include "dialog.h"

#define NUMCITIES 6

LRESULT CALLBACK WindowFunc(HWND, UINT, WPARAM, LPARAM);
BOOL CALLBACK DialogFunc(HWND, UINT, WPARAM, LPARAM);

char szWinName[] = "MyWin"; /* name of window class */

HINSTANCE hInst;

HWND hDlg; /* dialog box handle */

/* cities database */
struct citiesTag {
  char name[30];
  unsigned long size;
  char state[3];
  char timezone[30];
} cities[NUMCITIES] = {
  "New York", 7322564, "NY", "Eastern",
  "Atlanta", 394017, "GA", "Eastern",
  "Chicago", 2783726, "IL", "Central",
  "Houston", 1630553, "TX", "Central",
  "Denver", 467610, "CO", "Mountain",
  "Los Angeles", 3485398, "CA", "Pacific"
};


int WINAPI WinMain(HINSTANCE hThisInst, HINSTANCE hPrevInst,
                   LPSTR lpszArgs, int nWinMode)
{
  HWND hwnd;
  MSG msg;
  WNDCLASSEX wcl;
  HANDLE hAccel;

  /* Define a window class. */
  wcl.hInstance = hThisInst; /* handle to this instance */
  wcl.lpszClassName = szWinName; /* window class name */
  wcl.lpfnWndProc = WindowFunc; /* window function */
  wcl.style = 0; /* default style */

  wcl.cbSize = sizeof(WNDCLASSEX); /* set size of WNDCLASSEX */

  wcl.hIcon = LoadIcon(NULL, IDI_APPLICATION); /* Large icon */
  wcl.hIconSm = LoadIcon(NULL, IDI_APPLICATION); /* Small icon */
```

```
wcl.hCursor = LoadCursor(NULL, IDC_ARROW); /* cursor style */

/* specify name of menu resource */
wcl.lpszMenuName = "MYMENU"; /* main menu */

wcl.cbClsExtra = 0; /* no extra */
wcl.cbWndExtra = 0; /* information needed */

/* Make the window white. */
wcl.hbrBackground = GetStockObject(WHITE_BRUSH);

/* Register the window class. */
if(!RegisterClassEx(&wcl)) return 0;

/* Now that a window class has been registered, a window
   can be created. */
hwnd = CreateWindow(
  szWinName, /* name of window class */
  "Demonstrate a Modeless Dialog Box", /* title */
  WS_OVERLAPPEDWINDOW, /* window style - normal */
  CW_USEDEFAULT, /* X coordinate - let Windows decide */
  CW_USEDEFAULT, /* Y coordinate - let Windows decide */
  CW_USEDEFAULT, /* width - let Windows decide */
  CW_USEDEFAULT, /* height - let Windows decide */
  HWND_DESKTOP, /* no parent window */
  NULL, /* no menu */
  hThisInst, /* handle of this instance of the program */
  NULL /* no additional arguments */
);

hInst = hThisInst; /* save the current instance handle */

/* load accelerators */
hAccel = LoadAccelerators(hThisInst, "MYMENU");

/* Display the window. */
ShowWindow(hwnd, nWinMode);
UpdateWindow(hwnd);

/* Create the message loop. */
while(GetMessage(&msg, NULL, 0, 0))
{
  if(!IsDialogMessage(hDlg, &msg)) {
    /* not dialog box message */
    if(!TranslateAccelerator(hwnd, hAccel, &msg)) {
      TranslateMessage(&msg); /* allow use of keyboard */
```

```
        DispatchMessage(&msg); /* return control to Windows */
      }
    }
  }

  return msg.wParam;
}

/* This function is called by Windows 95 and is passed
   messages from the message queue.
*/
LRESULT CALLBACK WindowFunc(HWND hwnd, UINT message,
                           WPARAM wParam, LPARAM lParam)
{
  int response;

  switch(message) {
    case WM_COMMAND:
      switch(LOWORD(wParam)) {
        case IDM_DIALOG:
          /* create modeless dialog box */
          hDlg = CreateDialog(hInst, "MYDB", hwnd, DialogFunc);
          break;
        case IDM_EXIT:
          response = MessageBox(hwnd, "Quit the Program?",
                               "Exit", MB_YESNO);
          if(response == IDYES) PostQuitMessage(0);
          break;
        case IDM_HELP:
          MessageBox(hwnd, "No Help", "Help", MB_OK);
          break;
      }
      break;
    case WM_DESTROY: /* terminate the program */
      PostQuitMessage(0);
      break;
    default:
      /* Let Windows 95 process any messages not specified in
         the preceding switch statement. */
      return DefWindowProc(hwnd, message, wParam, lParam);
  }
  return 0;
}

/* A simple dialog function. */
BOOL CALLBACK DialogFunc(HWND hdwnd, UINT message,
                        WPARAM wParam, LPARAM lParam)
{
```

```
long i;
char str[80];

switch(message) {
  case WM_COMMAND:
    switch(LOWORD(wParam)) {
      case IDCANCEL:
        DestroyWindow(hdwnd);
        return 1;
      case IDD_SIZE:
        i = SendDlgItemMessage(hdwnd, IDD_LB1,
                LB_GETCURSEL, 0, 0);  /* get index */
        sprintf(str, "%lu", cities[i].size);
        MessageBox(hdwnd, str, "Size", MB_OK);
        return 1;
      case IDD_STATE:
        i = SendDlgItemMessage(hdwnd, IDD_LB1,
                LB_GETCURSEL, 0, 0);  /* get index */
        sprintf(str, "%s", cities[i].state);
        MessageBox(hdwnd, str, "State", MB_OK);
        return 1;
      case IDD_ZONE:
        i = SendDlgItemMessage(hdwnd, IDD_LB1,
                LB_GETCURSEL, 0, 0);  /* get index */
        sprintf(str, "%s", cities[i].timezone);
        MessageBox(hdwnd, str, "Zone", MB_OK);
        return 1;
      case IDD_DONE: /* Enter Cities button pressed */
        /* get current contents of edit box */
        GetDlgItemText(hdwnd, IDD_EB1, str, 80);

        /* find a matching string in the list box */
        i = SendDlgItemMessage(hdwnd, IDD_LB1, LB_FINDSTRING,
                0, (LPARAM) str);

        if(i != LB_ERR) { /* if match is found */
          /* select the matching city in list box */
          SendDlgItemMessage(hdwnd, IDD_LB1, LB_SETCURSEL, i, 0);

          /* get string associated with that index */
          SendDlgItemMessage(hdwnd, IDD_LB1, LB_GETTEXT,
              i, (LPARAM) str);

          /* update text in edit box */
          SetDlgItemText(hdwnd, IDD_EB1, str);
        }
        else MessageBox(hdwnd, str, "No Match With", MB_OK);
        return 1;
```

```
    case IDD_LB1: /* process a list box LBN_DBLCLK */
      /* see if user made a selection */
      if(HIWORD(wParam)==LBN_DBLCLK) {
        i = SendDlgItemMessage(hdwnd, IDD_LB1,
              LB_GETCURSEL, 0, 0);  /* get index */
        sprintf(str, "%s, %s\n%s Time Zone\nPop.:%lu",
              cities[i].name, cities[i].state,
              cities[i].timezone, cities[i].size);

        MessageBox(hdwnd, str, "Selection Made", MB_OK);

        /* get string associated with that index */
        SendDlgItemMessage(hdwnd, IDD_LB1, LB_GETTEXT,
            i, (LPARAM) str);

        /* update edit box */
        SetDlgItemText(hdwnd, IDD_EB1, str);
      }
      return 1;
    case IDD_SELECT: /* Select City button has been pressed */
      i = SendDlgItemMessage(hdwnd, IDD_LB1,
            LB_GETCURSEL, 0, 0);  /* get index */
      sprintf(str, "%s, %s\n%s Time Zone\nPop.:%lu",
            cities[i].name, cities[i].state,
            cities[i].timezone, cities[i].size);

      MessageBox(hdwnd, str, "Selection Made", MB_OK);

      /* get string associated with that index */
      SendDlgItemMessage(hdwnd, IDD_LB1, LB_GETTEXT,
          i, (LPARAM) str);

      /* update edit box */
      SetDlgItemText(hdwnd, IDD_EB1, str);
      return 1;
  }
  break;
case WM_INITDIALOG: /* initialize list box */
  for(i=0; i<NUMCITIES; i++)
    SendDlgItemMessage(hdwnd, IDD_LB1,
            LB_ADDSTRING, 0, (LPARAM)cities[i].name);

  /* select first item */
  SendDlgItemMessage(hdwnd, IDD_LB1, LB_SETCURSEL, 0, 0);

  /* initialize the edit box */
  SetDlgItemText(hdwnd, IDD_EB1, "New York");
```

4

```
      return 1;
    }
    return 0;
}
```

Sample output from this program is shown in Figure 4-4.

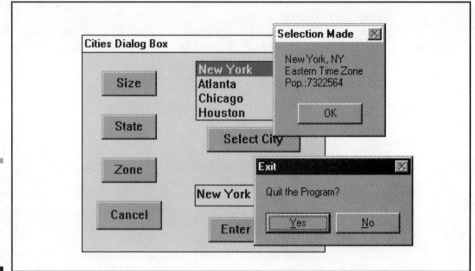

Sample output produced by the modeless dialog box program
Figure 4-4.

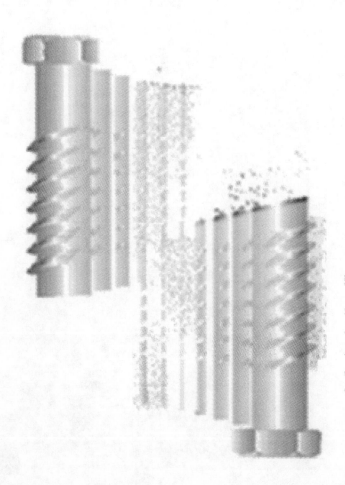

CHAPTER 5

More Controls

Controls were introduced in the preceding chapter, when dialog boxes were first discussed. This chapter continues the topic by examining three more of Windows 95's standard controls: scroll bars, check boxes, and radio buttons. As you will see, many of the techniques that you learned when using controls in Chapter 4 will apply to the controls discussed here.

This chapter begins with a discussion of the scroll bar and illustrates its use in a simple example program. Although scroll bars offer a bit more of a programming challenge than do the other standard controls, they are still quite easy to use. Next, check boxes and radio buttons are discussed. The chapter concludes with a demonstration program that requires the use of all three controls. The program implements a simple countdown timer. You could use such a program as a darkroom timer, for example. In the process of developing the countdown timer, Windows 95 timer interrupts and the **WM_TIMER** message are explored.

Scroll Bars

The scroll bar is one of Windows 95's most important controls. Scroll bars exist in two forms. The first type of scroll bar is an integral part of a normal window or dialog box. This is called a *standard scroll bar*. The other type of scroll bar exists separately as a control and is called a *scroll bar control*. Both types of scroll bars are managed in the same way. Since the standard window scroll bars are the most common, they will be examined here. However, the same general techniques also apply to scroll bar controls. Although many newcomers to Windows programming expect scroll bars to be difficult, this is not the case. As you will see, using a scroll bar is quite straightforward.

Generating Standard Scroll Bars

For a window to include standard scroll bars, you must explicitly request it. In the case of a dialog box, this means including the **WS_VSCROLL** and/or **WS_HSCROLL** styles in the dialog box's definition inside its resource file. As expected, the **WS_VSCROLL** causes a standard vertical scroll bar to be included, and **WS_HSCROLL** activates a horizontal scroll bar. After you have added these styles, the dialog box will automatically display the standard vertical and horizontal scroll bars.

Receiving Scroll Bar Messages

Unlike other controls, a scroll bar control does not generate a **WM_COMMAND** message. Instead, scroll bars send either a **WM_VSCROLL** or a **WM_HSCROLL** message when either a vertical or horizontal scroll bar is accessed, respectively. The value of the low-order word of **wParam** contains a code that describes the activity. For the standard window scroll bars, **lParam** is 0. However, if a scroll bar control generates the message, then **lParam** contains the handle of the scroll bar control.

As mentioned, the value in **LOWORD(wParam)** specifies what type of scroll bar action has taken place. Here are some common scroll bar values:

SB_LINEUP
SB_LINEDOWN
SB_PAGEUP
SB_PAGEDOWN
SB_LINELEFT
SB_LINERIGHT
SB_PAGELEFT
SB_PAGERIGHT
SB_THUMBPOSITION
SB_THUMBTRACK

For vertical scroll bars, each time the user moves the scroll bar up one position, **SB_LINEUP** is sent. Each time the scroll bar is moved down one position, **SB_LINEDOWN** is sent. **SB_PAGEUP** and **SB_PAGEDOWN** are sent when the scroll bar is moved up or down one page.

For horizontal scroll bars, each time the user moves the scroll bar left one position, **SB_LINELEFT** is sent. Each time the scroll bar is moved right one position, **SB_LINERIGHT** is sent. **SB_PAGELEFT** and **SB_PAGERIGHT** are sent when the scroll bar is moved left or right one page.

For both types of scroll bars, the **SB_THUMBPOSITION** value is sent each time the *slider box* (also called the *thumb*) is dragged to a new position. The **SB_THUMBTRACK** message also is sent when the thumb is dragged to a new position. In addition, however, it is sent each time the thumb *passes over* a new position. This allows you to "track" the movement of the thumb before it is released. When **SB_THUMBPOSITION** or **SB_THUMBTRACK** is received, the high-order word of **wParam** contains the current slider box position.

5

Note: Relative to scroll bar messages, the organization of **lParam** and **wParam** in Windows 95 differs substantially from that used by Windows 3.1. Refer to Appendix A for details.

SetScrollInfo( ) and GetScrollInfo( )

Scroll bars are, for the most part, manually managed controls. This means that in addition to responding to scroll bar messages, your program will also need to update various attributes associated with a scroll bar. For example, your program must update the position of the slider box manually.

Windows 95 contains two functions that help you manage scroll bars. The first is **SetScrollInfo( )**, which is used to set various attributes associated with a scroll bar. It has this prototype:

>   int SetScrollInfo(HWND *hwnd*, int *Which*,
>   LPSCROLLINFO *lpSI*, BOOL *repaint*);

Here, *hwnd* is the handle that identifies the scroll bar. For window scroll bars, this is the handle of the window that owns the scroll bar. For scroll bar controls, this is the handle of the scroll bar itself. The value of *Which* determines which scroll bar is affected. If you are setting the attributes of the vertical window scroll bar, then this parameter must be **SB_VERT**. If you are setting the attributes of the horizontal window scroll bar, this value must be **SB_HORZ**. However, to set a scroll bar control, this value must be **SB_CTL**, and *hwnd* must be the handle of the control. The attributes are set according to the information pointed to by *lpSI* (discussed shortly). If *repaint* is true, then the scroll bar is redrawn. If false, the bar is not redisplayed. The function returns the position of the slider box.

To obtain the attributes associated with a scroll bar, use **GetScrollInfo( )**, shown here:

>   BOOL GetScrollInfo(HWND *hwnd*, int *Which*, LPSCROLLINFO *lpSI)*;

The *hwnd* and *Which* parameters are the same as those just described for **SetScrollInfo( )**. The information obtained by **GetScrollInfo( )** is put into the structure pointed to by *lpSI*. The function returns nonzero if successful and zero on failure.

The *lpSI* parameter of both functions points to a structure of type **SCROLLINFO**, which is defined like this:

```
typedef struct tagSCROLLINFO
{
  UINT cbSize; /* size of SCROLLINFO */
  UINT fMask; /* Operation performed */
  int nMin; /* minimum range */
  int nMax; /* maximum range */
  UINT nPage; /* Page value */
  int nPos; /* slider box position */
  int nTrackPos; /* current tracking position */
} SCROLLINFO;
```

Here, **cbSize** must contain the size of the **SCROLLINFO** structure. The value or values contained in **fMask** determine which of the remaining members contain valid information. **fMask** must be one or more of these values. (To combine values, simply OR them together.)

SIF_ALL	Same as SIF_PAGE ¦ SIF_POS ¦ SIF_RANGE ¦ SIF_TRACKPOS
SIF_DISABLENOSCROLL	Scroll bar is disabled rather than removed if its range is set to zero
SIF_PAGE	**nPage** contains valid information
SIF_POS	**nPos** contains valid information
SIF_RANGE	**nMin** and **nMax** contain valid information
SIF_TRACKPOS	**nTrackPos** contains valid information

nPage contains the current page setting for proportional scroll bars. **nPos** contains the position of the slider box. **nMin** and **nMax** contain the minimum and maximum range of the scroll bar. **nTrackPos** contains the current tracking position. The tracking position is the current position of the slider box while it is being dragged by the user. This value cannot be set.

Working with Scroll Bars

As stated, scroll bars are manually managed controls. This means that your program will need to update the position of the slider box within the scroll bar each time it is moved. To do this, you will need to assign **nPos** the value of the new position, assign **fMask** the value **SIF_POS**, and then call **SetScrollInfo( )**. For example, to update the slider box for the vertical scroll bar, your program will need to execute a sequence like the following:

```
SCROLLINFO si;
/*
   .
   .
   .
*/
si.cbSize = sizeof(SCROLLINFO);
si.fMask = SIF_POS;
si.nPos = newposition;
SetScrollInfo(hwnd, SB_VERT, &si, 1);
```

The range of the scroll bar determines how many positions there are between one end and the other. By default, window scroll bars have a range of 0 to 100. However, you can set their range to meet the needs of your program. Control scroll bars have a default range of 0 to 0, which means that the range must be set before the scroll bar control can be used. (A scroll

5

bar that has a zero range is inactive.) Setting the range can make it easier for your application to maintain the position of the slider box.

A Sample Scroll Bar Program

The sample program in this section demonstrates both vertical and horizontal standard scroll bars. The scroll bar program requires the following resource file:

```
; Demonstrate scroll bars.
#include "scroll.h"
#include <windows.h>

MYMENU MENU
{
  POPUP "&Dialog"
  {
    MENUITEM "&Scroll Bars\tF2", IDM_DIALOG
    MENUITEM "&Exit\tF3", IDM_EXIT
  }
  MENUITEM "&Help", IDM_HELP
}

MYMENU ACCELERATORS
{
  VK_F2, IDM_DIALOG, VIRTKEY
  VK_F3, IDM_EXIT, VIRTKEY
  VK_F1, IDM_HELP, VIRTKEY
}

MYDB DIALOG 18, 18, 142, 92
CAPTION "Using Scroll Bars"
STYLE DS_MODALFRAME | WS_POPUP | WS_CAPTION | WS_SYSMENU
      | WS_VSCROLL | WS_HSCROLL
{
}
```

As you can see, the dialog box definition is empty. The scroll bars are added automatically because of the **WS_VSCROLL** and **WS_HSCROLL** style specifications.

You will also need to create this header file, called SCROLL.H:

```
#define IDM_DIALOG    100
#define IDM_EXIT      101
#define IDM_HELP      102
```

The vertical scroll bar in the following program responds to the **SB_LINEUP**, **SB_LINEDOWN**, **SB_PAGEUP**, **SB_PAGEDOWN**, **SB_THUMBPOSITION,** and **SB_THUMBTRACK** messages by moving the slider box appropriately. It also displays the current position of the thumb. The position will change as you move the slider. The horizontal scroll bar only responds to **SB_LINELEFT** and **SB_LINERIGHT**. Its thumb position is also displayed. (On your own, you might try adding the necessary code to make the horizontal scroll bar respond to other messages.) Notice that the range of both the horizontal and vertical scroll bars is set when the dialog box receives a **WM_INITDIALOG** message. You might want to try changing the range of the scroll bars and observing the results.

One other point: notice that the thumb position of each scroll bar is displayed by outputting text into the client area of the dialog box using **TextOut( )**. Although a dialog box performs a special purpose, it is still a window with the same basic characteristics as the main window.

The entire scroll bar demonstration program is shown here:

```
/* Demonstrate Scroll Bars */

#include <windows.h>
#include <string.h>
#include <stdio.h>
#include "scroll.h"

#define VERTRANGEMAX 200
#define HORZRANGEMAX  50

LRESULT CALLBACK WindowFunc(HWND, UINT, WPARAM, LPARAM);
BOOL CALLBACK DialogFunc(HWND, UINT, WPARAM, LPARAM);

char szWinName[] = "MyWin"; /* name of window class */

HINSTANCE hInst;

int WINAPI WinMain(HINSTANCE hThisInst, HINSTANCE hPrevInst,
                   LPSTR lpszArgs, int nWinMode)
{
  HWND hwnd;
  MSG msg;
  WNDCLASSEX wcl;
  HANDLE hAccel;

  /* Define a window class. */
  wcl.hInstance = hThisInst; /* handle to this instance */
  wcl.lpszClassName = szWinName; /* window class name */
```

5

```
wcl.lpfnWndProc = WindowFunc; /* window function */
wcl.style = 0; /* default style */

wcl.cbSize = sizeof(WNDCLASSEX); /* set size of WNDCLASSEX */

wcl.hIcon = LoadIcon(NULL, IDI_APPLICATION); /* large icon */
wcl.hIconSm = LoadIcon(NULL, IDI_APPLICATION); /* small icon */

wcl.hCursor = LoadCursor(NULL, IDC_ARROW); /* cursor style */

/* specify name of menu resource */
wcl.lpszMenuName = "MYMENU"; /* main menu */

wcl.cbClsExtra = 0; /* no extra */
wcl.cbWndExtra = 0; /* information needed */

/* Make the window white. */
wcl.hbrBackground = GetStockObject(WHITE_BRUSH);

/* Register the window class. */
if(!RegisterClassEx(&wcl)) return 0;

/* Now that a window class has been registered, a window
   can be created. */
hwnd = CreateWindow(
  szWinName, /* name of window class */
  "Managing Scroll Bars", /* title */
  WS_OVERLAPPEDWINDOW, /* window style - normal */
  CW_USEDEFAULT, /* X coordinate - let Windows decide */
  CW_USEDEFAULT, /* Y coordinate - let Windows decide */
  CW_USEDEFAULT, /* width - let Windows decide */
  CW_USEDEFAULT, /* height - let Windows decide */
  HWND_DESKTOP, /* no parent window */
  NULL, /* no menu */
  hThisInst, /* handle of this instance of the program */
  NULL /* no additional arguments */
);

hInst = hThisInst; /* save the current instance handle */

/* load accelerators */
hAccel = LoadAccelerators(hThisInst, "MYMENU");

/* Display the window. */
ShowWindow(hwnd, nWinMode);
UpdateWindow(hwnd);

/* Create the message loop. */
```

```
    while(GetMessage(&msg, NULL, 0, 0))
    {
      if(!TranslateAccelerator(hwnd, hAccel, &msg)) {
        TranslateMessage(&msg); /* allow use of keyboard */
        DispatchMessage(&msg); /* return control to Windows */
      }
    }
    return msg.wParam;
}

/* This function is called by Windows 95 and is passed
   messages from the message queue.
*/
LRESULT CALLBACK WindowFunc(HWND hwnd, UINT message,
                                 WPARAM wParam, LPARAM lParam)
{
  int response;

  switch(message) {
    case WM_COMMAND:
      switch(LOWORD(wParam)) {
        case IDM_DIALOG:
          DialogBox(hInst, "MYDB", hwnd, DialogFunc);
          break;
        case IDM_EXIT:
          response = MessageBox(hwnd, "Quit the Program?",
                                  "Exit", MB_YESNO);
          if(response == IDYES) PostQuitMessage(0);
          break;
        case IDM_HELP:
          MessageBox(hwnd, "Try the Scroll Bar", "Help", MB_OK);
          break;
      }
      break;
    case WM_DESTROY: /* terminate the program */
      PostQuitMessage(0);
      break;
    default:
      /* Let Windows 95 process any messages not specified in
         the preceding switch statement. */
      return DefWindowProc(hwnd, message, wParam, lParam);
  }
  return 0;
}

/* Dialog function */
BOOL CALLBACK DialogFunc(HWND hdwnd, UINT message,
                           WPARAM wParam, LPARAM lParam)
```

5

```
{
  char str[80];
  static int vpos = 0; /* vertical slider box position */
  static int hpos = 0; /* horizontal slider box position */
  static SCROLLINFO si; /* scroll bar info structure */

  HDC hdc;
  PAINTSTRUCT paintstruct;

  switch(message) {
    case WM_COMMAND:
      switch(LOWORD(wParam)) {
        case IDCANCEL:
          EndDialog(hdwnd, 0);
          return 1;
      }
      break;
    case WM_INITDIALOG:
      si.cbSize = sizeof(SCROLLINFO);
      si.fMask = SIF_RANGE;
      si.nMin = 0; si.nMax = VERTRANGEMAX;
      SetScrollInfo(hdwnd, SB_VERT, &si, 1);
      si.nMax = HORZRANGEMAX;
      SetScrollInfo(hdwnd, SB_HORZ, &si, 1);
      return 1;
    case WM_PAINT:
      hdc = BeginPaint(hdwnd, &paintstruct);
      sprintf(str, "Vertical: %d", vpos);
      TextOut(hdc, 1, 1, str, strlen(str));
      sprintf(str, "Horizontal: %d", hpos);
      TextOut(hdc, 1, 30, str, strlen(str));
      EndPaint(hdwnd, &paintstruct);
      return 1;
    case WM_VSCROLL:
      switch(LOWORD(wParam)) {
        case SB_LINEDOWN:
          vpos++;
          if(vpos>VERTRANGEMAX) vpos = VERTRANGEMAX;
          break;
        case SB_LINEUP:
          vpos--;
          if(vpos<0) vpos = 0;
          break;
        case SB_THUMBPOSITION:
          vpos = HIWORD(wParam); /* get current position */
          break;
        case SB_THUMBTRACK:
          vpos = HIWORD(wParam); /* get current position */
```

```
        break;
      case SB_PAGEDOWN:
        vpos += 5;
        if(vpos>VERTRANGEMAX) vpos = VERTRANGEMAX;
        break;
      case SB_PAGEUP:
        vpos -= 5;
        if(vpos<0) vpos = 0;
    }
    si.fMask = SIF_POS;
    si.nPos = vpos;
    SetScrollInfo(hdwnd, SB_VERT, &si, 1);
    hdc = GetDC(hdwnd);
    sprintf(str, "Vertical: %d   ", vpos);
    TextOut(hdc, 1, 1, str, strlen(str));
    ReleaseDC(hdwnd, hdc);
    return 1;
  case WM_HSCROLL:
    switch(LOWORD(wParam)) {
      case SB_LINERIGHT:
        hpos++;
        if(hpos>HORZRANGEMAX) hpos = HORZRANGEMAX;
        break;
      case SB_LINELEFT:
        hpos--;
        if(hpos<0) hpos = 0;
    }
    si.fMask = SIF_POS;
    si.nPos = hpos;
    SetScrollInfo(hdwnd, SB_HORZ, &si, 1);
    hdc = GetDC(hdwnd);
    sprintf(str, "Horizontal: %d   ", hpos);
    TextOut(hdc, 1, 30, str, strlen(str));
    ReleaseDC(hdwnd, hdc);
    return 1;
  }
  return 0;
}
```

5

Sample output from the program is shown in Figure 5-1.

Check Boxes

A *check box* is a control that is used to turn an option on or off. It consists of a small rectangle that can either contain a check mark or not. A check box has associated with it a label that describes what option the box represents. If the box contains a check mark, the box is said to be *checked* and the option is selected. If the box is empty, then the option will be deselected.

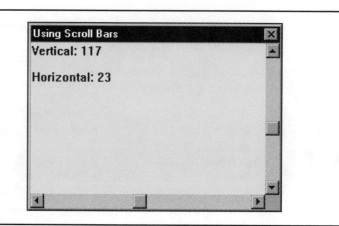

Sample output
from the
scroll bar
demonstration
program
Figure 5-1.

Creating a Scroll Bar Control

To create a scroll bar control in a dialog box, use the **SCROLLBAR**
statement, which has this general form:

   SCROLLBAR *SBID*, *X*, *Y*, *Width*, *Height* [, *Style*]

Here, *SBID* is the value associated with the scroll bar. The scroll bar's
upper-left corner will be at *X*, *Y*, and the scroll bar will have the dimensions
specified by *Width* × *Height*. *Style* determines the exact nature of the scroll
bar. Its default style is **SBS_HORZ**, which creates a horizontal scroll bar.
For a vertical scroll bar, specify the **SBS_VERT** style. If you want the scroll
bar to be able to receive keyboard focus, include the **WS_TABSTOP** style.
For example, the following dialog box definition

```
MYDB DIALOG 18, 18, 142, 92
CAPTION "Using Scroll Bars"
STYLE DS_MODALFRAME | WS_POPUP | WS_CAPTION | WS_SYSMENU
     | WS_VSCROLL | WS_HSCROLL
{
  SCROLLBAR ID_SB1, 110, 10, 10, 70, SBS_VERT | WS_TABSTOP
}
```

adds a vertical scroll bar control.

If you want to try the scroll bar control, you can do so by modifying the
scroll bar example program. First add the following line to SCROLL.H.

```
#define ID_SB1 200
```

Next, you will need to modify parts of the scroll bar example program so that it can distinguish between the standard scroll bars and the scroll bar control. To do this, just remember that a scroll bar control passes its handle in **lParam**. For standard scroll bars, **lParam** is zero. For example, here is one way to modify the **SB_LINEDOWN** case so that it can distinguish between the standard scroll bar and the control scroll bar.

```
case SB_LINEDOWN:
  if(lParam) { /* is scroll bar control */
    cntlpos++;
    if(cntlpos>VERTRANGEMAX) cntlpos = VERTRANGEMAX;
    si.fMask = SIF_POS;
    si.nPos = cntlpos;
    SetScrollInfo((HWND)lParam, SB_CTL, &si, 1);
    hdc = GetDC(hdwnd);
    sprintf(str, "Scroll Bar Control: %d   ", cntlpos);
    TextOut(hdc, 1, 60, str, strlen(str));
    ReleaseDC(hdwnd, hdc);
    return 1;
  }
  else { /* is window scroll bar */
    vpos++;
    if(vpos>VERTRANGEMAX) vpos = VERTRANGEMAX;
  }
  break;
```

The variable **cntlpos** holds the position of the slider box within the control scroll bar. It must be initially set to zero. You will also need to set the range of the control scroll bar when the dialog box is initialized. After making the appropriate changes, the program will produce the following dialog box:

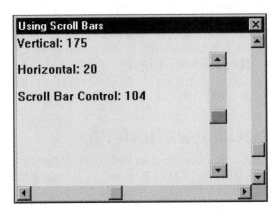

5

A check box is a control that is typically part of a dialog box and is generally defined within the dialog box's definition in your program's resource file. To add a check box to a dialog box definition, use either the **CHECKBOX** or **AUTOCHECKBOX** command. Their general forms are as follows:

CHECKBOX "*string*", *CBID*, *X*, *Y*, *Width*, *Height* [, *Style*]

AUTOCHECKBOX "*string*", *CBID*, *X*, *Y*, *Width*, *Height* [, *Style*]

Here, *string* is the text that will be shown alongside the check box. *CBID* is the value associated with the check box. The box's upper-left corner will be at *X*, *Y*, and the box plus its associated text will have the dimensions specified by *Width* × *Height*. *Style* determines the exact nature of the check box. If no explicit style is specified, then the check box defaults to displaying the *string* on the right and allowing the box to be tabbed to. When a check box is first created, it is unchecked.

As you know, check boxes are toggles. Each time you select a check box, its state changes from checked to unchecked, and vice versa. However, this is not necessarily accomplished automatically. When you use the **CHECKBOX** resource command, you are creating a *manual check box,* which your program must manage by checking and unchecking the box each time it is selected. (That is, a manual check box must be manually toggled by your program.) However, you can have Windows 95 perform this housekeeping function for you if you create an *automatic check box* by using **AUTOCHECKBOX**. When you use an automatic check box, Windows 95 automatically toggles its state (between checked and not checked) each time it is selected. Since most applications do not need to manually manage a check box, we will be using only **AUTOCHECKBOX** in the examples that follow.

Obtaining the State of a Check Box

A check box is either checked or unchecked. You can determine the status of a check box by sending it the message **BM_GETCHECK** by use of the **SendDlgItemMessage( )** API function. (**SendDlgItemMessage( )** is described in Chapter 4.) When you send this message, both *wParam* and *lParam* are 0. The check box returns 1 if the box is checked, and 0 otherwise.

Checking a Check Box

A check box can be checked by your program. To do this, send the check box a **BM_SETCHECK** message by using the **SendDlgItemMessage( )** API function. In this case, *wParam* determines whether the check box will be checked or cleared. If *wParam* is 1, the check box is checked. If it is 0, the box is cleared. In all cases, *lParam* is 0.

As mentioned, manual check boxes will need to be checked or cleared by your program each time they are toggled by the user. However, when using an automatic check box, your program will only need to explicitly check or clear the box during initialization. The state an automatic check box is changed automatically each time it is selected.

Remember: Check boxes are cleared (that is, unchecked) each time the dialog box containing them is activated. If you want the check boxes to reflect their previous state, then you must initialize them each time the dialog box is activated. The easiest way to do this is to send them the appropriate **BM_SETCHECK** messages when the dialog box is created. Keep in mind that each time a dialog box is activated, it is sent a **WM_INITDIALOG** message. When this message is received, you can set the state of the check boxes (and anything else) inside the dialog box.

Check Box Messages

Each time the user clicks on the check box or selects the check box and then presses the spacebar, a **WM_COMMAND** message is sent to the dialog function and the low-order word of **wParam** contains the identifier associated with that check box. If you are using a manual check box, then you will want to respond to this command by changing the state of the box.

Radio Buttons

The next control that we will examine is the *radio button*. Radio buttons are used to present mutually exclusive options. A radio button consists of a label and a small circular button. If the button is empty, then the option is not selected. If the button is filled, then the option is selected. Windows 95 supports two types of radio buttons: manual and automatic. The *manual radio button* (like the manual check box) requires that you perform all management functions. The *automatic radio button* performs the management functions for you. Because automatic radio buttons are used almost exclusively, they are the only ones examined here.

Like other controls, automatic radio buttons are defined in your program's resource file, within a dialog definition. To create an automatic radio button, use **AUTORADIOBUTTON**, which has this general form:

AUTORADIOBUTTON "*string*", *RBID, X, Y, Width, Height* [, *Style*]

Here, *string* is the text that will be shown alongside the button. *RBID* is the value associated with the radio button. The button's upper-left corner will be at *X, Y,* and the button plus its associated text will have the dimensions

5

FAST TRACK TIP

The Three-State Check Box

Windows 95 provides an interesting variation of the check box called the *three-state box*. This check box has three possible states: checked, cleared, or grayed. (When the control is grayed, it is disabled.) Like its check box relative, the three-state check box can be implemented as either an automatic or manually managed control—by use of the **AUTO3STATE** and **STATE3** resource commands, respectively. Their general forms are as follows:

STATE3 "*string*", *ID*, *X*, *Y*, *Width*, *Height* [, *Style*]

AUTO3STATE "*string*", *ID*, *X*, *Y*, *Width*, *Height* [, *Style*]

Here, *string* is the text that will be shown alongside the check box. *ID* is the value associated with the check box. The box's upper-left corner will be at *X*, *Y*, and the box plus its associated text will have the dimensions specified by *Width* × *Height*. *Style* determines the exact nature of the check box. If no explicit style is specified, then the check box defaults to displaying the *string* on the right and allowing the box to be tabbed to. When a three-state check box is first created, it is unchecked.

In response to a **BM_GETCHECK** message, three-state check boxes return 0 if unchecked, 1 if checked, and 2 if grayed. Correspondingly, when setting a three-state check box using **BM_SETCHECK**, use 0 to clear it, 1 to check it, and 2 to gray it.

specified by *Width* × *Height*. *Style* determines the exact nature of the radio button. If no explicit style is specified, then the button defaults to displaying the *string* on the right and allowing the button to be tabbed to. By default, a radio button is unchecked.

As stated, radio buttons are generally used to create groups of mutually exclusive options. When you use automatic radio buttons to create such a group, then Windows 95 automatically manages the buttons in a mutually exclusive manner. That is, each time you select one button, the previously selected button is turned off. Also, it is not possible to select more than one button at any one time.

You can set a radio button (even an automatic one) to a known state by using the **SendDlgItemMessage( )** function to send it the **BM_SETCHECK** message. The value of *wParam* determines whether the button will be checked or cleared. If *wParam* is 1, then the button will be checked. If it is 0, the box will be cleared. By default, all buttons are cleared.

Note: Even if you use automatic radio buttons, it is possible to manually set more than one option or to clear all options by using **SendDlgItemMessage( )**. However, normal Windows style dictates that radio buttons be used in a mutually exclusive fashion, with one (and only one) option selected. It is strongly suggested that you do not violate this rule.

You can obtain the status of a radio button by sending it the **BM_GETCHECK** message. The button returns 1 if the button is selected and 0 if it is not.

Demonstrating Check Boxes, Radio Buttons, and Scroll Bars

To conclude this chapter, a simple but useful program is developed. It implements a countdown timer. Using the timer, you can set the number of seconds that you want to delay. The program will then wait that number of seconds and notify you when the time is up. The countdown timer utilizes the three controls described in this chapter. Specifically, it uses a scroll bar to set the number of seconds to delay. It uses check boxes and radio buttons to set various options, such as whether the program will beep when the end of the time has been reached. However, before we can develop the program, you will need to learn about another feature of Windows 95: timers. The countdown program will use one of Windows 95's built-in timers to monitor the passage of time. As you will see, using a timer is straightforward. Also, as you begin to write your own applications, you will find that timers are useful in a variety of programming situations.

5

Generating Timer Messages

By using Windows 95, you can establish a timer that will interrupt your program at periodic intervals. Each time the timer goes off, Windows 95 sends a **WM_TIMER** message to your program. Using a timer is a good way for you to "wake up your program" every so often. This is particularly useful when your program is running as a background task.

To start a timer, use the **SetTimer( )** API function, which has this prototype:

```
UINT SetTimer(HWND hwnd, UINT nID, UINT wLength,
              TIMERPROC lpTFunc);
```

Here, *hwnd* is the handle of the window that uses the timer. Generally, this window will be either your program's main window or a dialog box window. The value of *nID* specifies a value that will be associated with this timer. (More than one timer can be active.) The value of *wLength* specifies the length of the period, in milliseconds. That is, *wLength* specifies how long there is between interrupts. The function pointed to by *lpTFunc* is the timer function that will be called when the timer goes off. However, if the value of *lpTFunc* is **NULL**, then the window function associated with the window specified by *hwnd* will be called each time the timer goes off, and there is no need to specify a separate timer function. In this case, each time the timer goes off, a **WM_TIMER** message is put into the message queue for your program and processed like any other message. This is the approach used by the example that follows. The **SetTimer( )** function returns *nID* if successful. If the timer cannot be allocated, zero is returned.

If you wish to define a separate timer function, it must be a callback function that has the following prototype. (Of course, the name of the function may be different.)

> VOID CALLBACK TFunc(HWND *hwnd*, UINT *msg*, UINT *TimerID*,
>   DWORD *SysTime*);

Here, *hwnd* will contain the handle of the timer window, *msg* will contain the message **WM_TIMER**, *TimerID* will contain the ID of the timer that went off, and *SysTime* will contain the current system time.

Once a timer has been started, it continues to interrupt your program until either you terminate the application, or until your program executes a call to the **KillTimer( )** API function, which has this prototype:

> BOOL KillTimer(HWND *hwnd*, UINT *nID*);

Here, *hwnd* is the window that contains the timer, and *nID* is the value that identifies that particular timer. The function returns nonzero if successful and zero on failure.

Each time a **WM_TIMER** message is generated, the value of **wParam** contains the ID of the timer, and **lParam** contains the address of the timer callback function (if one is used). For the example that follows, **lParam** will be **NULL**.

The Countdown Timer Resource and Header Files

The countdown timer uses the following resource file:

```
; Demonstrate scroll bars, check boxes, and radio buttons.
#include "cd.h"
#include <windows.h>

MYMENU MENU
{
  POPUP "&Dialog"
  {
    MENUITEM "&Timer\tF2", IDM_DIALOG
    MENUITEM "&Exit\tF3", IDM_EXIT
  }
  MENUITEM "&Help", IDM_HELP
}

MYMENU ACCELERATORS
{
  VK_F2, IDM_DIALOG, VIRTKEY
  VK_F3, IDM_EXIT, VIRTKEY
  VK_F1, IDM_HELP, VIRTKEY
}

MYDB DIALOG 18, 18, 152, 92
CAPTION "A Countdown Timer"
STYLE DS_MODALFRAME ¦ WS_POPUP ¦ WS_CAPTION ¦ WS_SYSMENU
     ¦ WS_VSCROLL
{
  PUSHBUTTON "Start", IDD_START, 10, 60, 30, 14,
             WS_CHILD ¦ WS_VISIBLE ¦ WS_TABSTOP
  PUSHBUTTON "Cancel", IDCANCEL, 60, 60, 30, 14,
             WS_CHILD ¦ WS_VISIBLE ¦ WS_TABSTOP
  AUTOCHECKBOX "Show Countdown", IDD_CB1, 1, 20, 70, 10
  AUTOCHECKBOX "Beep At End", IDD_CB2, 1, 30, 50, 10
  AUTORADIOBUTTON "Minimize", IDD_RB1, 80, 20, 50, 10
  AUTORADIOBUTTON "Maximize", IDD_RB2, 80, 30, 50, 10
  AUTORADIOBUTTON "As-Is", IDD_RB3, 80, 40, 50, 10
}
```

5

The header file required by the timer program is shown next. Call this file CD.H.

```
#define IDM_DIALOG    100
#define IDM_EXIT      101
#define IDM_HELP      102

#define IDD_START     300
#define IDD_TIMER     301

#define IDD_CB1       400
#define IDD_CB2       401
```

```
#define IDD_RB1      402
#define IDD_RB2      403
#define IDD_RB3      404
```

The Countdown Timer Program

The entire Countdown Timer program is shown here:

```
/* A Countdown Timer */

#include <windows.h>
#include <string.h>
#include <stdio.h>
#include "cd.h"

#define VERTRANGEMAX 200

LRESULT CALLBACK WindowFunc(HWND, UINT, WPARAM, LPARAM);
BOOL CALLBACK DialogFunc(HWND, UINT, WPARAM, LPARAM);

char szWinName[] = "MyWin"; /* name of window class */

HINSTANCE hInst;

HWND hwnd;

int WINAPI WinMain(HINSTANCE hThisInst, HINSTANCE hPrevInst,
                   LPSTR lpszArgs, int nWinMode)
{
  MSG msg;
  WNDCLASSEX wcl;
  HANDLE hAccel;

  /* Define a window class. */
  wcl.hInstance = hThisInst; /* handle to this instance */
  wcl.lpszClassName = szWinName; /* window class name */
  wcl.lpfnWndProc = WindowFunc; /* window function */
  wcl.style = 0; /* default style */

  wcl.cbSize = sizeof(WNDCLASSEX); /* set size of WNDCLASSEX */

  wcl.hIcon = LoadIcon(NULL, IDI_APPLICATION); /* large icon */
  wcl.hIconSm = LoadIcon(NULL, IDI_APPLICATION); /* small icon */

  wcl.hCursor = LoadCursor(NULL, IDC_ARROW); /* cursor style */

  /* specify name of menu resource */
```

```
wcl.lpszMenuName = "MYMENU"; /* main menu */

wcl.cbClsExtra = 0; /* no extra */
wcl.cbWndExtra = 0; /* information needed */

/* Make the window white. */
wcl.hbrBackground = GetStockObject(WHITE_BRUSH);

/* Register the window class. */
if(!RegisterClassEx(&wcl)) return 0;

/* Now that a window class has been registered, a window
   can be created. */
hwnd = CreateWindow(
  szWinName, /* name of window class */
  "Demonstrating Controls", /* title */
  WS_OVERLAPPEDWINDOW, /* window style - normal */
  CW_USEDEFAULT, /* X coordinate - let Windows decide */
  CW_USEDEFAULT, /* Y coordinate - let Windows decide */
  CW_USEDEFAULT, /* width - let Windows decide */
  CW_USEDEFAULT, /* height - let Windows decide */
  HWND_DESKTOP, /* no parent window */
  NULL, /* no menu */
  hThisInst, /* handle of this instance of the program */
  NULL /* no additional arguments */
);

hInst = hThisInst; /* save the current instance handle */

/* load accelerators */
hAccel = LoadAccelerators(hThisInst, "MYMENU");

/* Display the window. */
ShowWindow(hwnd, nWinMode);
UpdateWindow(hwnd);

/* Create the message loop. */
while(GetMessage(&msg, NULL, 0, 0))
{
  if(!TranslateAccelerator(hwnd, hAccel, &msg)) {
    TranslateMessage(&msg); /* allow use of keyboard */
    DispatchMessage(&msg); /* return control to Windows */
  }
}
return msg.wParam;
}

/* This function is called by Windows 95 and is passed
   messages from the message queue.
```

5

```
*/
LRESULT CALLBACK WindowFunc(HWND hwnd, UINT message,
                                WPARAM wParam, LPARAM lParam)
{
  int response;

  switch(message) {
    case WM_COMMAND:
      switch(LOWORD(wParam)) {
        case IDM_DIALOG:
          DialogBox(hInst, "MYDB", hwnd, DialogFunc);
          break;
        case IDM_EXIT:
          response = MessageBox(hwnd, "Quit the Program?",
                                "Exit", MB_YESNO);
          if(response == IDYES) PostQuitMessage(0);
          break;
        case IDM_HELP:
          MessageBox(hwnd, "Try the Timer", "Help", MB_OK);
          break;
      }
      break;
    case WM_DESTROY: /* terminate the program */
      PostQuitMessage(0);
      break;
    default:
      /* Let Windows 95 process any messages not specified in
         the preceding switch statement. */
      return DefWindowProc(hwnd, message, wParam, lParam);
  }
  return 0;
}

/* Dialog function */
BOOL CALLBACK DialogFunc(HWND hdwnd, UINT message,
                         WPARAM wParam, LPARAM lParam)
{
  char str[80];
  static int vpos = 0; /* vertical slider box position */
  static SCROLLINFO si; /* scroll bar info structure */

  HDC hdc;
  PAINTSTRUCT paintstruct;

  static int t;

  switch(message) {
```

```
case WM_COMMAND:
  switch(LOWORD(wParam)) {
    case IDCANCEL:
      EndDialog(hdwnd, 0);
      return 1;
    case IDD_START: /* start the timer */
      SetTimer(hdwnd, IDD_TIMER, 1000, NULL);
      t = vpos;
      if(SendDlgItemMessage(hdwnd,
                 IDD_RB1, BM_GETCHECK, 0, 0))
        ShowWindow(hwnd, SW_MINIMIZE);
      else
      if(SendDlgItemMessage(hdwnd,
                 IDD_RB2, BM_GETCHECK, 0, 0))
        ShowWindow(hwnd, SW_MAXIMIZE);
      return 1;
  }
  break;
case WM_TIMER: /* timer went off */
  if(t==0) {
    KillTimer(hdwnd, IDD_TIMER);
    if(SendDlgItemMessage(hdwnd,
                   IDD_CB2, BM_GETCHECK, 0, 0))
      MessageBeep(MB_OK);
    MessageBox(hdwnd, "Timer Went Off", "Timer", MB_OK);
    ShowWindow(hwnd, SW_RESTORE);
    return 1;
  }
  t--;

  /* see if countdown is to be displayed */
  if(SendDlgItemMessage(hdwnd,
                 IDD_CB1, BM_GETCHECK, 0, 0)) {
    hdc = GetDC(hdwnd);
    sprintf(str, "Counting: %d    ", t);
    TextOut(hdc, 1, 1, str, strlen(str));
    ReleaseDC(hdwnd, hdc);
  }
  return 1;
case WM_INITDIALOG:
  si.cbSize = sizeof(SCROLLINFO);
  si.fMask = SIF_RANGE;
  si.nMin = 0; si.nMax = VERTRANGEMAX;
  SetScrollInfo(hdwnd, SB_VERT, &si, 1);

  /* check the As-Is radio button */
  SendDlgItemMessage(hdwnd, IDD_RB3, BM_SETCHECK, 1, 0);
  return 1;
```

5

```
case WM_PAINT:
  hdc = BeginPaint(hdwnd, &paintstruct);
  sprintf(str, "Interval: %d", vpos);
  TextOut(hdc, 1, 1, str, strlen(str));
  EndPaint(hdwnd, &paintstruct);
  return 1;
case WM_VSCROLL:
  switch(LOWORD(wParam)) {
    case SB_LINEDOWN:
      vpos++;
      if(vpos>VERTRANGEMAX) vpos = VERTRANGEMAX;
      break;
    case SB_LINEUP:
      vpos--;
      if(vpos<0) vpos = 0;
      break;
    case SB_THUMBPOSITION:
      vpos = HIWORD(wParam); /* get current position */
      break;
    case SB_THUMBTRACK:
      vpos = HIWORD(wParam); /* get current position */
      break;
    case SB_PAGEDOWN:
      vpos += 5;
      if(vpos>VERTRANGEMAX) vpos = VERTRANGEMAX;
      break;
    case SB_PAGEUP:
      vpos -= 5;
      if(vpos<0) vpos = 0;
  }
  si.fMask = SIF_POS;
  si.nPos = vpos;
  SetScrollInfo(hdwnd, SB_VERT, &si, 1);
  hdc = GetDC(hdwnd);
  sprintf(str, "Interval: %d   ", vpos);
  TextOut(hdc, 1, 1, str, strlen(str));
  ReleaseDC(hdwnd, hdc);
  return 1;
}
return 0;
}
```

Sample output from this program is shown in Figure 5-2.

A Closer Look at the Countdown Program

To better understand how each control in the countdown program operates, let's take a closer look at it now. As you can see, the vertical scroll bar is used

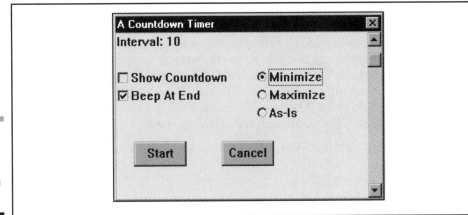

Figure 5-2.

to set the delay. It uses much of the same code that was described earlier in this chapter when scroll bars were examined, and no further explanation is needed. However, the code that manages the check boxes and radio buttons deserves detailed attention.

As mentioned, by default no radio button is checked when the buttons are first created. Thus, the program must manually select one each time the dialog box is activated. In this example, each time a **WM_INITDIALOG** message is received, the As-Is radio button (**IDD_RB3**) is checked by use of this statement.

5

```
SendDlgItemMessage(hdwnd, IDD_RB3, BM_SETCHECK, 1, 0);
```

To start the timer, the user presses the Start button. This causes the following code to execute.

```
case IDD_START: /* start the timer */
  SetTimer(hdwnd, IDD_TIMER, 1000, NULL);
  t = vpos;
  if(SendDlgItemMessage(hdwnd,
          IDD_RB1, BM_GETCHECK, 0, 0))
    ShowWindow(hwnd, SW_MINIMIZE);
  else
  if(SendDlgItemMessage(hdwnd,
        IDD_RB2, BM_GETCHECK, 0, 0))
    ShowWindow(hwnd, SW_MAXIMIZE);
  return 1;
```

Here, the timer is set to go off once every second (1,000 milliseconds). The value of the counter variable **t** is set to the value determined by the position of the vertical scroll bar. If the Minimize radio button is checked, the program windows are minimized. If the Maximize button is checked, they are maximized. Otherwise, the program windows are left unchanged. Notice that the main window handle, **hwnd**, is used in the call to **ShowWindow( )** and not the dialog box handle, **hdwnd**. To minimize or maximize the program, the main window handle must be used—not the handle of the dialog box. Also, notice that **hwnd** is a global variable in this program. This allows it to be used inside **DialogFunc( )**.

Each time a **WM_TIMER** message is received, the following code executes.

```
case WM_TIMER: /* timer went off */
  if(t==0) {
    KillTimer(hdwnd, IDD_TIMER);
    if(SendDlgItemMessage(hdwnd,
                IDD_CB2, BM_GETCHECK, 0, 0))
      MessageBeep(MB_OK);
    MessageBox(hdwnd, "Timer Went Off", "Timer", MB_OK);
    ShowWindow(hwnd, SW_RESTORE);
    return 1;
  }
  t--;

  /* see if countdown is to be displayed */
  if(SendDlgItemMessage(hdwnd,
              IDD_CB1, BM_GETCHECK, 0, 0)) {
    hdc = GetDC(hdwnd);
    sprintf(str, "Counting: %d   ", t);
    TextOut(hdc, 1, 1, str, strlen(str));
    ReleaseDC(hdwnd, hdc);
  }
  return 1;
```

If the countdown has reached zero, the timer is killed, a message box informing the user that the specified time has elapsed is displayed, and the window is restored to its former size, if necessary. If the Beep At End button is checked, then the computer's speaker is beeped.

If there is still time remaining, then the counter variable **t** is decremented. If the Show Countdown button is checked, then the time remaining in the countdown is displayed.

As you can see by looking at the program, since automatic check boxes and radio buttons are mostly managed by Windows 95, there is surprisingly little code within the countdown program that actually deals with these two controls. In fact, the convenience of check boxes and radio buttons helps make them two of the most commonly used control elements.

Static Controls

Although none of the standard controls are difficult to use, there is no question that the static controls are the easiest. The reason for this is simple: a *static control* is one that neither receives nor generates any messages. In short, the term *static control* is just a formal way of describing something that is simply displayed in a dialog box. Static controls include **CTEXT**, **RTEXT**, and **LTEXT**, which are static text controls, and **GROUPBOX**, which is used to visually group other controls.

The **CTEXT** control outputs a string that is centered within a predefined area. **LTEXT** displays the string left-justified. **RTEXT** outputs the string right-justified. The general forms for these controls are as follows:

CTEXT "*text*", *ID, X, Y, Width, Height* [, *Style*]

RTEXT "*text*", *ID, X, Y, Width, Height* [, *Style*]

LTEXT "*text*", *ID, X, Y, Width, Height* [, *Style*]

Here, *text* is the text that will be displayed. *ID* is the value associated with the text. The text will be shown in a box whose upper-left corner will be at *X, Y*, and dimensions are specified by *Width × Height*. *Style* determines the exact nature of the text box. Generally, the default style is sufficient. Understand that the box itself is not displayed. The box simply defines the space that the text is allowed to occupy.

The static text controls provide a convenient means of outputting text to a dialog box. Frequently, static text is used to label other dialog box controls or to provide simple directions to the user. You will want to experiment with the static text controls on your own.

A group box is simply a box the surrounds other dialog elements and is generally used to visually group other items. The box may contain a title. This is the general form for **GROUPBOX**:

GROUPBOX "*title*", *ID, X, Y, Width, Height* [, *Style*]

Here, *title* is the title to the box. *ID* is the value associated with the text. The upper-left corner will be at *X, Y,* and its dimensions are specified by *Width × Height*. *Style* determines the exact nature of the group box. Generally, the default setting is sufficient.

5

To see the effect of using a group box, add the following definition to the resource file you created for the countdown program.

```
GROUPBOX "Display As", 1, 72, 10, 60, 46
```

After you have added the group box, the dialog box will look like the one shown here. Remember that although the group box makes the dialog box look different, its function has not been changed.

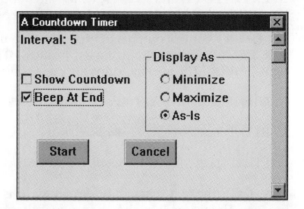

Stand-Alone Controls

One final aspect of controls must be briefly discussed. Although controls are most often used within a dialog box, they may also be freestanding within the client area of the main window. To create a freestanding control, simply use the **CreateWindow( )** or **CreateWindowEx( )** function, specifying the name of the control class and the style of control that you desire. For example, the following code creates a freestanding scroll bar and push button.

```
hsbwnd = CreateWindow(
  "SCROLLBAR", /* name of scroll bar class */
  "", /* no title */
  SBS_HORZ | WS_CHILD | WS_VISIBLE, /* horizontal scroll bar */
  10, 10, /* position */
  120, 20, /* dimensions */
  hwnd, /* parent window */
  NULL, /* no control ID needed for scroll bar */
  hThisInst, /* handle of this instance of the program */
  NULL /* no additional arguments */
);
```

```
hpbwnd = CreateWindow(
  "BUTTON", /* name of push button class */
  "Push Button", /* text inside button */
  BS_PUSHBUTTON | WS_CHILD | WS_VISIBLE, /* push button */
  10, 60, /* position */
  90, 30, /* dimensions */
  hwnd, /* parent window */
  (HWND) 500, /* control ID */
  hThisInst, /* handle of this instance of the program */
  NULL /* no additional arguments */
);
```

As the push button shows, when a freestanding control requires an associated ID, that ID is specified in the ninth parameter. Freestanding controls send their messages to the main window function and not to a dialog box function.

The standard control class names are listed here:

> BUTTON
> COMBOBOX
> EDIT
> LISTBOX
> SCROLLBAR
> STATIC

Each of these classes has several style macros associated with it. However, it is beyond the scope of this book to describe them. A list of these style macros can be found by examining WINDOWS.H (and its support files) or by referring to an API reference guide.

5

CHAPTER 6

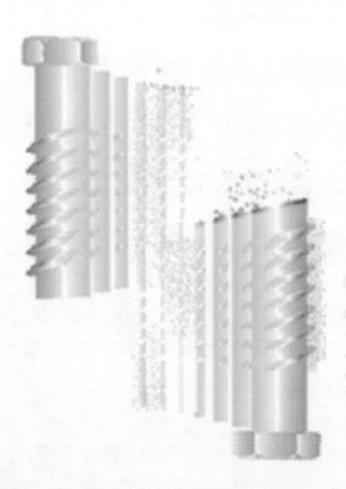

Managing the
Client Area

Although the dialog box is the place where most
user input takes place, the client area of your
program's main window is still where your
application will display most of its output.
Therefore, the effective use and management of
the client area is crucial to nearly all Windows 95
programs. The preceding chapters largely ignored
the client area, concentrating instead on other
Windows 95 fundamentals. However, now it is
time to learn some important techniques that
will help you better manage this resource.

Specifically, this chapter describes how to

♦ Display a bitmap image
♦ Repaint the client area
♦ Manage text output

As you will see, the methods used to accomplish these operations involve some of the most fundamental aspects of Windows 95. Virtually any program that you write will use them. We will begin with displaying a bitmap, because this will introduce several core concepts that will be used by the other operations.

Using a Bitmap

A *bitmap* is a graphics image. Since Windows is a graphics-based operating system, it makes sense that you can include graphics images in your applications. It is important to understand that you can draw graphical objects, such as lines, circles, and boxes, inside the client area of a window by using the rich set of graphics functions contained in the Windows API. (These functions are discussed in Chapter 10.) However, a bitmap, and the mechanism used to display one, is separate from those graphics. A bitmap is a self-contained graphical resource that your program utilizes as a single entity. A bitmap contains a bit-by-bit representation of the image that will ultimately be displayed on the screen. Put differently, a bitmap contains a complete image that your program generally displays in its totality.

Creating a Bitmap

If you wish to try the next example program, which displays a bitmap, you must first create a bitmap resource. To create a bitmap, you must use an image editor. (An image editor will be supplied with your compiler.) Some bitmaps, such as icons and cursors, have a fixed size. However, the size of a custom bitmap is under your control. For the example that follows, your bitmap must be 256×128 pixels. Call your bitmap file BP.BMP. After you have defined your bitmap, create a resource file called BP.RC that contains this line:

```
MYBP1 BITMAP BP.BMP
```

Displaying a Bitmap

Once you have created a bitmap and included it in your application's resource file, you can display it whenever you want in the client area of a window. However, displaying a bitmap requires a little work on your part. The following discussion explains the proper procedure.

Before you can use your custom bitmap, you must load it and store its handle. (This can be done inside **WinMain( )** or any other place that makes sense.) To load the bitmap, use the **LoadBitmap( )** API function, whose prototype is shown here:

HBITMAP LoadBitmap(HINSTANCE *hThisInst,* LPCSTR *lpszName*);

The instance handle is specified in *hThisInst,* and a pointer to the name of the bitmap as specified in the resource file is passed in *lpszName.* The function returns the handle to the bitmap or **NULL** if an error occurs. Here is an example:

```
HBITMAP hBit1; /* handle of bitmap */
/* ... */
hBit1 = LoadBitmap(hThisInst, "MYBP1"); /* load bitmap */
```

This fragment loads a bitmap called **MYBP1** and stores a handle to it in **hBit1**.

When it comes time to display the bitmap, your program must follow these four steps:

1. Obtain the device context so that your program can output to the window.
2. Obtain an equivalent memory device context that will hold the bitmap until it is displayed. (A bitmap is held in memory until it is copied to your window.)
3. Select the bitmap into the memory device context.
4. Finally, copy the bitmap from the memory device context to the window device context. This causes the bitmap to actually be displayed.

6

To see how the preceding four steps can be implemented, consider the following fragment. It causes a bitmap to be displayed at two locations each time a **WM_PAINT** message is received.

```
HDC DC, memDC;
PAINTSTRUCT paintstruct;

/* ... */

case WM_PAINT:
  DC = BeginPaint(hwnd, &paintstruct); /* get device context */

  memDC = CreateCompatibleDC(DC); /* create compatible DC */
  SelectObject(memDC, hBit1); /* select bitmap */
```

```
BitBlt(DC, 10, 10, 256, 128,
       memDC, 0, 0, SRCCOPY); /* display image */
BitBlt(DC, 300, 100, 256, 128,
       memDC, 0, 0, SRCCOPY); /* display image */

EndPaint(hwnd, &paintstruct); /* release DC */
DeleteDC(memDC); /* free the memory context */
break;
```

Let's examine this code, step by step.

First, two device context handles are declared. **DC** will hold the current window device context as obtained by **BeginPaint( )**. The other, called **memDC**, will hold the device context of the memory that stores the bitmap until it is drawn in the window.

Within the **case**, the window device context is obtained. This is necessary because the bitmap will be displayed in the client area of the window, and no output can occur until your program is granted a device context. Next, a memory context is created that will hold the bitmap. This memory device context will be compatible with the window device context. The compatible memory device context is created by use of the **CreateCompatibleDC( )** API function. Its prototype is shown here:

HDC CreateCompatibleDC(HDC *hdc*);

This function returns a handle to a region of memory that is compatible with the device context of the window, specified by *hdc*. This memory will be used to construct an image before it is actually displayed. The function returns **NULL** if an error occurs.

Before a bitmap can be displayed, it must be selected into the device context by use of the **SelectObject( )** API function. Since there can be several bitmaps associated with an application, you must select the one you want to display before it can actually be output to the window. This is the **SelectObject( )** prototype:

HGDIOBJ SelectObject(HDC *hdc*, HGDIOBJ *hObject*);

Here, *hdc* specifies the device context, and *hObject* is the handle of the object being selected into that context. The function returns the handle of the previously selected object, allowing it to be reselected later, if desired.

To actually display the object once it has been selected, use the **BitBlt( )** API function. This function copies a bitmap from one device context to another. Its prototype is as follows:

BOOL BitBlt(HDC *hDest*, int *X*, int *Y*, int *Width*,
int *Height*, HDC *hSource*, int *SourceX*,
int *SourceY*, DWORD *dwHow*);

Here, *hDest* is the handle of the target device context, and *X* and *Y* are the upper-left coordinates where the bitmap will be drawn. The width and height of the bitmap are specified in *Width* and *Height*. The *hSource* parameter contains the handle of the source device context, which in this case will be the memory context obtained by use of **CreateCompatibleDC( )**. The *SourceX* and *SourceY* parameters specify the upper-left coordinates within the bitmap at which the copy operation will begin. These values are usually 0. The value of *dwHow* determines how the bit-by-bit contents of the bitmap will actually be drawn on the screen. Some of its most common values are listed here:

Macro	Effect
SRCCOPY	Copies bitmap as is, overwriting any preexisting output
SRCAND	ANDs bitmap with current destination
SRCPAINT	ORs bitmap with current destination
SRCINVERT	XORs bitmap with current destination

These macros are defined by including WINDOWS.H. **BitBlt( )** returns nonzero if successful and zero on failure.

In the example, each call to **BitBlt( )** displays the entire bitmap by copying it to the client area of the window.

After the bitmap is displayed, both device contexts are released. In this case, **EndPaint( )** is called to release the device context obtained by calling **BeginPaint( )**. To release the memory device context obtained by using **CreateCompatibleDC( )**, you must use **DeleteDC( )**, which takes as its parameter the handle of the device context to release. You cannot use **ReleaseDC( )** for this purpose. (Only a device context obtained through a call to **GetDC( )** can be released by a call to **ReleaseDC( )**.)

A bitmap is a resource that must be removed before your application ends. To remove it, your program must call **DeleteObject( )**, either when the bitmap is no longer needed or when a **WM_DESTROY** message is received. **DeleteObject( )** has this prototype:

BOOL DeleteObject(HGDIOBJ *hObj*);

Here, *hObj* is the handle to the object being deleted. The function returns nonzero if successful and zero on failure.

6

The Complete Bitmap Example Program

Here is the complete bitmap program:

```c
/*  Display a bitmap. */

#include <windows.h>
#include <string.h>
#include <stdio.h>

LRESULT CALLBACK WindowFunc(HWND, UINT, WPARAM, LPARAM);

char szWinName[] = "MyWin"; /* name of window class */

HBITMAP hBit1; /* handle of bitmap */

int WINAPI WinMain(HINSTANCE hThisInst, HINSTANCE hPrevInst,
                   LPSTR lpszArgs, int nWinMode)
{
  HWND hwnd;
  MSG msg;
  WNDCLASSEX wcl;

  /* Define a window class. */
  wcl.hInstance = hThisInst; /* handle to this instance */
  wcl.lpszClassName = szWinName; /* window class name */
  wcl.lpfnWndProc = WindowFunc; /* window function */
  wcl.style = 0; /* default style */

  wcl.cbSize = sizeof(WNDCLASSEX); /* set size of WNDCLASSEX */

  wcl.hIcon = LoadIcon(NULL, IDI_APPLICATION); /* large icon */
  wcl.hIconSm = LoadIcon(NULL, IDI_APPLICATION); /* small icon */

  wcl.hCursor = LoadCursor(NULL, IDC_ARROW); /* cursor style */

  wcl.lpszMenuName = NULL; /* no main menu */

  wcl.cbClsExtra = 0; /* no extra */
  wcl.cbWndExtra = 0; /* information needed */

  /* Make the window white. */
  wcl.hbrBackground = GetStockObject(WHITE_BRUSH);

  /* Register the window class. */
  if(!RegisterClassEx(&wcl)) return 0;
```

```
    /* Now that a window class has been registered, a window
       can be created. */
    hwnd = CreateWindow(
      szWinName, /* name of window class */
      "Displaying a Bitmap", /* title */
      WS_OVERLAPPEDWINDOW, /* window style - normal */
      CW_USEDEFAULT, /* X coordinate - let Windows decide */
      CW_USEDEFAULT, /* Y coordinate - let Windows decide */
      CW_USEDEFAULT, /* width - let Windows decide */
      CW_USEDEFAULT, /* height - let Windows decide */
      HWND_DESKTOP, /* no parent window */
      NULL, /* no menu */
      hThisInst, /* handle of this instance of the program */
      NULL /* no additional arguments */
    );

    /* load the bitmap */
    hBit1 = LoadBitmap(hThisInst, "MYBP1"); /* load bitmap */

    /* Display the window. */
    ShowWindow(hwnd, nWinMode);
    UpdateWindow(hwnd);

    /* Create the message loop. */
    while(GetMessage(&msg, NULL, 0, 0))
    {
      TranslateMessage(&msg); /* allow use of keyboard */
      DispatchMessage(&msg); /* return control to Windows */
    }
    return msg.wParam;
}

/* This function is called by Windows 95 and is passed
   messages from the message queue.
*/
LRESULT CALLBACK WindowFunc(HWND hwnd, UINT message,
                            WPARAM wParam, LPARAM lParam)
{
  HDC DC, memDC;
  PAINTSTRUCT paintstruct;

  switch(message) {
    case WM_PAINT:
      DC = BeginPaint(hwnd, &paintstruct); /* get device context */

      memDC = CreateCompatibleDC(DC); /* create compatible DC */
      SelectObject(memDC, hBit1); /* select bitmap */
```

6

```
          BitBlt(DC, 10, 10, 256, 128,
                  memDC, 0, 0, SRCCOPY); /* display image */
          BitBlt(DC, 300, 100, 256, 128,
                  memDC, 0, 0, SRCCOPY); /* display image */

          EndPaint(hwnd, &paintstruct); /* release DC */
          DeleteDC(memDC); /* free the memory context */
          break;
      case WM_DESTROY: /* terminate the program */
        DeleteObject(hBit1); /* remove the bitmap */
        PostQuitMessage(0);
        break;
      default:
        /* Let Windows 95 process any messages not specified in
            the preceding switch statement. */
        return DefWindowProc(hwnd, message, wParam, lParam);
    }
    return 0;
}
```

Sample output is shown in Figure 6-1.

You might want to experiment with the bitmap program before continuing. For example, try using different copy options with **BitBlt( )**. Also, try different size bitmaps.

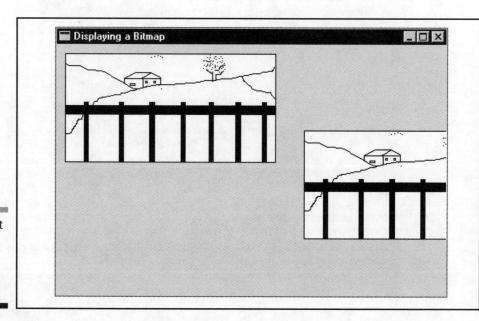

Sample output produced by the custom bitmap

Figure 6-1.

Solving the Repaint Problem

Now that you know how to copy a bitmap to the client area of a window, you can use that knowledge to solve one of the most fundamental problems encountered when writing a Windows 95 program: restoring the contents of a window when a **WM_PAINT** message is received. As you know, in Windows 95 (and all versions of Windows) it is the application's responsibility to redraw the contents of the client area of a window each time a **WM_PAINT** message is received. In general, windows need to be redrawn each time one is uncovered. That is, when you run a program, display something in the client area of a window, and then overlay the window with another, your output is lost. Thus, when the window is uncovered, its contents will need to be repainted. As you will see, the same techniques used to display a bitmap form the basis by which you can solve the repaint problem.

Let's start by reviewing the three basic methods that you can use to repaint a window. First, you can regenerate the output if that output is created by some computational method. Second, you can store a record of display events and "replay" those events. Third, you can maintain a virtual window and simply copy the contents of the virtual window to the physical window each time a **WM_PAINT** message is received. The most general of these is, of course, the third. This is the method that will be developed here.

Here is how output will be accomplished by use of a *virtual window*. First, a virtual device context and bitmap (that is, the virtual window) are created that are compatible with the actual device context used by your application. Thus, a virtual window is simply a compatible bitmap that has the same characteristics as your program's actual window. Once you have created a virtual window, all output intended for the client area of the main window must also be written to the virtual window. This causes the virtual window to contain a complete and current copy of whatever you output to the physical window. Each time a **WM_PAINT** message is received, the contents of the virtual window are copied into the actual window, restoring its contents. Therefore, a window that has been covered and then uncovered will automatically be redrawn when it receives the **WM_PAINT** message.

6

Some Additional API Functions

To implement a virtual window requires the use of several API functions. Four have been discussed already. These are **CreateCompatibleDC( )**, **SelectObject( )**, **GetStockObject( )**, and **BitBlt( )**. We will also be using **CreateCompatibleBitmap( ), PatBlt( ), and GetSystemMetrics( )**, which are described here.

CreateCompatibleBitmap( )

The **CreateCompatibleBitmap( )** function creates a bitmap that is compatible with the specified device context. This bitmap can be used by any memory device context (created by **CreateCompatibleDC( )**) that is compatible with the specified device context. The function's prototype is as follows:

> HBITMAP CreateCompatibleBitmap(HDC *hdc*, int *width*, int *height*);

Here, *hdc* is the handle for the device context with which the bitmap will be compatible. The dimensions of the bitmap are specified in *width* and *height*. These values are in pixels. The function returns a handle to the compatible bitmap or **NULL** on failure.

PatBlt( )

The **PatBlt( )** function fills a rectangle with the color and pattern of the currently selected *brush*. A brush is an object that specifies how a window (or region) will be filled. Filling an area by use of a brush is also commonly referred to as *painting* the region. **PatBlt( )** has this prototype:

> BOOL PatBlt(HDC *hdc*, int *X*, int *Y*, int *width*, int *height*,
>   DWORD *dwHow*);

Here, *hdc* is the handle of the device context. The coordinates *X* and *Y* specify the upper-left corner of the region to be filled. The width and height of the region are specified in *width* and *height.* The value passed in *dwHow* determines how the brush will be applied. It must be one of these macros:

Macro	Meaning
BLACKNESS	Region is black (brush is ignored)
WHITENESS	Region is white (brush is ignored)
PATCOPY	Brush is copied to region
PATINVERT	Brush is ORed to region
DSTINVERT	Region is inverted (brush is ignored)

Therefore, if you wish to apply the current brush unaltered, you would select **PATCOPY** for the value of *dwHow*. The function returns nonzero if successful, zero otherwise.

Obtaining the System Metrics

To create a virtual window requires that we know how big to make the bitmap that will be used as the virtual window. One way to do this is to obtain the size, in pixels, of the screen and use its dimensions for the bitmap. (Actually, a window can be larger than the screen, but this situation is left for you to resolve.) To obtain the size of the screen, and other information, use the **GetSystemMetrics( )** API function, which has this prototype:

    int GetSystemMetrics(int *what*);

Here, *what* specifies the value that you want to obtain. **GetSystemMetrics( )** can obtain many different values. The values for screen coordinates are returned in pixel units. Here are the macros for some common values:

Value	Metric Obtained
SM_CXFULLSCREEN	Width of maximized client area
SM_CYFULLSCREEN	Height of maximized client area
SM_CXICON	Width of large icon
SM_CYICON	Height of large icon
SM_CXSMICON	Width of small icon
SM_CYSMICON	Height of small icon
SM_CXSCREEN	Width of entire screen
SM_CYSCREEN	Height of entire screen

Now that you know about the functions that will be used, it is time to see how to implement a virtual window.

Creating and Using a Virtual Window

Let's begin by restating the procedure that will be implemented. To create an easy and convenient means of restoring a window after a **WM_PAINT** message has been received, a virtual window will be maintained. This means that all output intended for the client area will be written both to the virtual window and to the physical window. Therefore, the virtual window will always contain a complete copy of whatever has been output to the physical window. Each time a repaint request is received, the contents of the virtual window are copied into the window that is physically on the screen. Now, let's implement this approach.

The first step you must follow to create a virtual window is to obtain a virtual device context that is compatible with the current device context. This will be done only once, when the program begins execution. This compatible device context will stay in existence the entire time the program is executing. Here is the code that performs this function.

6

```
case WM_CREATE:
  /* get screen coordinates */
  maxX = GetSystemMetrics(SM_CXSCREEN);
  maxY = GetSystemMetrics(SM_CYSCREEN);

  /* make a compatible memory image */
  hdc = GetDC(hwnd);
  memdc = CreateCompatibleDC(hdc);
  hbit = CreateCompatibleBitmap(hdc, maxX, maxY);
  SelectObject(memdc, hbit);
  hbrush = GetStockObject(WHITE_BRUSH);
  SelectObject(memdc, hbrush);
  PatBlt(memdc, 0, 0, maxX, maxY, PATCOPY);
  ReleaseDC(hwnd, hdc);
  break;
```

Let's examine this code closely. First, the dimensions of the screen are obtained. They will be used to create a compatible bitmap. Then, the current device context is obtained. Next, a compatible device context is created in memory, by use of **CreateCompatibleDC( )**. The handle to this device context is stored in **memdc**, which is a global variable. Then, a compatible bitmap is created. This establishes a one-to-one mapping between the virtual window and the physical window. The dimensions of the bitmap are those of the maximum screen size. This ensures that the bitmap will always be large enough to fully restore the window no matter how large the physical window is. (Actually, slightly smaller values could be used, since the borders aren't repainted, but this minor improvement is left to you, as an exercise.) The handle to the bitmap is stored in the global variable **hbit**. It is also selected into the memory device context. Next, a stock white brush is obtained, and its handle is stored in the global variable **hbrush**. This brush is selected into the memory device context, and then **PatBlt( )** paints the entire virtual window using the brush. Thus, the virtual window will have a white background, which matches the background of the physical window in the example program that follows. (Remember, these colors are under your control. The colors used here are arbitrary.) Finally, the physical device context is released. However, the memory device context exists until the program ends.

Once the virtual window has been created, output can be directed to it. You can also concurrently output to the physical window, but you must make sure that a complete copy of all output is also written to the virtual window. Each time a **WM_PAINT** message is received, you will use the contents of the virtual window to restore the contents of the physical window. You will do this in much the same way that you copied a bitmapped image to the window in the preceding section: by using the **BitBlt( )** function.

The Entire Virtual Window Demonstration Program

Here is the complete program that demonstrates using a virtual window to solve the repaint problem. The program responds to **WM_CHAR** messages by outputting each character to both the virtual window and the physical windows. (That is, it echoes the characters you type to both windows.) When a **WM_PAINT** message is received, the contents of the virtual window are used to restore the physical window.

```c
/* Repaint using a virtual window. */

#include <windows.h>
#include <string.h>
#include <stdio.h>

LRESULT CALLBACK WindowFunc(HWND, UINT, WPARAM, LPARAM);

char szWinName[] = "MyWin"; /* name of window class */

char str[255]; /* holds output strings */

int X=0, Y=0; /* current output location */
int maxX, maxY; /* screen dimensions */

HDC memdc; /* store the virtual device handle */
HBITMAP hbit; /* store the virtual bitmap */
HBRUSH hbrush; /* store the brush handle */

int WINAPI WinMain(HINSTANCE hThisInst, HINSTANCE hPrevInst,
                   LPSTR lpszArgs, int nWinMode)
{
  HWND hwnd;
  MSG msg;
  WNDCLASSEX wcl;

  /* Define a window class. */
  wcl.hInstance = hThisInst; /* handle to this instance */
  wcl.lpszClassName = szWinName; /* window class name */
  wcl.lpfnWndProc = WindowFunc; /* window function */
  wcl.style = 0; /* default style */

  wcl.cbSize = sizeof(WNDCLASSEX); /* set size of WNDCLASSEX */ .

  wcl.hIcon = LoadIcon(NULL, IDI_APPLICATION); /* large icon */
  wcl.hIconSm = LoadIcon(NULL, IDI_APPLICATION); /* small icon */

  wcl.hCursor = LoadCursor(NULL, IDC_ARROW); /* cursor style */
```

```
wcl.lpszMenuName = NULL; /* no main menu */

wcl.cbClsExtra = 0; /* no extra */
wcl.cbWndExtra = 0; /* information needed */

/* Make the window white. */
wcl.hbrBackground = GetStockObject(WHITE_BRUSH);

/* Register the window class. */
if(!RegisterClassEx(&wcl)) return 0;

/* Now that a window class has been registered, a window
   can be created. */
hwnd = CreateWindow(
  szWinName, /* name of window class */
  "Using a Virtual Window", /* title */
  WS_OVERLAPPEDWINDOW, /* window style - normal */
  CW_USEDEFAULT, /* X coordinate - let Windows decide */
  CW_USEDEFAULT, /* Y coordinate - let Windows decide */
  CW_USEDEFAULT, /* width - let Windows decide */
  CW_USEDEFAULT, /* height - let Windows decide */
  HWND_DESKTOP, /* no parent window */
  NULL, /* no menu */
  hThisInst, /* handle of this instance of the program */
  NULL /* no additional arguments */
);

/* Display the window. */
ShowWindow(hwnd, nWinMode);
UpdateWindow(hwnd);

/* Create the message loop. */
while(GetMessage(&msg, NULL, 0, 0))
{
  TranslateMessage(&msg); /* allow use of keyboard */
  DispatchMessage(&msg); /* return control to Windows */
}
return msg.wParam;
}

/* This function is called by Windows 95 and is passed
   messages from the message queue.
*/
LRESULT CALLBACK WindowFunc(HWND hwnd, UINT message,
                            WPARAM wParam, LPARAM lParam)
{
  HDC hdc;
```

```
      PAINTSTRUCT paintstruct;

switch(message) {
  case WM_CREATE:
    /* get screen coordinates */
    maxX = GetSystemMetrics(SM_CXSCREEN);
    maxY = GetSystemMetrics(SM_CYSCREEN);

    /* make a compatible memory image */
    hdc = GetDC(hwnd);
    memdc = CreateCompatibleDC(hdc);
    hbit = CreateCompatibleBitmap(hdc, maxX, maxY);
    SelectObject(memdc, hbit);
    hbrush = GetStockObject(WHITE_BRUSH);
    SelectObject(memdc, hbrush);
    PatBlt(memdc, 0, 0, maxX, maxY, PATCOPY);
    ReleaseDC(hwnd, hdc);
    break;
  case WM_CHAR:
    hdc = GetDC(hwnd);
    sprintf(str, "%c", (char) wParam); /* stringize character */

    /* a "primitive" carriage return, linefeed sequence */
    if((char)wParam == '\r') {
      Y += 14; /* advance to next line */
      X = 0; /* reset to start of line */
    }
    else {
      TextOut(memdc, X, Y, str, strlen(str)); /* output to memory */
      TextOut(hdc, X, Y, str, strlen(str)); /* output to window */
      X += 10;
    }
    ReleaseDC(hwnd, hdc);
    break;
  case WM_PAINT: /* process a repaint request */
    hdc = BeginPaint(hwnd, &paintstruct); /* get DC */

    /* copy memory image onto screen */
    BitBlt(hdc, 0, 0, maxX, maxY, memdc, 0, 0, SRCCOPY);
    EndPaint(hwnd, &paintstruct); /* release DC */
    break;
  case WM_DESTROY: /* terminate the program */
    DeleteDC(memdc); /* delete the memory device */
    PostQuitMessage(0);
    break;
  default:
```

6

```
        /* Let Windows 95 process any messages not specified in
            the preceding switch statement. */
        return DefWindowProc(hwnd, message, wParam, lParam);
    }
    return 0;
}
```

Sample output is shown in Figure 6-2.

Let's look at this program in detail. First, examine the code associated with the **WM_CHAR** message. It is shown here for your convenience.

```
case WM_CHAR:
  hdc = GetDC(hwnd);
  sprintf(str, "%c", (char) wParam); /* stringize character */

  /* a "primitive" carriage return, linefeed sequence */
  if((char)wParam == '\r') {
    Y += 14; /* advance to next line */
    X = 0; /* reset to start of line */
  }
  else {
    TextOut(memdc, X, Y, str, strlen(str)); /* output to memory */
    TextOut(hdc, X, Y, str, strlen(str)); /* output to window */
    X += 10;
  }
  ReleaseDC(hwnd, hdc);
  break;
```

The variables **X** and **Y** are two global integers that are used to maintain the coordinates at which the next character will be displayed. They are initially zero. Each time a character is typed, it is "stringized" and output to both the physical window and the virtual window. Thus, a complete copy of each keystroke is maintained in the virtual window.

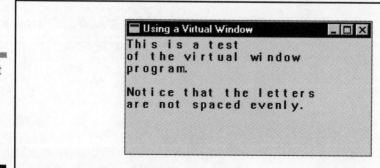

Sample output
from the
virtual
window
program
Figure 6-2.

As you can see, **X** is advanced by 10 for each character typed, and **Y** is increased by 14 to advance to the next line each time ENTER is pressed. This method of determining the proper X, Y location is a crude, temporary measure. In the next section, you will learn the proper way to manage these operations.

Each time a **WM_PAINT** message is received, the contents of the virtual device are copied into the physical device. This is accomplished by the following code:

```
case WM_PAINT: /* process a repaint request */
  hdc = BeginPaint(hwnd, &paintstruct); /* get DC */

  /* copy memory image onto screen */
  BitBlt(hdc, 0, 0, maxX, maxY, memdc, 0, 0, SRCCOPY);
  EndPaint(hwnd, &paintstruct); /* release DC */
  break;
```

As you can see, the **BitBlt( )** function is used to copy the image from **memdc** into **hdc**. Remember, the parameter **SRCCOPY** simply means to copy the image as-is, without alteration directly from the source to the target. Because all output has been stored in **memdc**, this statement causes the window to be restored. You should try this by entering some characters, covering, and then uncovering the window. As you will see, the characters that you typed are redisplayed.

As stated earlier, there are many ways to restore a window, but the method just developed is applicable to a wide range of situations and is, generally, quite efficient. Also, since your program is passed the coordinates of the region that must be repainted, you can actually make the preceding routine more efficient by simply restoring that part of the window that had been destroyed. (You might want to try implementing this enhancement on your own.)

Managing Text

As mentioned, the mechanism used by the preceding program to advance the current X, Y location as each character is entered, and to advance to the next line when ENTER is pressed, was a temporary and imprecise solution. Because Windows 95 allows the use of proportional character fonts and adjustable font sizes, it is not possible to "hard code" the information necessary to properly space characters. Instead, you must dynamically compute the size of each character and line position. In this section, you will learn the correct way to perform these operations and to properly manage text output. As with most other aspects of the Windows 95 environment, you, the programmer, have virtually unlimited control over the way that

6

Routing All Output Through WM_PAINT

There is a variation on the virtual window mechanism that you might find useful in some situations. Instead of outputting information twice—once to the physical window and once to the virtual window—your program can simply write all information to the virtual window and then call **InvalidateRect( )** to cause the information to actually be displayed. (Remember, **InvalidateRect( )** generates a **WM_PAINT** message.) For example, here is another way that the **WM_CHAR** message could be handled by the virtual window program.

```
case WM_CHAR:
  sprintf(str, "%c", (char) wParam); /* stringize character */

  /* a "primitive" carriage return, linefeed sequence */
  if((char)wParam == '\r') {
    Y += 14; /* advance to next line */
    X = 0; /* reset to start of line */
  }
  else {
    TextOut(memdc, X, Y, str, strlen(str)); /* output string */
    InvalidateRect(hwnd, NULL, 1); /* generate WM_PAINT */
    X += 10;
  }
  break;
```

As you can see, each time a key is pressed, output is sent only to the memory device context. However, **InvalidateRect( )** is also called, causing a **WM_PAINT** message to be generated. This, of course, causes the contents of the physical window to be restored—which will include the new character.

If you try this approach in the example program, you will find that the window seems to "flash" each time you press a key because the entire window is being updated with each keypress. Therefore, this approach is inappropriate for this example. However, for programs that perform infrequent output, such an approach may make sense.

text is displayed and managed within the client area of a window. For this reason, it is far beyond the scope of this chapter to cover all aspects of text manipulation supported by Windows. However, you will be able to easily explore other aspects of text manipulation after understanding the basics introduced in this chapter.

Let's begin with a discussion of several text and screen API functions. These functions help you control and manage text output to the client area of a window. Then, a sample program is developed that illustrates how to apply these functions and how to properly manage the spacing of text output within the client area.

Setting the Text and Background Color

By default, when you output text to a window by using **TextOut( )**, it is shown as black text against the current background. However, you can determine both the color of the text and the background color using the API functions **SetTextColor( )** and **SetBkColor( )**, whose prototypes are shown here:

COLORREF SetTextColor(HDC *hdc*, COLORREF *color*);

COLORREF SetBkColor(HDC *hdc*, COLORREF *color*);

The **SetTextColor( )** function sets the current text color of the device context associated with *hdc* to that specified by *color* (or the closest color that the display device is capable of displaying). The **SetBkColor( )** function sets the current text background color to that specified by *color* (or as near as possible). For both functions, the previous color setting is returned. If an error occurs, then the value **CLR_INVALID** is returned.

The color is specified as a value of type **COLORREF**, which is a 32-bit integer. Windows allows colors to be specified in three ways. First, and by far most common, is as an RGB (red, green, blue) value. In an RGB value, the relative intensities of the three colors are combined to produce the actual color. The second way a color can be specified is as an index into a logical palette. The third is as an RGB value relative to a palette. In this chapter, only the first way will be discussed.

A long integer value that holds an RGB color is passed to either **SetTextColor( )** or **SetBkColor( )** using the following encoding:

6

Byte	Color
Byte 0 (low-order byte)	Red
Byte 1	Green
Byte 2	Blue
Byte 3 (high-order byte)	Must be zero

Each color in an RGB value is in the range 0 through 255, with 0 being the lowest intensity and 255 being the brightest intensity.

Although you are free to manually construct a **COLORREF** value, Windows defines the macro **RGB( )** that does this for you. It has this general form:

COLORREF RGB(int *red*, int *green*, int *blue*);

Here, *red, green,* and *blue* must be values in the range 0 through 255. Therefore, to create magenta, use **RGB(255, 0, 255)**. To create white, use **RGB(255, 255, 255)**. To create the color black, use **RGB(0, 0, 0)**. To create other colors, you combine the three basic colors in varying intensities. For example, this creates a light aqua: **RGB(0, 100, 100)**. You can experiment to determine which colors are best for your application.

Setting the Background Display Mode

You can control the way that the background is affected when text is displayed on the screen by using the **SetBkMode( )** API function, whose prototype is shown here:

int SetBkMode(HDC *hdc*, int *mode*);

This function determines what happens to the current background color when text (and some other types of output) is displayed. The handle of the device context affected is specified by *hdc*. The background mode is specified in *mode* and must be one of these two macros: **OPAQUE** or **TRANSPARENT**. The function returns the previous setting or 0 if an error occurs.

If *mode* is **OPAQUE**, then each time text is output, the background is changed to that of the current background color. If *mode* is **TRANSPARENT**, then the background is not altered. In this case, any effects of a call to **SetBkColor( )** are essentially ignored. By default, the background mode is **OPAQUE**.

Obtaining the Text Metrics

As you know, characters are not all the same dimension. That is, in Windows, most text fonts are proportional. Therefore, the character *i* is not as wide as the character *w*. Also, the height of each character and length of descenders vary among fonts. The amount of space between horizontal lines is also changeable. That these (and other) attributes are variable would not be of much consequence except that Windows demands that you, the programmer, manually manage virtually all text output.

Windows provides only minimal support for text output to the client area of a window. The main output function is **TextOut( )**. This function will only display a string of text beginning at a specified location. It will not format output or even automatically perform a carriage return/linefeed sequence, for example. Instead, managing output to the client window is completely your job.

The fact that the size of each font may be different (and that fonts may be changed while your program is executing) implies that there must be some way to determine the dimensions and various other attributes of the currently selected font. For example, to write one line of text after another implies that you have some way of knowing how tall the font is and how many pixels are between lines. The API function that obtains information about the current font is called **GetTextMetrics( )**, and it has this prototype:

    BOOL GetTextMetrics(HDC *hdc*, LPTEXTMETRIC *lpTAttrib*);

Here, *hdc* is the handle of the device context, which is generally obtained by use of **GetDC( )** or **BeginPaint( ),** and *lpTAttrib* is a pointer to a structure of type **TEXTMETRIC,** which will, upon return, contain the text metrics for the currently selected font. The **TEXTMETRIC** structure is defined as shown here:

```
typedef struct tagTEXTMETRIC
{
  LONG tmHeight; /* total height of font */
  LONG tmAscent; /* height above base line */
  LONG tmDescent; /* length of descenders */
  LONG tmInternalLeading; /* space above characters */
  LONG tmExternalLeading; /* space between rows */
  LONG tmAveCharWidth; /* average width */
  LONG tmMaxCharWidth; /* maximum width */
  LONG tmWeight; /* weight */
  LONG tmOverhang; /* extra width added to special fonts */
  LONG tmDigitizedAspectX; /* horizontal aspect */
  LONG tmDigitizedAspectY; /* vertical aspect */
  BYTE tmFirstChar; /* first character in font */
  BYTE tmLastChar; /* last character in font */
  BYTE tmDefaultChar; /* default character */
  BYTE tmBreakChar; /* character used to break words */
  BYTE tmItalic; /* nonzero if italic */
  BYTE tmUnderlined; /* nonzero if underlined */
  BYTE tmStruckOut; /* nonzero if struck out */
  BYTE tmPitchAndFamily; /* pitch and family of font */
  BYTE tmCharSet; /* character set identifier */
} TEXTMERIC;
```

6

While most of the values obtained by this function will not be used in this chapter, two are very important because they are used to compute the vertical distance between lines of text. This value is needed if you want to output more than one line of text to a window. Unlike a console-based application in which there is only one font and its size is fixed, there may be several Windows fonts and they may vary in size. Specifically, each font defines the height of its characters and the amount of space required between lines. This means that it is not possible to know in advance the vertical (Y) coordinate of the next line of text. To determine where the next line of text will begin, you must call **GetTextMetrics( )** to acquire two values: the character height and the amount of space between lines. These values are given in the **tmHeight** and **tmExternalLeading** fields, respectively. By adding together these two values, you obtain the number of vertical units between lines.

Keep in mind that the value **tmExternalLeading** contains, in essence, the number of vertical units that should be left blank between lines of text. This value is separate from the height of the font. Thus, both values are needed to compute where the next line of text will begin. You will see this applied shortly.

Computing the Length of a String

Because characters in the current font are not the same size, it is not possible to know the length of a string, in logical units, by simply knowing how

---

FAST TRACK TIP

NEWTEXTMETRIC

There is an enhanced version of **TEXTMETRIC**, called **NEWTEXT-METRIC**. **NEWTEXTMETRIC** is exactly the same as **TEXTMETRIC,** except that it adds four fields at the end. These fields provide support for *TrueType* fonts. (TrueType fonts are fonts that have superior scalability features.) The new fields in **NEWTEXTMETRIC** are shown here:

```
DWORD ntmFlags; /* indicates type of font */
UINT ntmSizeEM; /* size of an em */
UINT ntmCellHeight; /* font height */
UINT ntmAvgWidth; /* average character width */
```

For the purposes of this chapter, none of these fields are needed. However, they may be of value to applications that you create. You should consult your API reference manual for details.

many characters are in it. That is, the result returned by **strlen( )** is not meaningful to managing output to a window because characters are of differing widths. To solve this problem, Windows 95 includes the API function **GetTextExtentPoint32( )**, which has this prototype:

BOOL GetTextExtentPoint32(HDC *hdc*, LPCSTR *lpszString*, int *len*,
                          LPSIZE *lpSize*);

Here, *hdc* is the handle of the output device. The string that you want the length of is pointed to by *lpszString*. The number of characters in the string is specified in *len*. The width and height of the string, in logical units, are returned in the **SIZE** structure pointed to by *lpSize*. The **SIZE** structure is defined as shown here:

```
typedef struct tagSIZE {
  LONG cx; /* width */
  LONG cy; /* height */
} SIZE;
```

Upon return from a call to **GetTextExtentPoint32( )**, the **cx** field will contain the length of the string. Therefore, this value can be used to determine the starting point for the next string to be displayed if you want to continue from where the previous output left off.

GetTextExtentPoint32( ) returns nonzero if successful, and zero on failure.

A Short Text Demonstration

The following program demonstrates text output and the text-based functions just described.

6

```
/* Managing Text Output */

#include <windows.h>
#include <string.h>
#include <stdio.h>

LRESULT CALLBACK WindowFunc(HWND, UINT, WPARAM, LPARAM);

char szWinName[] = "MyWin"; /* name of window class */

char str[255]; /* holds output strings */

int X=0, Y=0; /* current output location */

int WINAPI WinMain(HINSTANCE hThisInst, HINSTANCE hPrevInst,
                   LPSTR lpszArgs, int nWinMode)
```

```c
{
  HWND hwnd;
  MSG msg;
  WNDCLASSEX wcl;

  /* Define a window class. */
  wcl.hInstance = hThisInst; /* handle to this instance */
  wcl.lpszClassName = szWinName; /* window class name */
  wcl.lpfnWndProc = WindowFunc; /* window function */
  wcl.style = 0; /* default style */

  wcl.cbSize = sizeof(WNDCLASSEX); /* set size of WNDCLASSEX */

  wcl.hIcon = LoadIcon(NULL, IDI_APPLICATION); /* large icon */
  wcl.hIconSm = LoadIcon(NULL, IDI_APPLICATION); /* small icon */

  wcl.hCursor = LoadCursor(NULL, IDC_ARROW); /* cursor style */

  wcl.lpszMenuName = NULL; /* no main menu */

  wcl.cbClsExtra = 0; /* no extra */
  wcl.cbWndExtra = 0; /* information needed */

  /* Make the window white. */
  wcl.hbrBackground = GetStockObject(WHITE_BRUSH);

  /* Register the window class. */
  if(!RegisterClassEx(&wcl)) return 0;

  /* Now that a window class has been registered, a window
     can be created. */
  hwnd = CreateWindow(
    szWinName, /* name of window class */
    "Managing Text Output", /* title */
    WS_OVERLAPPEDWINDOW, /* window style - normal */
    CW_USEDEFAULT, /* X coordinate - let Windows decide */
    CW_USEDEFAULT, /* Y coordinate - let Windows decide */
    CW_USEDEFAULT, /* width - let Windows decide */
    CW_USEDEFAULT, /* height - let Windows decide */
    HWND_DESKTOP, /* no handle of parent window */
    NULL, /* no menu */
    hThisInst, /* handle of this instance of the program */
    NULL /* no additional arguments */
  );

  /* Display the window. */
  ShowWindow(hwnd, nWinMode);
```

```
    UpdateWindow(hwnd);

    /* Create the message loop. */
    while(GetMessage(&msg, NULL, 0, 0))
    {
      TranslateMessage(&msg); /* allow use of keyboard */
      DispatchMessage(&msg); /* return control to Windows */
    }
    return msg.wParam;
}

/* This function is called by Windows 95 and is passed
   messages from the message queue.
*/
LRESULT CALLBACK WindowFunc(HWND hwnd, UINT message,
                            WPARAM wParam, LPARAM lParam)
{
  HDC hdc;
  TEXTMETRIC tm;
  SIZE size;
  PAINTSTRUCT paintstruct;

  switch(message) {
    case WM_PAINT:
      hdc = BeginPaint(hwnd, &paintstruct);

      /* get text metrics */
      GetTextMetrics(hdc, &tm);

      X = Y = 0;

      sprintf(str, "This is on the first line.");
      TextOut(hdc, X, Y, str, strlen(str)); /* output string */
      Y = Y + tm.tmHeight + tm.tmExternalLeading; /* next line */

      strcpy(str, "This is on the second line.");
      TextOut(hdc, X, Y, str, strlen(str)); /* output string */
      Y = Y + tm.tmHeight + tm.tmExternalLeading; /* next line */

      strcpy(str, "This is on the third line.");
      TextOut(hdc, X, Y, str, strlen(str)); /* output string */

      /* compute length of a string */
      GetTextExtentPoint32(hdc, str, strlen(str), &size);
      sprintf(str, "The preceding sentence is %ld units long",
              size.cx);
      X = size.cx; /* advance to end of previous string */
      TextOut(hdc, X, Y, str, strlen(str));
```

6

```
      Y = Y + tm.tmHeight + tm.tmExternalLeading; /* next line */
      X = 0; /* return to start of line */

      sprintf(str, "The space between lines is %ld pixels.",
              tm.tmExternalLeading+tm.tmHeight);
      TextOut(hdc, X, Y, str, strlen(str)); /* output string */
      Y = Y + tm.tmHeight + tm.tmExternalLeading; /* next line */

      sprintf(str, "Average character width is %ld pixels",
              tm.tmAveCharWidth);
      TextOut(hdc, X, Y, str, strlen(str));
      Y = Y + tm.tmHeight + tm.tmExternalLeading; /* next line */

      /* set text color to red */
      SetTextColor(hdc, RGB(255, 0, 0));
      /* set background color to blue */
      SetBkColor(hdc, RGB(0, 0, 255));

      sprintf(str, "This line is red on blue background.");
      TextOut(hdc, X, Y, str, strlen(str));

      EndPaint(hwnd, &paintstruct);
      break;
    case WM_DESTROY: /* terminate the program */
      PostQuitMessage(0);
      break;
    default:
      /* Let Windows 95 process any messages not specified in
         the preceding switch statement. */
      return DefWindowProc(hwnd, message, wParam, lParam);
  }
  return 0;
}
```

Sample output is shown in Figure 6-3.

Now let's take a closer look at this program. The program declares two global variables called **X** and **Y** and initializes both to 0. These variables will contain the current window location at which text will be displayed. They will be continually updated by the program after each output sequence.

The interesting part of this program is mostly contained within the **WM_PAINT** message. Each time a **WM_PAINT** message is received, a device context is obtained and the text metrics are acquired. Next, the first line of text is output. Notice that it is constructed by use of **sprintf( )** and then actually output by use of **TextOut( )**. As you know from earlier in this book, neither **TextOut( )** nor any other API function performs text formatting. It is up to you, the programmer, to construct your output first and then display it by using **TextOut( )**. After the string is displayed, the **Y**

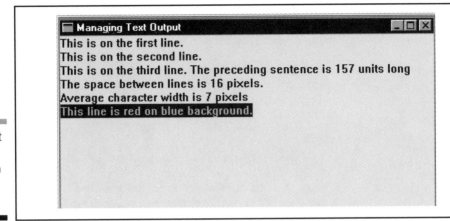

coordinate is advanced to the next line by adding the font height to the
distance between rows.

The program continues by next outputting the lines "This is on the second
line." and "This is on the third line." each on their own lines. Then, the
length of the third line is computed by use of a call to **GetTextExtent-
Point32( )**. This value is then used to advance the **X** coordinate to the
end of the previous line before the next line is printed. Notice that here,
the **Y** coordinate is unchanged. This causes the next string to be displayed
immediately after the previous one. Before continuing, the program advances
Y to the next line and resets **X** to 0, which is the leftmost coordinate. This
causes subsequent output once again to be started at the beginning of the
next line.

Next, some information about the currently selected character font is displayed.
Finally, the background color is set to blue, the text color is set to red, and a
line of text is displayed.

6

Fixing the Virtual Window Program

Now that you know the proper way to space characters and to advance
to the next line when outputting text, try fixing the virtual window
demonstration program so that it properly spaces characters and lines. To
correctly space characters, use **GetTextExtentPoint32( )** to determine
the width of each character typed, adding that value to the X coordinate.
To correctly advance to the next line, add the font height and the amount
of external leading to the Y coordinate each time ENTER is pressed. For
example, try replacing the **WM_CHAR** code sequence in the virtual
window example program with the following:

```
case WM_CHAR:
      hdc = GetDC(hwnd);

      /* get text metrics */
      GetTextMetrics(hdc, &tm);

      sprintf(str, "%c", (char) wParam); /* stringize
                                              character */

      /* a correct carriage return, linefeed sequence */
      if((char)wParam == '\r') {
        Y = Y + tm.tmHeight + tm.tmExternalLeading;
        X = 0; /* reset to start of line */
      }
      else {
        TextOut(memdc, X, Y, str, strlen(str)); /* output
                                                    to memory */
        TextOut(hdc, X, Y, str, strlen(str)); /* output
                                                  to window */

        /* compute length of character */
        GetTextExtentPoint32(memdc, str, strlen(str),
                             &size);
        X += size.cx; /* advance to end of character */
      }
      ReleaseDC(hwnd, hdc);
      break;
```

You will also need to add these variables to **WindowFunc( )**.

```
TEXTMETRIC tm;
SIZE size;
```

Now, when you enter text, it will appear properly spaced. For example, compare the following sample output with that shown earlier.

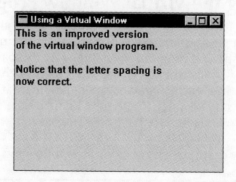

CHAPTER 7

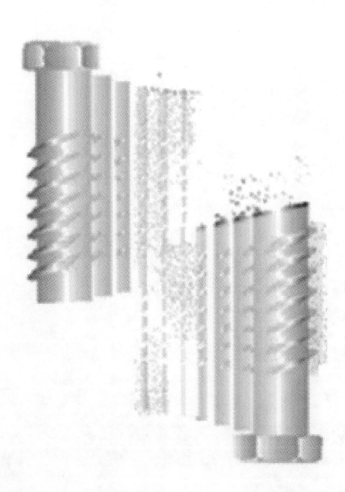

The Windows 95 Common Controls

This chapter introduces one of the most exciting new features of Windows 95: common controls. As you know, Windows 95 supports several standard controls. The standard controls are supported by all versions of Windows. However, the new common controls have been added by Windows 95. They are sophisticated, high-power controls that expand the types of user interactions that your program may have. They also add excitement and "freshness" to your application and greatly enhance the interface to any application.

The common controls supported by Windows 95 are listed in the following table:

Control	Description
Animation control	Displays an AVI file
Drag list box	Allows items to be dragged
Header control	Column heading
Hot key control	Supports user-created hot keys
Image list	List of graphical images
List view control	List of icons and labels
Progress bar	Visual gauge used for indicating the degree to which a task is completed
Property sheet	Properties dialog box
Rich edit control	Sophisticated edit box
Status window	Bar that displays information related to an application
Tab control	Tab-based menu (looks like tabs on file folders)
Toolbar	Graphics-based menu
Tooltip	Small pop-up text boxes (typically used to describe toolbar buttons)
Trackbar	Slider-based control (similar in concept to scroll bar, but looks like fader control on a stereo)
Tree view control	Tree-structured display
Up/down (spin) control	Up and down arrows (called spin control when linked with an edit box)

These controls are called *common controls* because they represent an extended set of controls that will be used by many applications. You have certainly encountered several (if not all) of these controls if you have been using Windows 95 for very long. While it won't be possible in this book to discuss all of the common controls, several of the most important and representative will be examined. This chapter begins by discussing the theory and general procedure for using a common control in your program. It then explores toolbars and tooltips.

Including and Initializing the Common Controls

Before you can use the common controls, you must include the standard header file COMMCTRL.H in your program. You must also make sure that the common controls library is linked into your program. (At this writing, the name of the common controls library is COMCTL32.LIB, but you should check your compiler's user manual.)

Applications that use one or more common controls must call **InitCommonControls( )** before using the first common control. This ensures that the common controls dynamic link library (DLL) is loaded and that the common controls subsystem is initialized. The prototype for **InitCommonControls( )** is shown here:

    void InitCommonControls(void);

A good place to call **InitCommonControls( )** is after your main window class has been registered.

Common Controls Are Windows

All of the common controls are child windows. They will be created by one of three methods: calling **CreateWindow( )**, calling **CreateWindowEx( )**, or calling a control-specific API function. (The **CreateWindowEx( )** function allows extended style attributes to be specified.) Because the common controls are windows, they can be managed in more or less the same way as you manage other windows used by your program.

Many common controls send your program either **WM_COMMAND** or **WM_NOTIFY** messages when they are accessed by the user. For many common controls, your program communicates by using the **SendMessage( )** API function, which has the following prototype, to send the control a message.

    LRESULT SendMessage(HWND *hwnd*, UINT *Msg*, WPARAM *wParam*,
                        LPARAM *lParam*);

Here, *hwnd* is the handle of the control, *Msg* is the message that you want to send to the control, and *wParam* and *lParam* contain any additional information associated with the message. The function returns the control's response, if any.

7

Using a Toolbar

One of the most important common controls is the toolbar because it can speed up menu selection when you are using a mouse. A *toolbar* is, essentially, a graphical menu. In the toolbar, menu items are represented by icons, which form graphical buttons. Often, a toolbar is used in conjunction with a standard menu. As such, it provides another way to make a menu selection. In a sense, a toolbar is a menu accelerator for the mouse.

To create a toolbar, use the **CreateToolbarEx( )** function, which has this general form:

HWND CreateToolbarEx(HWND *hwnd*, DWORD *dwStyle*, WORD *ID*,
                   int *NumBitmaps*, HINSTANCE *hInst*,
                   WORD *BmpID*, LPCTBBUTTON *Buttons*,
                   int *NumButtons*,
                   int *ButtonWidth*, int *ButtonHeight*,
                   int *BmpWidth*, int *BmpHeight*,
                   UINT *Size*);

Here, *hwnd* is the handle of the parent window that owns the toolbar.

The style of the toolbar is passed in *dwStyle*. The toolbar style must always include **WS_CHILD**. It can also include other standard styles, such as **WS_BORDER** or **WS_VISIBLE**. There are two toolbar-specific styles that are commonly used. The first is **TBSTYLE_TOOLTIPS**. This style allows tooltips to be used. (Tooltips are discussed later in this chapter.) The second is **TBSTYLE_WRAPABLE**. This allows a long toolbar to be wrapped to the next line.

The identifier associated with the toolbar is passed in *ID*. The identifier of the bitmap resource that forms the toolbar is passed in *BmpID*. This bitmap contains all of the images displayed within the individual toolbar buttons. The number of individual bitmap images contained in the bitmap specified by *BmpID* is passed in *NumBitmaps*. The instance handle of the application is passed in *hInst*.

Information about each button is passed in an array of **TBBUTTON** structures pointed to by *Buttons*. The number of buttons in the toolbar is specified in *NumButtons*. The width and height of the buttons are passed in *ButtonWidth* and *ButtonHeight*. The width and height of the images within each button are passed in *BmpWidth* and *BmpHeight*. If *ButtonWidth* and *ButtonHeight* are zero, then appropriate button dimensions that fit the bitmap size are supplied automatically. The size of the **TBBUTTON** structure is passed in *Size*. The function returns a handle to the toolbar window. It returns **NULL** on failure.

Each button has a **TBBUTTON** structure associated with it that defines its various characteristics. The **TBBUTTON** structure is shown here:

```
typedef struct _TBBUTTON {
  int iBitmap;
```

```
      int idCommand;
      BYTE fsState;
      BYTE fsStyle;
      DWORD dwData;
      int iString;
} TBBUTTON;
```

The index of the bitmap image associated with the button is contained in **iBitmap**. The buttons begin their indexing at zero and are displayed left to right.

The ID associated with the button is stored in **idCommand**. Each time the button is pressed, a **WM_COMMAND** message will be generated and sent to the parent window. The value of **idCommand** will be contained in the low-order word of **wParam**.

The initial state of the button is stored in **fsState**. It can be one (or more) of the following values:

State	Meaning
TBSTATE_CHECKED	Button is pressed.
TBSTATE_ENABLE	Button can be pressed.
TBSTATE_HIDDEN	Button is hidden and inactive.
TBSTATE_INDETERMINATE	Button is gray and inactive.
TBSTATE_PRESSED	Button is pressed.
TBSTATE_WRAP	Following buttons are on a new line.

The style of the button is contained in **fsStyle**. It can be any valid combination of the following values:

Style	Meaning
TBSTYLE_BUTTON	A standard button.
TBSTYLE_CHECK	Button toggles between checked and unchecked each time it is pressed.
TBSTYLE_CHECKGROUP	A check button that is part of a mutually exclusive group.
TBSTYLE_GROUP	A standard button that is part of a mutually exclusive group.
TBSTYLE_SEP	Separates buttons (**idCommand** must be zero when this style is used).

7

Notice the **TBSTYLE_SEP** style. This style is used to provide a gap between buttons on the toolbar. This allows you to visually group buttons into clusters.

In the **TBBUTTON** structure, the **dwData** field contains user-defined data. The **iString** field is the index of an optional string associated with the button. These fields should be zero if they are unused.

In their default configuration, toolbars are fully automated controls and require virtually no management by your program to use them. However, you can manually manage a toolbar if you like by sending it explicit control messages. These messages are sent to the toolbar by use of **SendMessage( )**. Three common toolbar messages are listed in the following table. (You will want to explore the other toolbar messages on your own.)

Message	Meaning
TB_CHECKBUTTON	Presses or clears a toolbar button. *wParam* must contain the ID of the button. *lParam* must be nonzero to press or zero to clear.
TB_ENABLEBUTTON	Enables or disables a toolbar button. *wParam* must contain the ID of the button. *lParam* must be nonzero to enable or zero to disable.
TB_HIDEBUTTON	Hides or shows a toolbar button. *wParam* must contain the ID of the button. *lParam* must be nonzero to hide or zero to show.

Toolbars can also generate notification messages that inform your program about various activities related to the toolbar. For simple toolbars, you won't need to worry about these messages. (The notification messages all begin with **TBN_**, and you can find information on them by examining the COMMCTRL.H header file or your API library reference.)

Adding Tooltips

As you have probably already seen when using Windows 95, some toolbars automatically pop up small text windows after the mouse pointer has paused for about one second over a toolbar button. These small text windows are called *tooltips*. Although not technically required, tooltips should be included with most toolbars because users will expect to see them.

To add tooltips to a toolbar, you must first include the **TBSTYLE_TOOLTIPS** style when you create the toolbar. This enables **WM_NOTIFY** messages to be sent when the mouse pointer lingers over a button for more than about one second. When a **WM_NOTIFY** message is received, **lParam** will point to a **TOOLTIPTEXT** structure, which is defined like this:

```
typedef struct {
  NMHDR hdr;
  LPSTR lpszText;
  char szText[80];
  HINSTANCE hinst;
  UINT uFlags;
} TOOLTIPTEXT;
```

The first member of **TOOLTIPTEXT** is an **NMHDR** structure, which is defined like this:

```
typedef struct tagNMHDR
{
  HWND   hwndFrom; /* handle of control */
  UINT   idFrom; /* control ID */
  UINT   code; /* notification code */
} NMHDR;
```

If a tooltip is being requested, then **code** will contain **TTN_NEEDTEXT** and **idFrom** will contain the ID of the button for which the tip is needed. There are three ways to supply the required tooltip. You can copy the tooltip text into the **szText** array of **TOOLTIPTEXT**, point **lpszText** to the text, or supply the resource ID of a string resource. When you use a string resource, the string ID is assigned to **lpszText,** and **hinst** must be the handle of the string resource. By far the easiest way is to point **lpszText** to a string supplied by your program. For example, the following case responds to tooltip requests for the tooltips example program shown later.

```
case WM_NOTIFY: /* respond to tooltip request */
  TTtext = (LPTOOLTIPTEXT) lParam;
  if(TTtext->hdr.code == TTN_NEEDTEXT)
    switch(TTtext->hdr.idFrom) {
      case IDM_OPEN: TTtext->lpszText = "Open File";
        break;
      case IDM_UPPER: TTtext->lpszText = "Uppercase";
        break;
      case IDM_LOWER: TTtext->lpszText = "Lowercase";
        break;
      case IDM_SAVE: TTtext->lpszText = "Save File";
        break;
      case IDM_HELP: TTtext->lpszText = "Help";
        break;
    }
  break;
```

7

Once the tooltip text has been set and control passes back to Windows, the tooltip will automatically be displayed. Your program need perform no further action. As you can see, tooltips are largely automated and easy to add to your application.

Creating a Toolbar Bitmap

Before you can use a toolbar, you must create the bitmaps that form the graphics images inside each button. To do this, you must use an image editor. (The process is similar to that which you used when working with bitmaps in Chapter 6.) However, there is one important point to remember: there is only one bitmap associated with the toolbar, and this bitmap must contain *all* of the button images. Thus, if your toolbar will have six buttons, then the bitmap associated with your toolbar must define six images. For example, if your toolbar images are each 16 × 16 bits and your toolbar has six buttons, then your toolbar bitmap will have to be 96 (6 times 16) bits long by 16 bits high.

For the toolbar example presented in this chapter, you will need five images. Each image must be 16 × 16 bits. This means that you will need to create a bitmap that is 80 × 16. Figure 7-1 shows how the toolbar bitmap used by the sample programs in this chapter looks inside the image editor. Store your bitmap in a file called TOOLBAR.BMP.

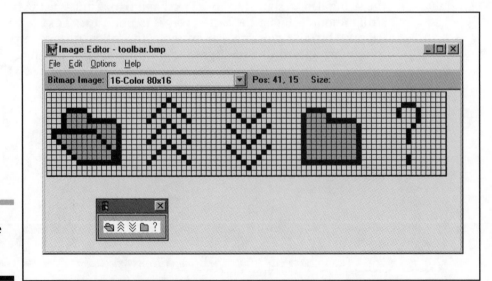

The toolbar bitmap while being edited

Figure 7-1.

A Toolbar Sample Program

The following program demonstrates a toolbar. It implements a very simple set of text file utilities. The program can perform the following operations:

♦ Load and display a file

♦ Convert a file to uppercase

♦ Convert a file to lowercase

♦ Save the file

Once the file has been loaded, it is displayed within the client area. A vertical scroll bar is included that allows you to scroll through the file. The toolbar duplicates the menu options and includes tooltips.

When you load or save a file, the program uses one of two Windows 95 API functions to obtain the name of the file that you wish to use. These functions are called **GetOpenFileName( )** and **GetSaveFileName( )**. They activate the standard Open and Save As dialog boxes. These functions are described later in this chapter.

The toolbar program is shown here:

```
/* Demonstrate a toolbar. */

#include <windows.h>
#include <commctrl.h>
#include <string.h>
#include <stdio.h>
#include <ctype.h>
#include "tb.h"

#define NUMBUTTONS 6
#define MAXSIZE 25000

void InitToolbar(); /* initialize the toolbar */

LRESULT CALLBACK WindowFunc(HWND, UINT, WPARAM, LPARAM);

char szWinName[] = "MyWin"; /* name of window class */

TBBUTTON tbButtons[NUMBUTTONS];

HWND tbwnd; /* toolbar handle */

void display(int startY, HDC hdc);
```

7

```
FILE *fp; /* file pointer */
char buf[MAXSIZE];  /* buffer to hold the file */

TEXTMETRIC tm;
SIZE size;

int SBPos = 0; /* scroll bar position */
int X = 5, Y = 32; /* scroll coordinates */
int NumLines;

int ToolBarActive = 1;

HWND hwnd;

int WINAPI WinMain(HINSTANCE hThisInst, HINSTANCE hPrevInst,
                   LPSTR lpszArgs, int nWinMode)
{
  MSG msg;
  WNDCLASSEX wcl;
  HANDLE hAccel;

  /* Define a window class. */
  wcl.hInstance = hThisInst; /* handle to this instance */
  wcl.lpszClassName = szWinName; /* window class name */
  wcl.lpfnWndProc = WindowFunc; /* window function */
  wcl.style = 0; /* default style */

  wcl.cbSize = sizeof(WNDCLASSEX);

  wcl.hIcon = LoadIcon(NULL, IDI_APPLICATION);
  wcl.hIconSm = LoadIcon(NULL, IDI_APPLICATION);
  wcl.hCursor = LoadCursor(NULL, IDC_ARROW);

  /* specify name of menu resource */
  wcl.lpszMenuName = "MYMENU"; /* main menu */

  wcl.cbClsExtra = 0; /* no extra */
  wcl.cbWndExtra = 0; /* information needed */

  /* Make the window white. */
  wcl.hbrBackground = GetStockObject(WHITE_BRUSH);

  /* Register the window class. */
  if(!RegisterClassEx(&wcl)) return 0;

  /* Now that a window class has been registered, a window
     can be created. */
  hwnd = CreateWindow(
```

```
      szWinName, /* name of window class */
      "Using a Toolbar", /* title */
      WS_OVERLAPPEDWINDOW ¦ WS_VSCROLL, /* window style */
      CW_USEDEFAULT, /* X coordinate - let Windows decide */
      CW_USEDEFAULT, /* Y coordinate - let Windows decide */
      CW_USEDEFAULT, /* width - let Windows decide */
      CW_USEDEFAULT, /* height - let Windows decide */
      HWND_DESKTOP, /* no parent window */
      NULL, /* no menu */
      hThisInst, /* handle of this instance of the program */
      NULL /* no additional arguments */
    );

    /* load accelerators */
    hAccel = LoadAccelerators(hThisInst, "MYMENU");

    InitToolbar(); /* initialize the toolbar */

    InitCommonControls(); /* activate the common controls */

    tbwnd = CreateToolbarEx(hwnd,
                            WS_VISIBLE ¦ WS_CHILD ¦
                            WS_BORDER ¦ TBSTYLE_TOOLTIPS,
                            IDM_TOOLBAR,
                            NUMBUTTONS,
                            hThisInst,
                            IDTB_BMP,
                            tbButtons,
                            NUMBUTTONS,
                            0, 0, 16, 16,
                            sizeof(TBBUTTON));

    /* Display the window. */
    ShowWindow(hwnd, nWinMode);
    UpdateWindow(hwnd);

    /* Create the message loop. */
    while(GetMessage(&msg, NULL, 0, 0))
    {
      if(!TranslateAccelerator(hwnd, hAccel, &msg)) {
        TranslateMessage(&msg); /* allow use of keyboard */
        DispatchMessage(&msg); /* return control to Windows */
      }
    }
    return msg.wParam;
}
```

7

```
/* This function is called by Windows 95 and is passed
   messages from the message queue.
*/
LRESULT CALLBACK WindowFunc(HWND hwnd, UINT message,
                            WPARAM wParam, LPARAM lParam)
{
  HDC hdc;
  PAINTSTRUCT paintstruct;
  int i, response;
  SCROLLINFO si;
  OPENFILENAME fname;
  char filename[64]; /* filename */
  static char fn[256]; /* full path name */
  char filefilter[] = {
        'C','\0', '*', '.', 'C','\0',
        'C', '+', '+', '\0', '*', '.', 'C', 'P', 'P', '\0',
        '\0','\0'};
  LPTOOLTIPTEXT TTtext;

  switch(message) {
    case WM_NOTIFY: /* respond to tooltip request */
      TTtext = (LPTOOLTIPTEXT) lParam;
      if(TTtext->hdr.code == TTN_NEEDTEXT)
        switch(TTtext->hdr.idFrom) {
          case IDM_OPEN: TTtext->lpszText = "Open File";
            break;
          case IDM_UPPER: TTtext->lpszText = "Uppercase";
            break;
          case IDM_LOWER: TTtext->lpszText = "Lowercase";
            break;
          case IDM_SAVE: TTtext->lpszText = "Save File";
            break;
          case IDM_HELP: TTtext->lpszText = "Help";
            break;
        }
      break;
    case WM_VSCROLL:
      switch(LOWORD(wParam)) {
        case SB_LINEDOWN:
          SBPos++;
          if(SBPos>NumLines) SBPos = NumLines;
          si.cbSize = sizeof(SCROLLINFO);
          si.fMask = SIF_POS;
          si.nPos = SBPos;
          SetScrollInfo(hwnd, SB_VERT, &si, 1);
          InvalidateRect(hwnd, NULL, 1);
          break;
        case SB_LINEUP:
```

```
          SBPos--;
          if(SBPos<0) SBPos = 0;
          si.cbSize = sizeof(SCROLLINFO);
          si.fMask = SIF_POS;
          si.nPos = SBPos;
          SetScrollInfo(hwnd, SB_VERT, &si, 1);
          InvalidateRect(hwnd, NULL, 1);
          break;
      case SB_THUMBTRACK:
          SBPos = HIWORD(wParam); /* get current position */
          if(SBPos<0) SBPos = 0;
          si.cbSize = sizeof(SCROLLINFO);
          si.fMask = SIF_POS;
          si.nPos = SBPos;
          SetScrollInfo(hwnd, SB_VERT, &si, 1);
          InvalidateRect(hwnd, NULL, 1);
          break;
    }
    break;
  case WM_COMMAND:
    switch(LOWORD(wParam)) {
      case IDM_OPEN:
        /* initialize the OPENFILENAME struct */
        memset(&fname, 0, sizeof(OPENFILENAME));
        fname.lStructSize = sizeof(OPENFILENAME);
        fname.hwndOwner = hwnd;
        fname.lpstrFilter = filefilter;
        fname.nFilterIndex = 1;
        fname.lpstrFile = fn;
        fname.nMaxFile = sizeof(fn);
        fname.lpstrFileTitle = filename;
        fname.nMaxFileTitle = sizeof(filename)-1;
        fname.Flags = OFN_FILEMUSTEXIST | OFN_HIDEREADONLY;

        if(!GetOpenFileName(&fname)) /* get the filename */
          break;

        if((fp=fopen(fn, "r"))==NULL) {
          MessageBox(hwnd, fn, "Cannot Open File", MB_OK);
          break;
        }

        for(i=0; !feof(fp) && (i < MAXSIZE-1); i++) {
          fread(&buf[i], sizeof (char), 1, fp);
        }
        buf[i] = '\0';
        fclose(fp);
```

7

```
      /* count the number of lines */
      for(NumLines=0, i=0; buf[i]; i++)
        if(buf[i] == '\n') NumLines++;

      /* set scrollbar range to number of lines */
      si.cbSize = sizeof(SCROLLINFO);
      si.fMask = SIF_RANGE | SIF_POS;
      si.nMin = 0; si.nMax = NumLines;
      si.nPos = 0;
      SetScrollInfo(hwnd, SB_VERT, &si, 1);

      SBPos = 0;

      if(ToolBarActive) Y = 32;
      else Y = 0;

      InvalidateRect(hwnd, NULL, 1);
      break;
    case IDM_UPPER: /* uppercase file */
      for(i=0; buf[i]; i++) buf[i] = toupper(buf[i]);
      InvalidateRect(hwnd, NULL, 1);
      break;
    case IDM_LOWER: /* lowercase file */
      for(i=0; buf[i]; i++) buf[i] = tolower(buf[i]);
      InvalidateRect(hwnd, NULL, 1);
      break;
    case IDM_SAVE:
      /* initialize the OPENFILENAME struct */
      memset(&fname, 0, sizeof(OPENFILENAME));
      fname.lStructSize = sizeof(OPENFILENAME);
      fname.hwndOwner = hwnd;
      fname.lpstrFilter = filefilter;
      fname.nFilterIndex = 1;
      fname.lpstrFile = fn;
      fname.nMaxFile = sizeof(fn);
      fname.lpstrFileTitle = filename;
      fname.nMaxFileTitle = sizeof(filename)-1;
      fname.Flags = OFN_HIDEREADONLY;

      if(!GetSaveFileName(&fname)) /* get the filename */
        break;

      if((fp=fopen(fn, "w"))==NULL) {
        MessageBox(hwnd, fn, "Cannot Open File", MB_OK);
        break;
      }
```

```
          for(i=0; buf[i]; i++) {
            fwrite(&buf[i], sizeof (char), 1, fp);
          }

          fclose(fp);
          InvalidateRect(hwnd, NULL, 1);
          break;
        case IDM_SHOW: /* show toolbar */
          ToolBarActive = 1;
          Y = 32; /* advance past toolbar */
          ShowWindow(tbwnd, SW_RESTORE);
          InvalidateRect(hwnd, NULL, 1);
          break;
        case IDM_HIDE: /* hide toolbar */
          ToolBarActive = 0;
          Y = 0;
          ShowWindow(tbwnd, SW_HIDE);
          InvalidateRect(hwnd, NULL, 1);
          break;
        case IDM_HELP:
          /* show help button as pressed */
          SendMessage(tbwnd, TB_CHECKBUTTON,
                      (LPARAM) IDM_HELP, (WPARAM) 1);

          MessageBox(hwnd, "F2: Open\nF3: Uppercase\n"
                      "F4: Lowercase\nF5: Save\n"
                      "F6: Show Toolbar\n"
                      "F7: Hide Toolbar",
                      "File Utilities", MB_OK);

          /* reset the help button */
          SendMessage(tbwnd, TB_CHECKBUTTON,
                      (LPARAM) IDM_HELP, (WPARAM) 0);
          break;
        case IDM_EXIT:
          response = MessageBox(hwnd, "Quit the Program?",
                                "Exit", MB_YESNO);
          if(response == IDYES) PostQuitMessage(0);
          break;
      }
      break;
    case WM_PAINT: /* process a repaint request */
      hdc = BeginPaint(hwnd, &paintstruct); /* get DC */
      GetTextMetrics(hdc, &tm);
      display(SBPos, hdc);
```

7

```
      EndPaint(hwnd, &paintstruct); /* release DC */
      break;
    case WM_DESTROY: /* terminate the program */
      PostQuitMessage(0);
      break;
    default:
    /* Let Windows 95 process any messages not specified in
       the preceding switch statement. */
      return DefWindowProc(hwnd, message, wParam, lParam);
  }
  return 0;
}

/* Initialize the toolbar structures. */
void InitToolbar()
{
  tbButtons[0].iBitmap = 0;
  tbButtons[0].idCommand = IDM_OPEN;
  tbButtons[0].fsState = TBSTATE_ENABLED;
  tbButtons[0].fsStyle = TBSTYLE_BUTTON;
  tbButtons[0].dwData = 0L;
  tbButtons[0].iString = 0;

  tbButtons[1].iBitmap = 1;
  tbButtons[1].idCommand = IDM_UPPER;
  tbButtons[1].fsState = TBSTATE_ENABLED;
  tbButtons[1].fsStyle = TBSTYLE_BUTTON;
  tbButtons[1].dwData = 0L;
  tbButtons[1].iString = 0;

  tbButtons[2].iBitmap = 2;
  tbButtons[2].idCommand = IDM_LOWER;
  tbButtons[2].fsState = TBSTATE_ENABLED;
  tbButtons[2].fsStyle = TBSTYLE_BUTTON;
  tbButtons[2].dwData = 0L;
  tbButtons[2].iString = 0;

  tbButtons[3].iBitmap = 3;
  tbButtons[3].idCommand = IDM_SAVE;
  tbButtons[3].fsState = TBSTATE_ENABLED;
  tbButtons[3].fsStyle = TBSTYLE_BUTTON;
  tbButtons[3].dwData = 0L;
  tbButtons[3].iString = 0;

  /* button separator */
  tbButtons[4].iBitmap = 0;
  tbButtons[4].idCommand = 0;
  tbButtons[4].fsState = TBSTATE_ENABLED;
```

```
      tbButtons[4].fsStyle = TBSTYLE_SEP;
      tbButtons[4].dwData = 0L;
      tbButtons[4].iString = 0;

      tbButtons[5].iBitmap = 4;
      tbButtons[5].idCommand = IDM_HELP;
      tbButtons[5].fsState = TBSTATE_ENABLED;
      tbButtons[5].fsStyle = TBSTYLE_BUTTON;
      tbButtons[5].dwData = 0L;
      tbButtons[5].iString = 0;
}

/* Display the file. */
void display(int startline, HDC hdc)
{
  register int i, j;
  int linelim;
  int lines;
  char line[256];
  RECT coords;
  int tempY;

  GetClientRect(hwnd, &coords); /* get size of window */

  lines = (coords.bottom / tm.tmHeight) + 1;

  /* find first line */
  for(i=0; startline && buf[i]; i++)
    if(buf[i] == '\n')  startline--;

  tempY = Y;

  /* erase old contents */
  PatBlt(hdc, X, Y, coords.right, coords.bottom, PATCOPY);

  /* display file */
  for(linelim=lines; linelim && buf[i]; i++) {
    for(j=0; j<256 && buf[i] && buf[i]!='\n'; j++, i++)
      line[j] = buf[i];

    if(!buf[i]) break;

    TextOut(hdc, X, Y, line, j);
    Y = Y + tm.tmHeight + tm.tmExternalLeading; /* next line */
    linelim--;
  }
  Y = tempY;
}
```

7

This program requires the following resource file:

```
#include <windows.h>
#include "tb.h"

IDTB_BMP BITMAP "toolbar.bmp"

MYMENU MENU
{
  POPUP "&File"
  {
    MENUITEM "&Open", IDM_OPEN
    MENUITEM "&Uppercase", IDM_UPPER
    MENUITEM "&Lowercase", IDM_LOWER
    MENUITEM "&Save", IDM_SAVE
    MENUITEM "&Exit", IDM_EXIT
  }
  POPUP "&Options"
  {
    MENUITEM "&Show Toolbar", IDM_SHOW
    MENUITEM "&Hide Toolbar", IDM_HIDE
  }
  MENUITEM "&Help", IDM_HELP
}

MYMENU ACCELERATORS
{
  VK_F2, IDM_OPEN, VIRTKEY
  VK_F3, IDM_UPPER, VIRTKEY
  VK_F4, IDM_LOWER, VIRTKEY
  VK_F5, IDM_SAVE, VIRTKEY
  VK_F6, IDM_SHOW, VIRTKEY
  VK_F7, IDM_HIDE, VIRTKEY
  VK_F1, IDM_HELP, VIRTKEY
}
```

The TB.H header file is shown here:

```
#define IDM_OPEN     100
#define IDM_UPPER    101
#define IDM_LOWER    102
#define IDM_SHOW     103
#define IDM_HIDE     104
#define IDM_SAVE     105
#define IDM_HELP     106
#define IDM_EXIT     107
```

```
#define IDM_TOOLBAR    200

#define IDTB_BMP       300
```

Sample output from the Toolbar program is shown in Figure 7-2.

A Closer Look at the Toolbar Program

The toolbar program implements a very simple set of file operations. It works like this. When you select the Open option (either from the menu or the toolbar), a file is opened and its contents are read into the **buf** array. The size of **buf** is arbitrary and can be changed if you like. A window's worth of this buffer is displayed each time a **WM_PAINT** message is received by calling the **display( )** function. Some of the code within **display( )** should be familiar because it uses the same techniques as those described in Chapter 6 to output text to the window. By selecting Uppercase, you convert the contents of the buffer to uppercase. By selecting Lowercase, you convert the buffer to lowercase. You can save the contents of the buffer by selecting Save. Each of these operations can be initiated by use of the menu or the toolbar.

The toolbar information is held in the **tbButtons** array. This array is initialized in **InitToolbar( )**. Notice that the fifth structure is simply a

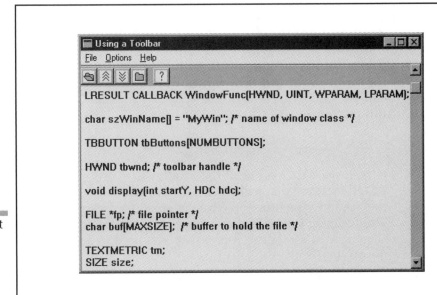

Sample output from the Toolbar program

Figure 7-2.

7

button separator. In **WinMain( )**, the **InitCommonControls( )** function is called. Next, the toolbar is created, and a handle to it is assigned to **tbwnd**.

Each button in the toolbar corresponds to a menu entry in the main menu. Specifically, each of the buttons (other than the separator) is associated with a menu ID. When a button is pressed, its associated ID will be sent to the program as part of a **WM_COMMAND** message, just as if a menu item had been selected. In fact, the same **case** statement handles both toolbar button presses and menu selections.

Since a toolbar is a window, it can be displayed or hidden like any other window by use of the **ShowWindow( )** function. To hide the window, select Hide Toolbar in the Options menu. To redisplay the toolbar, select Show Toolbar. Since the toolbar overlays part of the client area of the main window, you should always allow the user to remove the toolbar if it is not needed. As the program illustrates, this is very easy to do.

Notice the code inside the **IDM_HELP** case. When Help is selected (either through the main menu or by pressing the Help button), the Help toolbar button is manually pressed by sending it a **TB_CHECKBUTTON** message. After the user closes the Help message box, the button is manually released. Thus, the Help button remains pressed while the Help message box is displayed. This is an example of how a toolbar can be manually managed by your program when necessary.

The file can be scrolled in the window by use of the vertical scroll bar. The operation of the scroll bar was described in Chapter 5. The function **display( )** actually displays the file. It only outputs sufficient text to fill the window as it is currently sized. (This is more efficient than outputting a screen full of information and letting Windows clip it.) The current size of the window is obtained by calling **GetClientRect( )**, which returns the current window coordinates in a **RECT** structure. **GetClientRect( )** has this prototype:

```
BOOL GetClientRect(HWND hwnd, LPRECT rect);
```

Here, *hwnd* is the handle of the window in question, and *rect* is a pointer to a **RECT** structure that will receive the current coordinates of the client area of the window. The function returns nonzero if successful and zero on failure. This function is useful whenever you need to know the current size of the client area of a window. In this case, it is used to determine how much of the file can be displayed.

Passing Along WM_SIZE Messages

Try the following experiment with the toolbar program. Execute the program and then increase its horizontal size. As you will see, the toolbar is *not* automatically expanded to the new size. The reason is that a toolbar is a child window of the program's main window. Therefore, it does not automatically receive resize messages. Instead, if you want a child window (in this case, a toolbar) to receive resize messages, you must pass that message along to it. For example, to do this in the toolbar program, add the following **case** to **WindowFunc( )**.

```
case WM_SIZE:
  /* pass resize message along to toolbar */
  SendMessage(tbwnd, WM_SIZE, wParam, lParam);
  break;
```

After you add this code, when you expand the main window, the toolbar will automatically be resized appropriately.

As a general rule, if your program contains a child window, your main window function will need to pass appropriate messages along to the child window.

GetOpenFileName( ) and GetSaveFileName( )

As mentioned in the toolbar example, the name of the file to open or to save to is obtained by use of the functions **GetOpenFileName( )** and **GetSaveFileName( )**, respectively. These functions activate standard, built-in dialog boxes, called Open and Save As, which perform these functions. Let's take a close look at these functions.

7

The Open dialog box is used to input the name of a file to be opened. It allows a user to select a filename either by typing it or by selecting it from a list. The user can also change directories or drives. The Open dialog box is activated by calling the **GetOpenFileName( )** API function. When called, it displays a dialog box similar to that shown here:

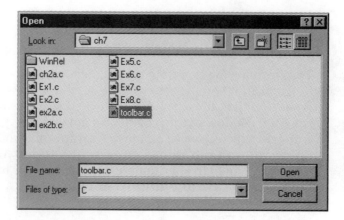

The Save As dialog box allows the user to select a file into which output will be written. The Save As dialog box looks like this:

The **GetOpenFileName( )** and **GetSaveFileName( )** functions have these prototypes:

  BOOL GetOpenFileName(LPOPENFILENAME *lpbuf*);

  BOOL GetSaveFileName(LPOPENFILENAME *lpbuf*);

Here, *lpbuf* is a pointer to a structure of type **OPENFILENAME**. These functions return nonzero if a valid filename is specified by the user and zero otherwise.

The **OPENFILENAME** structure pointed to by *lpbuf* must be initialized before calling either function. Upon return, the filename specified by the user, and several other pieces of information, will be contained in that structure.

The **OPENFILENAME** structure is defined like this:

```
typedef struct tagOFN
{
  DWORD lStructSize;
  HWND hwndOwner;
  HINSTANCE hInstance;
  LPCSTR lpstrFilter;
  LPSTR lpstrCustomFilter;
  DWORD nMaxCustFilter;
  DWORD nFilterIndex;
  LPSTR lpstrFile;
  DWORD nMaxFile;
  LPSTR lpstrFileTitle;
  DWORD nMaxFileTitle;
  LPCSTR lpstrInitialDir;
  LPCSTR lpstrTitle;
  DWORD Flags;
  WORD nFileOffset;
  WORD nFileExtension;
  LPCSTR lpstrDefExt;
  LPARAM lCustData;
  LPOFNHOOKPROC lpfnHook;
  LPCSTR lpTemplateName;
} OPENFILENAME;
```

 FAST TRACK TIP

Using Files in a Windows Program

Files are easily used in a Windows 95 program. Because any C/C++ compiler that can create a Windows 95 program will supply Windows 95-compatible file functions, such as **fopen( )** or **fclose( )**, you can generally use those functions to perform file I/O without any further worry. However, if you wish, you can create or open a file by using the API function **CreateFile( )**. This function returns a handle to the file. **CreateFile( )** may give you more control over how a file is created or opened in certain situations. (This will be especially true where file sharing and security attributes are involved.) To close a file that has been opened with **CreateFile( )**, call **CloseHandle( )**. If the low-level control of files is important to your application, you will want to think about using these functions.

7

Each element of **OPENFILENAME** is described here:

lStructSize must contain the size of the **OPENFILENAME** structure. **hwndOwner** must contain the handle of the window that will contain the dialog box. **hInstance** is the handle to a region of data that defines an alternative dialog box design or *template*. This element is only used if the **Flags** element enables a template by including **OFN_ENABLETEMPLATE**.

lpstrFilter must point to an array that contains pairs of strings that define a filename filter. The pairs of strings must be organized like this: "*description*""*mask*", where the *description* identifies the type of files matched by the *mask*. For example, "C Files""C.*" specifies the description *C Files* and the mask *C.*. The last two strings in the array must be null in order to terminate the list. The names of the filters are displayed in a drop-down list from which the user can choose. If this element is **NULL**, then no filename filter is used.

lpstrCustomFilter must point to an array that also contains a filename filter as just described. This array must initially contain a valid description and file filter. However, after the user selects a filename, the filter and description are copied into the array. If **lpstrCustomFilter** is **NULL**, then this element is ignored. The array must be 40 characters (or more) long.

nMaxCustFilter specifies the size of the array pointed to by **lpstrCustomFilter**. This value is only needed if **lpstrCustomFilter** is not **NULL**.

nFilterIndex specifies which pair of strings pointed to by **lpstrFilter** will provide the initial file filter and description when the dialog box is first displayed. The value 1 corresponds to the first pair. The second pair is specified by the value 2, and so on. This value is ignored if **lpstrFilter** is **NULL**.

lpstrFile points to an array that will receive the complete file, path, and drive of the filename selected by the user. The array may contain an initial filename that will be used to initialize the filename edit box, or it may point to a null string.

nMaxFile specifies the size of the array pointed to by **lpstrFile**. The array should be at least 256 bytes long to accommodate the longest possible filename.

lpstrFileTitle points to an array that receives the filename (without path or drive information) of the file selected by the user.

nMaxFileTitle specifies the size of the array pointed to by **lpstrFileTitle**.

lpstrInitialDir points to an array that contains the directory that will first be used when the dialog box is activated. If **lpstrInitialDir** is **NULL**, then the current directory is used.

lpstrTitle points to a string that will be used as the title for the dialog box. The default title is used if **lpstrTitle** is **NULL**. For the **GetOpenFileName( )** function, the default title is "Open"; for **GetSaveFileName( )**, the default title is "Save As".

The **Flags** element is used to set various options inside the dialog box. Several commonly used flags are listed here. You can OR together two or more flags if necessary.

Flags	Effect
OFN_ENABLEHOOK	Allows the function pointed to by **lpfnHook** to be used.
OFN_ENABLETEMPLATE	Allows an alternative dialog box template to be used.
OFN_FILEMUSTEXIST	User can only specify existent files.
OFN_HIDEREADONLY	Causes the read-only check box to be suppressed.
OFN_NOCHANGEDIR	Current directory remains unchanged by user selection.
OFN_OVERWRITEPROMPT	Causes the confirmation window to be displayed if user selects a file that already exists.
OFN_PATHMUSTEXIST	User can only specify existent paths.

The **nFileOffset** element receives the index of the start of the filename within the string returned in the array pointed to by **lpstrFile**. (Remember, this array will contain drive and path information in addition to the filename.)

nFileExtension receives the index of the file extension within the string returned in the array pointed to by **lpstrFile**.

lpstrDefExt points to an array that contains a default extension that is appended to the filename entered by the user when no extension is included. (The extension should be specified without a leading period.)

lCustData contains data that is passed to the optional function pointed to by **lpfnHook**.

lpfnHook is a pointer to a function that preempts and processes messages intended for the dialog box. This element is only used if **Flags** contains the value **OFN_ENABLEHOOK**.

7

You can use a different layout (template) for the dialog box. To do so, assign **lpTemplateName** the address of an array that contains the name of the resource file that contains the new layout. **lpTemplateName** is ignored unless **Flags** contains the value **OFN_ENABLETEMPLATE.**

Notice how the **OPENFILENAME** structure (**fname**) is initialized within the toolbars program. Since many of the elements of the structure must be set to **NULL** if not used, it is common practice to first zero the entire structure by using **memset( )**, as is done in the program. After **fname** has been zeroed, the essential elements are set. Pay special attention to how the array **filefilter** is initialized. Remember that the array pointed to by **lpstrFilter** must contain *pairs of strings*.

Once a filename has been obtained, it is used to open the file. Notice that in this case, the entire drive, path, and filename contained in **fn** and pointed to by **lpstrFile** are used. If you wanted to restrict files to the current directory, then the contents of **filename** (pointed to by **lpstrFileTitle**) could have been used.

You might want to try experimenting with **GetOpenFileName( )** and **GetSaveFileName( )** on your own, by trying different options. These are two important built-in dialog boxes which nearly all applications will need to use.

FAST TRACK TIP

The Common Dialog Boxes

The functions **GetOpenFileName( )** and **GetSaveFileName( )** are two examples of a general class of built-in dialog boxes called *common dialog boxes*. Common dialog boxes are system-defined dialog boxes that your application can use for performing various common input tasks, such as obtaining a filename, choosing a font, or setting a color. Unlike the common controls, which are new to Windows 95, the common dialog boxes are also available in earlier versions of Windows, such as Windows 3.1.

A common dialog box is activated by calling an API function. (This differs from the common controls, which are windows that must be created.) The common dialog boxes supported by Windows 95 are listed in the following table:

Function	Dialog Box Activated
ChooseColor( )	The Color dialog box, which allows the user to choose a color or create a custom control
ChooseFont( )	The Font dialog box, which allows the user to select a font
FindText( )	The Find dialog box, which supports text searches
GetOpenFileName( )	The Open dialog box, which allows the user to select a file to open
GetSaveFileName( )	The Save As dialog box, which allows the user to select a file into which information will be saved
PrintDlg( )	The Print dialog box, which is used to print files
ReplaceText( )	The Replace dialog box, which supports text replacements

While there is no technical reason that you cannot create your own dialog boxes to handle the types of input managed by the common dialog boxes, generally you should not. Instead, the common dialog boxes should be used by your program whenever one of the operations that they can perform is required. The reason is easy to understand: the users expect it. The common dialog boxes provide easy to use solutions to several fairly complex input situations.

7

CHAPTER 8

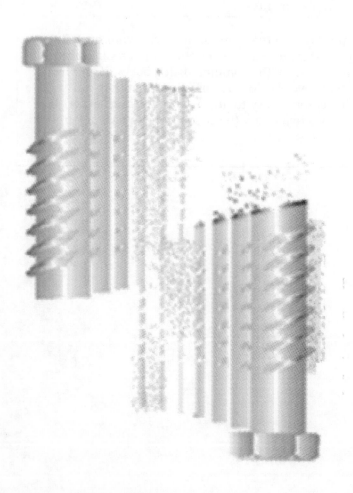

Up-Down Controls and Trackbars

This chapter explores two more of Windows 95 common controls: the *up-down control* and the *trackbar.* The up-down control and the trackbar are particularly important for three reasons. First, they are visually appealing. Second, they are easily incorporated into any new application. Third, they make a convenient means of enhancing an existing program when it is ported to Windows 95.

As a means of demonstrating up-down controls and trackbars, the countdown timer program developed in Chapter 5 is modified so that it utilizes these two new controls.

Using Up-Down Controls

An up-down control is essentially a compressed scroll bar. That is, it consists only of the arrows found on the ends of a scroll bar; there is no bar between them. As you may have seen while using various Windows 95 applications, some scroll bars are so small that the bar is essentially pointless. Also, some situations don't lend themselves to the concept of the bar, but do benefit from the use of the up and down arrows. To accommodate these situations, the designers of Windows 95 decided to define the up-down control.

An up-down control may be employed two ways. First, it may be used more or less like a stand-alone scroll bar. Second, it can be used in conjunction with another control, called its *buddy window*. The most common buddy window is an edit box. When this is the case, a *spin control* (or *spinner*) is created. Here is the way these two controls appear. (The spin control is on the right.)

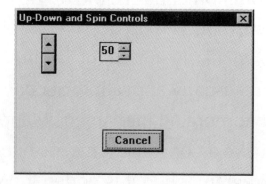

When you use a spin control, almost all of the overhead required to manage the control is provided automatically by Windows 95. This makes the spin control easy to add to your application. The methods of creating and managing both a stand-alone up-down control and a spin control are discussed here.

Creating an Up-Down Control

To create an up-down control, use the **CreateUpDownControl( )** function, which has this general form:

```
HWND CreateUpDownControl(DWORD Style, int X, int Y,
                int Width, int Height, HWND hParent,
                int ID, HINSTANCE hInst,
                HWND hBuddy, int Max, int Min, int StartPos);
```

Here, *Style* specifies the style of the up-down control. This parameter must include the standard styles **WS_CHILD**, **WS_VISIBLE**, and **WS_BORDER**. It may also include one or more of the up-down styles shown in Table 8-1.

Style	Meaning
UDS_ALIGNLEFT	Aligns the up-down control to the left of its buddy window.
UDS_ALIGNRIGHT	Aligns the up-down control to the right of its buddy window.
UDS_ARROWKEYS	Enables arrow keys (that is, arrow keys can be used to move a control).
TBS_AUTOBUDDY	Buddy window is the previous window in z-order.
UDS_HORZ	Up-down control is horizontal. (Up-down controls are vertical by default.)
UDS_NOTHOUSANDS	Commas are not used in large values. (Applies to spin controls only.)
UDS_SETBUDDYINT	Automatically sets the text within the buddy window when the control position is changed. This allows the buddy window to show the current position of the up-down control.
UDS_WRAP	Position of the up-down control will "wrap around" when moved past an end.

The Up-Down
Control Styles
Table 8-1.

The location of the upper-left corner of the up-down control is passed in *X* and *Y*. The width and height of the control is specified in *Width* and *Height*.

The handle of the parent window is passed in *hParent*. The ID associated with the up-down control is specified in *ID*. The instance handle of the application is passed in *hInst*. The handle of the buddy window is passed in *hBuddy*. If there is no buddy window, then this parameter must be **NULL**.

The range of the control is passed in Max and Min. If Max is less than *Min*, the control runs backwards. The initial position of the control (which must be within the specified range) is passed in *StartPos*. This value determines the control's initial value. It is important to understand that an up-down control maintains an internal counter that is incremented or decremented each time one of the arrows is pressed. This internal value will always be within the range specified when the control is created.

The function returns a handle to the control. It returns **NULL** on failure.

8

Up-Down Control Messages

When one of the arrows of an up-down control is pressed, it sends a **WM_VSCROLL** message to its parent window. The handle of the up-down control will be in *lParam*. Since there may be more than one control that generates **WM_VSCROLL** messages, you will need to check the handle in *lParam* to determine if it is that of the up-down control. To obtain the new value of the control (that is, its new position), send the control a **UDM_GETPOS** message. You can send the control messages by using **SendMessage( )**. The current position of the control is returned.

In addition to the **UDM_GETPOS** message, up-down controls respond to several others. Commonly used up-down messages are shown in Table 8-2. For example, your program can set the position of an up-down control by using the **UDM_SETPOS** message.

Creating a Spin Control

While there is nothing wrong with creating and using a stand-alone up-down control, the up-down control is most commonly linked with an edit box. As mentioned, this combination is called a spin control. Because the spin control is such a common use of an up-down control, Windows 95 provides special support for it. In fact, a spin control is a completely automated control—your program incurs virtually no management overhead.

To create a spin control, you must specify an edit control as a buddy window to an up-down control. After you have done this, each time the up-down

Message	Meaning
UDM_GETBUDDY	Obtains the handle of the buddy window. The handle is in the low-order word of the return value. *wParam* is zero. *lParam* is zero.
UDM_GETPOS	Obtains the current position. The current position is in the low-order word of the return value. *wParam* is zero. *lParam* is zero.
UDM_GETRANGE	Obtains the current range. The maximum value is in the low-order word of the return value, and the minimum value is in the high-order word of the return value. *wParam* is zero. *lParam* is zero.
UDM_SETBUDDY	Specifies a new buddy window. The handle of the old buddy window is returned. *wParam* is the handle of the new buddy window. *lParam* is zero.
UDM_SETPOS	Sets the current position. *wParam* is zero. *lParam* is the new current position.
UDM_SETRANGE	Sets the current range. *wParam* is zero. *lParam* is the range. Its low-order word contains the maximum value; its high-order word contains the minimum.

Common Up-Down Messages Table 8-2.

control is changed, its new position is automatically displayed in the edit box. Further, if you manually change the value in the edit box, the up-down control is automatically set to reflect that value. Typically, you will define the edit box within your program's resource file. You will see an example of a spin control later in this chapter.

Before showing an example of an up-down control, let's examine the trackbar.

Using a Trackbar

One of the most visually appealing of the common controls is the trackbar (sometimes called a *slider control*). A trackbar resembles the slide control found on various types of electronic equipment, such as stereos. It consists of a pointer that moves within a track. Although it looks quite different from a scroll bar, a trackbar is handled in much the same way by your program. Trackbars are particularly useful when your program is emulating a real device. For example, if your program is controlling a graphic equalizer, then trackbars are an excellent choice for representing and setting the frequency curve.

To create a trackbar, use either **CreateWindow( )** or **CreateWindowEx( )**. **CreateWindowEx( )** allows some extended style specifications. For the trackbar example in this chapter we won't need to use any extended styles, but you may find them useful in your own applications. The window class of a trackbar is **TRACKBAR_CLASS**.

Trackbar Styles

When you create the trackbar, you can specify various style options. The most common ones are shown in Table 8-3. You will almost always want to include **TBS_AUTOTICKS** because this style causes small tick marks to be automatically shown on the bar. The tick marks provide a scale for the bar.

Style	Effect
TBS_AUTOTICKS	Automatically adds tick marks to the trackbar.
TBS_HORZ	Trackbar is horizontal (default).
TBS_VERT	Trackbar is vertical.
TBS_BOTTOM	Tick marks appear on bottom of bar (default).
TBS_TOP	Tick marks appear on top of bar.
TBS_LEFT	Tick marks appear on left side of bar.
TBS_RIGHT	Tick marks appear on right side of bar (default).
TBS_BOTH	Tick marks appear on both sides of bar.

Common Trackbar Style Options
Table 8-3.

8

FAST TRACK TIP

Managing Power

Windows 95 provides a set of power management functions that help your application manage and monitor the power consumption of the computer. In the past, power management was something that most programmers did not worry about. However, as laptops and other types of portable computers become increasingly common, the issue of power management has moved to the forefront. Fortunately, Windows 95 provides two API functions that help you with power management. They are as follows:

BOOL GetSystemPowerStatus(LPSYSTEM_POWER_STATUS *lpPower*);

BOOL SetSystemPowerState(BOOLEAN *State*, BOOLEAN *NoPermission*);

The **GetSystemPowerStatus( )** function obtains information about the power supply, such as whether the computer is running on AC or on a battery. It puts the current power status into the **SYSTEM_POWER_STATUS** structure pointed to by *lpPower*. The **SYSTEM_POWER_STATUS** structure is defined like this:

```
typedef struct _SYSTEM_POWER_STATUS {
  BYTE ACLineStatus; /* AC or battery */
  BYTE BatteryFlag; /* current battery status */
  BYTE BatteryLifePercent; /* remaining battery power */
  BYTE Reserved1;
  DWORD BatteryLifeTime; /* seconds of battery time left */
  DWORD BatteryFullLifeTime; /* fully charged battery life */
} SYSTEM_POWER_STATUS;
```

To conserve battery power, your application can call **SetSystemPowerState( )** to suspend operation. If *State* is nonzero, then the system is suspended, but memory is kept in a "RAM-alive" state. If *State* is zero, then the system enters a "hibernate" state. If *NoPermission* is nonzero, then the powered-down state is entered unconditionally. If *NoPermission* is false, then each currently executing application must grant permission for the system to be powered down.

If power management is important to your application, you will want to incorporate Windows 95's power management system.

Message	Meaning
TBM_GETPOS	Obtains the current position. *wParam* is zero. *lParam* is zero.
TBM_GETRANGEMAX	Obtains the maximum trackbar range. *wParam* is zero. *lParam* is zero.
TBM_GETRANGEMIN	Obtains the minimum trackbar range. *wParam* is zero. *lParam* is zero.
TBM_SETPOS	Sets the current position. *wParam* is nonzero to redraw trackbar and zero otherwise. *lParam* contains the new position.
TBM_SETRANGE	Sets the trackbar range. *wParam* is nonzero to redraw the trackbar and zero otherwise. *lParam* contains the range. The minimum value is in the low-order word. The maximum value is in the high-order word.
TBM_SETRANGEMAX	Sets the maximum range. *wParam* is nonzero to redraw the trackbar and zero otherwise. *lParam* contains the maximum range value.
TBM_SETRANGEMIN	Sets the minimum range. *wParam* is nonzero to redraw the trackbar and zero otherwise. *lParam* contains the minimum range value.

Common
Trackbar
Messages
Table 8-4.

Sending Trackbar Messages

As with the other common controls examined, you send a trackbar a message by using the **SendMessage( )** function. Common trackbar messages are shown in Table 8-4. Two messages that you will almost always need to send to a trackbar are **TBM_SETRANGE** and **TBM_SETPOS**. These set the range of the trackbar and establish its initial position, respectively. These items cannot be set when the trackbar is created.

Processing Trackbar Notification Messages

When a trackbar is accessed, it generates a **WM_HSCROLL** scroll message. A value describing the nature of the activity is passed in the low-order word of *wParam*. This value is called a *notification message*. The handle of the trackbar that generated the message is in *lParam*. Common trackbar notification messages are described in the following table:

8

Message	Meaning
TB_BOTTOM	The END key is pressed. Slider is moved to the minimum value.
TB_ENDTRACK	End of trackbar activity.
TB_LINEDOWN	The RIGHT ARROW or DOWN ARROW key is pressed.
TB_LINEUP	The LEFT ARROW or UP ARROW key is pressed.
TB_PAGEDOWN	The PAGE DOWN key is pressed or the mouse is clicked before the slider.
TB_PAGEUP	The PAGE UP key is pressed or the mouse is clicked after the slider.
TB_THUMBPOSITION	Slider is moved by use of the mouse.
TB_THUMBTRACK	Slider is dragged by use of the mouse.
TB_TOP	The HOME key is pressed. Slider is moved to the maximum value.

Demonstrating a Spin Control and a Trackbar

The following program demonstrates a spin control and a trackbar by modifying the countdown timer program first developed in Chapter 5. Specifically, it uses the spin control to set the number of seconds to delay. It uses the trackbar to set the number of beeps that will be sounded when the timer goes off. The enhanced countdown timer program is shown here:

```
/* Add a spin control and a trackbar to
   the countdown timer. */

#include <windows.h>
#include <commctrl.h>
#include <string.h>
#include <stdio.h>
#include "timer.h"

#define BEEPMAX 10
#define MAXTIME 99

LRESULT CALLBACK WindowFunc(HWND, UINT, WPARAM, LPARAM);
BOOL CALLBACK DialogFunc(HWND, UINT, WPARAM, LPARAM);

char szWinName[] = "MyWin"; /* name of window class */

HINSTANCE hInst;

HWND hwnd;
```

```
int WINAPI WinMain(HINSTANCE hThisInst, HINSTANCE hPrevInst,
                   LPSTR lpszArgs, int nWinMode)
{
  MSG msg;
  WNDCLASSEX wcl;
  HANDLE hAccel;

  /* Define a window class. */
  wcl.hInstance = hThisInst; /* handle to this instance */
  wcl.lpszClassName = szWinName; /* window class name */
  wcl.lpfnWndProc = WindowFunc; /* window function */
  wcl.style = 0; /* default style */

  wcl.cbSize = sizeof(WNDCLASSEX); /* set size of WNDCLASSEX */

  wcl.hIcon = LoadIcon(NULL, IDI_APPLICATION); /* large icon */
  wcl.hIconSm = LoadIcon(NULL, IDI_APPLICATION); /* small icon */

  wcl.hCursor = LoadCursor(NULL, IDC_ARROW); /* cursor style */

  /* specify name of menu resource */
  wcl.lpszMenuName = "MYMENU"; /* main menu */

  wcl.cbClsExtra = 0; /* no extra */
  wcl.cbWndExtra = 0; /* information needed */

  /* Make the window white. */
  wcl.hbrBackground = GetStockObject(WHITE_BRUSH);

  /* Register the window class. */
  if(!RegisterClassEx(&wcl)) return 0;

  /* Now that a window class has been registered, a window
     can be created. */
  hwnd = CreateWindow(
    szWinName, /* name of window class */
    "Spin Controls and Trackbars", /* title */
    WS_OVERLAPPEDWINDOW, /* window style - normal */
    CW_USEDEFAULT, /* X coordinate - let Windows decide */
    CW_USEDEFAULT, /* Y coordinate - let Windows decide */
    CW_USEDEFAULT, /* width - let Windows decide */
    CW_USEDEFAULT, /* height - let Windows decide */
    HWND_DESKTOP, /* no parent window */
    NULL, /* no menu */
    hThisInst, /* handle of this instance of the program */
    NULL /* no additional arguments */
  );
```

8

```
  hInst = hThisInst; /* save the current instance handle */

  /* load accelerators */
  hAccel = LoadAccelerators(hThisInst, "MYMENU");

  /* Display the window. */
  ShowWindow(hwnd, nWinMode);
  UpdateWindow(hwnd);

  /* Create the message loop. */
  while(GetMessage(&msg, NULL, 0, 0))
  {
    if(!TranslateAccelerator(hwnd, hAccel, &msg)) {
      TranslateMessage(&msg); /* allow use of keyboard */
      DispatchMessage(&msg); /* return control to Windows */
    }
  }
  return msg.wParam;
}

/* This function is called by Windows 95 and is passed
   messages from the message queue.
*/
LRESULT CALLBACK WindowFunc(HWND hwnd, UINT message,
                            WPARAM wParam, LPARAM lParam)
{
  int response;

  switch(message) {
    case WM_COMMAND:
      switch(LOWORD(wParam)) {
        case IDM_DIALOG:
          DialogBox(hInst, "MYDB", hwnd, DialogFunc);
          break;
        case IDM_EXIT:
          response = MessageBox(hwnd, "Quit the Program?",
                                "Exit", MB_YESNO);
          if(response == IDYES) PostQuitMessage(0);
          break;
        case IDM_HELP:
          MessageBox(hwnd, "Try the Timer", "Help", MB_OK);
          break;
      }
      break;
    case WM_DESTROY: /* terminate the program */
      PostQuitMessage(0);
      break;
```

```
      default:
        /* Let Windows 95 process any messages not specified in
           the preceding switch statement. */
        return DefWindowProc(hwnd, message, wParam, lParam);
    }
    return 0;
}

/* Dialog function */
BOOL CALLBACK DialogFunc(HWND hdwnd, UINT message,
                         WPARAM wParam, LPARAM lParam)
{
  char str[80];

  HDC hdc;
  PAINTSTRUCT paintstruct;
  static int t;
  int i;

  static long udpos = 1;
  static long trackpos = 1;
  static HWND hEboxWnd;
  static HWND hTrackWnd;
  static HWND udWnd;
  int low=1, high=BEEPMAX;

  switch(message) {
    case WM_INITDIALOG:
      hEboxWnd = GetDlgItem(hdwnd, IDD_EB1);
      udWnd = CreateUpDownControl(
                  WS_CHILD | WS_BORDER | WS_VISIBLE |
                  UDS_SETBUDDYINT | UDS_ALIGNRIGHT,
                  10, 10, 50, 50,
                  hdwnd,
                  IDD_UPDOWN,
                  hInst,
                  hEboxWnd,
                  MAXTIME, 1, udpos);

      /* Create a trackbar */
      hTrackWnd = CreateWindow(TRACKBAR_CLASS,
                  "",
                  WS_CHILD | WS_VISIBLE | WS_TABSTOP |
                  TBS_AUTOTICKS | WS_BORDER,
                  0, 50,
                  200, 30,
                  hdwnd,
                  NULL,
```

8

```
                    hInst,
                    NULL
    );
    SendMessage(hTrackWnd, TBM_SETRANGE,
                1, MAKELONG(low, high));
    SendMessage(hTrackWnd, TBM_SETPOS,
                1, trackpos);

    /* check the As-Is radio button */
    SendDlgItemMessage(hdwnd, IDD_RB3, BM_SETCHECK, 1, 0);

    /* set number of beeps box */
    SetDlgItemInt(hdwnd, IDD_EB2, trackpos, 1);
    return 1;
case WM_VSCROLL: /* process up-down control */
    if(udWnd==(HWND)lParam)
      udpos = GetDlgItemInt(hdwnd, IDD_EB1, NULL, 1);
    return 1;
case WM_HSCROLL: /* trackbar was activated */
    if(hTrackWnd != (HWND)lParam) break; /* not trackbar */

    switch(LOWORD(wParam)) {
      case TB_TOP:
      case TB_BOTTOM:        /* For this example */
      case TB_LINEUP:        /* all messages will be */
      case TB_LINEDOWN:      /* processed in the same */
      case TB_THUMBPOSITION: /* way. */
      case TB_THUMBTRACK:
      case TB_PAGEUP:
      case TB_PAGEDOWN:
        trackpos = SendMessage(hTrackWnd, TBM_GETPOS,
                       0, 0);
        SetDlgItemInt(hdwnd, IDD_EB2, trackpos, 1);
        return 1;
    }
    break;
case WM_COMMAND:
    switch(LOWORD(wParam)) {
      case IDCANCEL:
        EndDialog(hdwnd, 0);
        return 1;
      case IDD_EB2:
        /* Update trackbar if user enters number
           of beeps into the Beeps edit box. */
        trackpos = GetDlgItemInt(hdwnd, IDD_EB2, NULL, 1);
```

```
          SendMessage(hTrackWnd, TBM_SETPOS,
                    1, trackpos);
          return 1;
        case IDD_START: /* start the timer */
          SetTimer(hdwnd, IDD_TIMER, 1000, NULL);

          /* get number of seconds to delay */
          t = udpos = GetDlgItemInt(hdwnd, IDD_EB1, NULL, 1);

          if(SendDlgItemMessage(hdwnd,
                  IDD_RB1, BM_GETCHECK, 0, 0))
            ShowWindow(hwnd, SW_MINIMIZE);
          else
          if(SendDlgItemMessage(hdwnd,
                  IDD_RB2, BM_GETCHECK, 0, 0))
            ShowWindow(hwnd, SW_MAXIMIZE);
          return 1;
      }
      break;
    case WM_TIMER: /* timer went off */
      if(t==0) {
        KillTimer(hdwnd, IDD_TIMER);
        if(SendDlgItemMessage(hdwnd,
                    IDD_CB2, BM_GETCHECK, 0, 0)) {

          /* beep and move trackbar with each beep */
          for(i=trackpos ; i; i--) {
            SendMessage(hTrackWnd, TBM_SETPOS, 1, i);
            MessageBeep(MB_OK);
            Sleep(250);
          }

          /* reset trackbar after countdown */
          SendMessage(hTrackWnd, TBM_SETPOS, 1, trackpos);
        }

        MessageBox(hdwnd, "Timer Went Off", "Timer", MB_OK);
        SetDlgItemInt(hdwnd, IDD_EB1, udpos, 1);
        ShowWindow(hwnd, SW_RESTORE);
        return 1;
      }
      t--;

      /* see if countdown is to be displayed */
      if(SendDlgItemMessage(hdwnd,
```

8

```
                    IDD_CB1, BM_GETCHECK, 0, 0)) {
          SetDlgItemInt(hdwnd, IDD_EB1, t, 1);
      }
      return 1;
    case WM_PAINT:
      hdc = BeginPaint(hdwnd, &paintstruct);
      sprintf(str, "Seconds");
      TextOut(hdc, 44, 6, str, strlen(str));
      sprintf(str, "Beeps");
      TextOut(hdc, 182, 6, str, strlen(str));
      sprintf(str, "Set Number of Beeps");
      TextOut(hdc, 30, 32, str, strlen(str));
      EndPaint(hdwnd, &paintstruct);
      return 1;
  }
  return 0;
}
```

This program uses the following resource file. The edit box identified as **IDD_EB1** will be linked to the up-down control to form the spin control.

```
; Demonstrate a Spin Control and a Trackbar
#include <windows.h>
#include "timer.h"
MYMENU MENU
{
  POPUP "&Options"
  {
    MENUITEM "&Timer\tF2", IDM_DIALOG
    MENUITEM "&Exit\tF3", IDM_EXIT
  }
  MENUITEM "&Help", IDM_HELP
}


MYMENU ACCELERATORS
{
  VK_F2, IDM_DIALOG, VIRTKEY
  VK_F3, IDM_EXIT, VIRTKEY
  VK_F1, IDM_HELP, VIRTKEY
}


MYDB DIALOG 18, 18, 144, 100
CAPTION "A Countdown Timer"
STYLE DS_MODALFRAME | WS_POPUP | WS_CAPTION | WS_SYSMENU
```

```
{
  PUSHBUTTON "Start", IDD_START, 30, 80, 30, 14,
          WS_CHILD | WS_VISIBLE | WS_TABSTOP
  PUSHBUTTON "Cancel", IDCANCEL, 70, 80, 30, 14,
          WS_CHILD | WS_VISIBLE | WS_TABSTOP
  EDITTEXT IDD_EB1, 1, 1, 20, 12, ES_LEFT | WS_CHILD |
          WS_VISIBLE | WS_BORDER
  EDITTEXT IDD_EB2, 80, 1, 10, 12, ES_LEFT | WS_CHILD |
          WS_VISIBLE | WS_BORDER
  AUTOCHECKBOX "Show Countdown", IDD_CB1, 1, 48, 70, 10
  AUTOCHECKBOX "Beep At End", IDD_CB2, 1, 58, 50, 10
  AUTORADIOBUTTON "Minimize", IDD_RB1, 80, 48, 50, 10
  AUTORADIOBUTTON "Maximize", IDD_RB2, 80, 58, 50, 10
  AUTORADIOBUTTON "As-Is", IDD_RB3, 80, 68, 50, 10
}
```

The header file TIMER.H is shown here.

```
#define IDM_DIALOG   100
#define IDM_EXIT     101
#define IDM_HELP     102

#define IDD_START    300
#define IDD_TIMER    301

#define IDD_CB1      400
#define IDD_CB2      401
#define IDD_RB1      402
#define IDD_RB2      403
#define IDD_RB3      404

#define IDD_EB1      500
#define IDD_EB2      501

#define IDD_UPDOWN   602
```

Sample output from the program is shown in Figure 8-1. When the timer is started (by pressing Start), the currently specified delay time is retrieved from the spin control. If the Show Countdown option is checked, then the time remaining is updated in the spin control each time the timer goes off. When the end of the time has been reached, the specified number of beeps is sounded (if the Beep At End option was selected). Also, the trackbar is moved left one position each time a beep sounds. Let's take a closer look at the enhanced countdown program now.

8

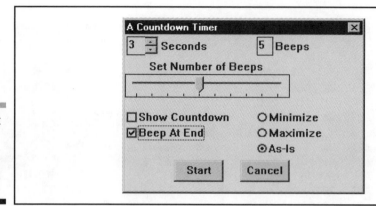

Sample output
from the
enhanced
timer program
Figure 8-1.

The Sleep( ) Function

In the countdown program, the **Sleep( )** function is used to provide a slight
delay between beeps when the timer goes off. If a short delay does not
separate each beep, then only one long, continuous sound is heard. In the
past, such a delay was generally achieved through the use of some sort of
software-based delay loop, such as

```
for(x=0; x<100000; x++) ; /* a simple delay loop */
```

However, such software methods are problematic for two main reasons.
First, software delay loops are imprecise–the length of the delay is affected
by the speed of the CPU. On a fast computer, the delay will be shorter. On
a slow computer, the delay will be longer. Further, even with equivalent
CPU speeds, different compilers will use different machine instructions when
they compile the preceding loop. This could lead to differences in the length
of the delay. The second reason software delay loops can cause problems is
that they are CPU intensive. That is, even though they do nothing, they are
using CPU time that could be allocated to other processes running in your
system. To prevent inconsistent delays and CPU-intensive code, your
Windows 95 programs should use the **Sleep( )** function to provide a delay.

The **Sleep( )** function suspends the execution of the thread that calls it for
a specified number of milliseconds. (For single-threaded programs, this
means that the entire program is suspended.) This is the prototype of the
Sleep( ) function:

VOID Sleep(DWORD *delay*);

Here, *delay* specifies the number of milliseconds that the calling thread will
suspend. While your program is asleep, CPU time is allocated to other
processes running in the system.

Creating the Spin Control and Trackbar

Both the spin control and the trackbar are created each time **DialogFunc( )** receives a **WM_INITDIALOG** message, using the code shown here:

```
case WM_INITDIALOG:
  hEboxWnd = GetDlgItem(hdwnd, IDD_EB1);
  udWnd = CreateUpDownControl(
              WS_CHILD | WS_BORDER | WS_VISIBLE |
              UDS_SETBUDDYINT | UDS_ALIGNRIGHT,
              10, 10, 50, 50,
              hdwnd,
              IDD_UPDOWN,
              hInst,
              hEboxWnd,
              MAXTIME, 1, udpos);

  /* Create a trackbar */
  hTrackWnd = CreateWindow(TRACKBAR_CLASS,
              "",
              WS_CHILD | WS_VISIBLE | WS_TABSTOP |
              TBS_AUTOTICKS | WS_BORDER,
              0, 50,
              200, 30,
              hdwnd,
              NULL,
              hInst,
              NULL
  );
  SendMessage(hTrackWnd, TBM_SETRANGE,
              1, MAKELONG(low, high));
  SendMessage(hTrackWnd, TBM_SETPOS,
              1, trackpos);

  /* check the As-Is radio button */
  SendDlgItemMessage(hdwnd, IDD_RB3, BM_SETCHECK, 1, 0);

  /* set number of beeps box */
  SetDlgItemInt(hdwnd, IDD_EB2, trackpos, 1);
  return 1;
```

Look first at the call to **CreateUpDownControl( )**. This creates a spin control that is at location 10, 10 within the dialog box. The control is 50 pixels wide and 50 pixels tall. Because the control is a child window of the dialog box, the dialog box's handle (**hdwnd**) is passed as the parent handle. The ID of the up-down control is **IDD_UPDOWN**. **hInst** is the instance handle of the program. The buddy window is specified by **hEboxWnd**. This

8

is the handle of the edit box that will be linked to the up-down control. The range of the up-down control is 1 to **MAXTIME**, and the initial position is 1.

Since the dialog box that is part of the spin control is defined in the resource file, the program must call **GetDlgItem( )** to obtain its handle. (**GetDlgItem( )** was described in Chapter 4.) Once the handle of the dialog box has been obtained, it is passed as the buddy window to the **CreateUpDownControl( )** function. After the up-down control has been created with an edit box as its buddy window, the two controls are automatically linked together, forming the spin control.

Next, examine how the trackbar is created. It is located at 0, 50 and is 200 pixels long by 30 pixels high. The handle of the trackbar is stored in **hTrackWnd**. After the trackbar is created, its range is set to 1 through **BEEPMAX**. (These are the values contained in **low** and **high**.) Its initial position is set at 1. Notice that the range is set by the macro **MAKELONG( )**. This macro assembles two integers into a long integer. It has this prototype:

DWORD MAKELONG(WORD *low*, WORD *high*);

The low-order part of the double-word value is specified in *low,* and the high-order portion is specified in *high.* **MAKELONG( )** is quite useful when you need to encode two word values into a long integer.

Using the Spin Control

Each time the spin control is accessed, a **WM_VSCROLL** message is sent to the dialog box. The handle of the up-down control is contained in **lParam**. This handle is tested against that returned by **CreateUpDownControl( )** to confirm that it is the up-down control that generated the message. While there is only one control in this example, real-world applications may have several controls capable of generating a **WM_VSCROLL** message, so you should always confirm which control has been accessed.

The current value of the spin control is most easily retrieved by obtaining the value of the integer inside its edit box. Remember, the value in the edit box always reflects the current value of the spin control. To retrieve this value, use **GetDlgItemInt( )**. This function is similar to **GetDlgItemText( )**, which you learned about in Chapter 4. However, instead of obtaining the text from an edit box, it returns the integer equivalent of the contents of the box. For example, if the box contains the string 102, then **GetDlgItemInt( )** will return the value 102. For obvious reasons, this function only applies to edit boxes that contain numeric values. The prototype for **GetDlgItemInt( )** is shown here:

INT GetDlgItemInt(HWND *hDialog*, int *ID*, BOOL **error*, BOOL *signed*);

The handle of the dialog box that contains the edit control is passed in *hDialog*. The ID of the edit box is passed in *ID*. If the edit box does not contain a valid numeric string, zero is returned. However, zero is also a valid value. For this reason, the success or failure of the function is returned in the variable pointed to by *error*. After the call, the variable pointed to by *error* will be nonzero if the return value is valid. It will be zero if an error occurred. If you don't care about errors, you can use **NULL** for this parameter. If *signed* is a nonzero value, then a signed value will be returned by **GetDlgItemInt( )**. Otherwise, an unsigned value is returned.

Managing the Trackbar

Whenever the trackbar is moved, a **WM_HSCROLL** message is received and processed by the following code:

```
case WM_HSCROLL: /* trackbar was activated */
  if(hTrackWnd != (HWND)lParam) break; /* not trackbar */

  switch(LOWORD(wParam)) {
    case TB_TOP:
    case TB_BOTTOM:        /* For this example */
    case TB_LINEUP:        /* all messages will be */
    case TB_LINEDOWN:      /* processed in the same */
    case TB_THUMBPOSITION: /* way. */
    case TB_THUMBTRACK:
    case TB_PAGEUP:
    case TB_PAGEDOWN:
      trackpos = SendMessage(hTrackWnd, TBM_GETPOS,
                   0, 0);
      SetDlgItemInt(hdwnd, IDD_EB2, trackpos, 1);
      return 1;
  }
  break;
```

When the user moves the slider within the trackbar, the trackbar's position is automatically updated—your program does not have to do this itself. After the trackbar has been moved, the program obtains its new value and then uses this value to update the edit box that displays the number of beeps.

8

The current value of the trackbar is displayed inside the Beeps edit box by use of **SetDlgItemInt( )**. This function is essentially the reverse of **GetDlgItemInt( )** just discussed. It has the following prototype:

BOOL SetDlgItemInt(HWND *hDialog*, int *ID*, UINT *value*, BOOL *signed*);

The handle of the dialog box that contains the edit control is passed in *hDialog*. The ID of the edit box is passed in *ID*. The value to put into the edit box is passed in *value*. If *signed* is a nonzero value, then negative values are allowed. Otherwise, an unsigned value is assumed. The function returns nonzero if successful and zero on failure.

The user can also manually set the number of beeps by using the Beeps edit box. When this is done, the trackbar is automatically adjusted to reflect the value entered by the user.

In this example, the trackbar can be moved by use of either the mouse or the keyboard. In fact, the reason that so many **TB_** messages are included is to support the keyboard interface. You might want to try taking some of these messages out and observing the results.

The Progress Bar

A progress bar is another of Windows 95's common controls. It is a small, horizontal window that depicts the degree of completion of a task. As the task proceeds, the bar is filled from left to right. When the bar is filled, the task is finished. The progress bar is one of the simplest of the common controls, and you have likely seen one in action. Progress bars are created by use of either **CreateWindow( )** or **CreateWindowEx( )** by specifying the **PROGRESS_CLASS** window class.

Your program sends a progress bar a message by using the standard **SendMessage( )** function. Progress bars do not generate messages. Generally, you will send messages to set a progress bar's range and to increment its progress. A few of the most common progress bar messages are described in the following table:

Message	Meaning
PBM_SETPOS	Sets the progress bar's position. The old position is returned. *wParam* contains the new position. *lParam* is zero.
PBM_SETRANGE	Sets the progress bar's range. The old range is returned, with the maximum value in the high-order word and the minimum value in the low-order word. *wParam* is zero. *lParam* contains the range. The maximum value is in the high-order word. The minimum value is in the low-order word.
PBM_SETSTEP	Sets the increment (or step) value. The old increment is returned. *wParam* contains the new increment. *lParam* is zero.
PBM_STEPIT	Advances the bar's progress by the step value. *wParam* is zero. *lParam* is zero.

By default, a progress bar has the range 0 through 100. However, you can set it to any value from 0 through 65,535. Typically, you will advance the bar by sending it a **PBM_STEPIT** message. This causes the bar's current position to advance by a predetermined increment called a *step*. By default, the step increment is 10, but it can be any value you like. As you increment the bar's position, more of the bar is filled. Since a progress bar is used to display the degree of completion of a long task, the task should end when the bar is fully filled.

To try a progress bar, change **DialogFunc( )** in the countdown program as follows. First, declare this progress bar handle:

```
static HWND hProgWnd;
```

Next, add these statements to the **INIT_DIALOG** case:

```
/* create progress bar */
hProgWnd = CreateWindow(PROGRESS_CLASS,
            "",
            WS_CHILD | WS_VISIBLE | WS_BORDER,
            0, 84,
            200, 12,
            hdwnd,
            NULL,
```

8

```
                               hInst,
                               NULL);

           /* set step increment to 1 */
           SendMessage(hProgWnd, PBM_SETSTEP, 1, 0);
```

Add the following statements to the **IDD_START** case. This sets the range
of the progress bar so that it matches the number of seconds to delay. It
also resets the progress bar position so that it starts each countdown fresh.

```
           /* initialize progress bar */
           SendMessage(hProgWnd, PBM_SETRANGE, 0,
                       MAKELONG(0, udpos));
           SendMessage(hProgWnd, PBM_SETPOS, 0, 0);
```

Finally, add the following statement to the **WM_TIMER** case so that it is
executed each time the timer goes off.

```
           /* advance progress bar */
           SendMessage(hProgWnd, PBM_STEPIT, 0, 0);
```

After you make these changes, the dialog box will look like that shown here,
and the progress bar will automatically show the progress of the countdown.

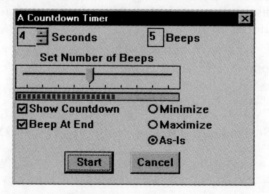

CHAPTER 9

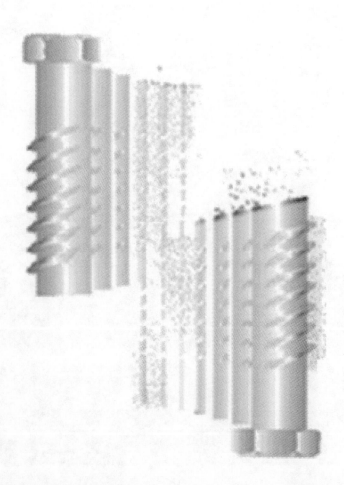

Thread-based Multitasking

This chapter describes Windows 95's thread-based multitasking system. As mentioned at the start of this book, Windows 95 supports two forms of multitasking. The first type is *process-based*. This is the type of multiprocessing that Windows has supported from its inception. A *process* is, essentially, a program that is executing. In process-based multitasking, two or more processes can execute concurrently. The second type of multitasking is *thread-based*. Thread-based multitasking will be new to most Windows users and programmers because it was not available for general use before Windows 95. (Windows NT supports thread-based multitasking. However, Windows NT is not widely used.) A thread is a path (or *thread*) of execution within a process.

In Windows 95, every process has at least one thread, but it may have two or more. Thread-based multitasking allows two or more parts of a single program to execute concurrently. This allows you to write extremely efficient programs because you can define the threads of execution and thus manage the way your program executes.

The inclusion of thread-based multitasking has increased the need for a special type of multitasking feature called *synchronization,* which allows the execution of threads (and processes) to be coordinated in certain well-defined ways. Windows 95 has added a complete subsystem devoted to synchronization, and several of its key features are discussed in this chapter.

Creating Multithreaded Programs

If you have never programmed for a multithreaded environment before, then you are in for a pleasant surprise. Multithreaded multitasking adds a new dimension to your programming by letting you more fully control how pieces of your program execute. For example, you could assign one thread of a program the job of sorting a file, another thread the job of gathering information from some remote source, and another thread the task of performing user input. Because of multithreaded multitasking, each thread could execute concurrently, and no CPU time would be wasted.

It is important to understand that all processes have at least one thread of execution. For the sake of discussion, this is called the *main thread.* However, it is possible to create one or more other threads of execution within the same process. In general, once a new thread is created, it also begins execution. Thus, each process starts with one thread of execution and may create one or more additional threads. In this way, thread-based multitasking is supported.

In this section you will see how to create a multithreaded program.

Creating a Thread

To create a thread, use the API function **CreateThread( )**, which has this prototype:

```
HANDLE CreateThread(LPSECURITY_ATTRIBUTES lpAttr,
                    DWORD dwStack,
                    LPTHREAD_START_ROUTINE lpFunc,
                    LPVOID lpParam,
                    DWORD dwFlags,
                    LPDWORD lpdwID);
```

Here, *lpAttr* is a pointer to a set of security attributes pertaining to the thread. However, if *lpAttr* is **NULL**, as should be the case for Windows 95, then no security is used.

Each thread has its own stack. You can specify the size of the new thread's stack, in bytes, by using the *dwStack* parameter. If this value is 0, then the thread will be given a stack that is the same size as the main thread of the process that creates it. In this case, the stack will be expanded, if necessary. (Specifying 0 is the common approach taken to thread stack size.)

Each thread of execution begins with a call to a function, called a *thread function,* within the process. Execution of the thread continues until the thread function returns. The address of this function (that is, the entry point to the thread) is specified in *lpFunc*. All thread functions must have this prototype:

```
DWORD threadfunc(LPVOID param);
```

Any argument that you need to pass to the new thread is specified in **CreateThread( )**'s *lpParam*. This 32-bit value is received by the thread's entry function in its parameter. This parameter can be used for any purpose.

The *dwFlags* parameter determines the execution state of the thread. If it is 0, the thread begins execution immediately. If it is **CREATE_SUSPEND**, the thread is created in a suspended state, awaiting execution. (It can be started by a call to **ResumeThread( )**.)

The identifier associated with a thread is returned in the double word pointed to by *lpdwID*.

The function returns a handle to the thread if successful or **NULL** if a failure occurs.

Terminating a Thread

As stated, a thread of execution terminates when its entry function returns. The process may also terminate the thread manually by using either **TerminateThread( )** or **ExitThread( )**, whose prototypes are shown here:

```
BOOL TerminateThread(HANDLE hThread, DWORD dwStatus);
```

```
VOID ExitThread(DWORD dwStatus);
```

For **TerminateThread( )**, *hThread* is the handle of the thread to be terminated. **ExitThread( )** can only be used to terminate the thread that calls **ExitThread( )**. For both functions, *dwStatus* is the termination status. **TerminateThread( )** returns nonzero if successful and zero otherwise.

9

Calling **ExitThread( )** is functionally equivalent to allowing a thread function to return normally. This means that the stack is properly reset. When a thread is terminated by use of **TerminateThread( )**, it is stopped immediately and does not perform any special cleanup activities. Also, **TerminateThread( )** may stop a thread during an important operation. For these reasons, it is usually best (and easiest) to let a thread terminate normally when its entry function returns. This is the approach used by the example programs in this chapter.

Note: Some C/C++ compilers designed for Windows 95 provide their own thread management functions. For example, Microsoft provides the functions **beginthread( )** and **endthread( )**. When this is the case, you may need to use those functions rather than **CreateThread( )** and **ExitThread( )**. You will need to check your compiler's user manual for details.

Suspending and Resuming a Thread

A thread of execution can be suspended by a call to **SuspendThread( )**. It can be resumed by a call to **ResumeThread( )**. The prototypes for these functions are shown here:

DWORD SuspendThread(HANDLE *hThread*);

DWORD ResumeThread(HANDLE *hThread*);

For both functions, the handle to the thread is passed in *hThread*.

Each thread of execution has associated with it a *suspend count*. If this count is zero, then the thread is not suspended. If it is nonzero, the thread is in a suspended state. Each call to **SuspendThread( )** increments the suspend count. Each call to **ResumeThread( )** decrements the suspend count. A suspended thread will only resume after its suspend count has reached zero. Therefore, to resume a suspended thread implies that there must be the same number of calls to **ResumeThread( )** as there have been calls to **SuspendThread( )**.

Both functions return the thread's previous suspend count or –1 if an error occurs.

A Multithreaded Example

The following program creates two threads each time the Demonstrate Thread menu option is selected. Each thread iterates a **for** loop 5,000 times, displaying the number of the iteration each time it repeats. As you will see when you run the program, both threads appear to execute concurrently.

```c
/* A simple multithreaded program. */

#include <windows.h>
#include <string.h>
#include <stdio.h>
#include "thread.h"

#define MAX 5000

LRESULT CALLBACK WindowFunc(HWND, UINT, WPARAM, LPARAM);
DWORD MyThread1(LPVOID param);
DWORD MyThread2(LPVOID param);

char szWinName[] = "MyWin"; /* name of window class */

char str[255]; /* holds output strings */

DWORD Tid1, Tid2; /* thread IDs */

int WINAPI WinMain(HINSTANCE hThisInst, HINSTANCE hPrevInst,
                   LPSTR lpszArgs, int nWinMode)
{
  HWND hwnd;
  MSG msg;
  WNDCLASSEX wcl;
  HANDLE hAccel;

  /* Define a window class. */
  wcl.hInstance = hThisInst; /* handle to this instance */
  wcl.lpszClassName = szWinName; /* window class name */
  wcl.lpfnWndProc = WindowFunc; /* window function */
  wcl.style = 0; /* default style */

  wcl.cbSize = sizeof(WNDCLASSEX); /* set size of WNDCLASSEX */

  wcl.hIcon = LoadIcon(NULL, IDI_APPLICATION); /* large icon */
  wcl.hIconSm = LoadIcon(NULL, IDI_APPLICATION); /* small icon */

  wcl.hCursor = LoadCursor(NULL, IDC_ARROW); /* cursor style */

  /* specify name of menu resource */
```

9

```
wcl.lpszMenuName = "MYMENU"; /* main menu */

wcl.cbClsExtra = 0; /* no extra */
wcl.cbWndExtra = 0; /* information needed */

/* Make the window white. */
wcl.hbrBackground = GetStockObject(WHITE_BRUSH);

/* Register the window class. */
if(!RegisterClassEx(&wcl)) return 0;

/* Now that a window class has been registered, a window
   can be created. */
hwnd = CreateWindow(
  szWinName, /* name of window class */
  "Demonstrate Threads", /* title */
  WS_OVERLAPPEDWINDOW, /* window style - normal */
  CW_USEDEFAULT, /* X coordinate - let Windows decide */
  CW_USEDEFAULT, /* Y coordinate - let Windows decide */
  CW_USEDEFAULT, /* width - let Windows decide */
  CW_USEDEFAULT, /* height - let Windows decide */
  HWND_DESKTOP, /* no parent window */
  NULL, /* no menu */
  hThisInst, /* handle of this instance of the program */
  NULL /* no additional arguments */
);

/* load accelerators */
hAccel = LoadAccelerators(hThisInst, "MYMENU");

/* Display the window. */
ShowWindow(hwnd, nWinMode);
UpdateWindow(hwnd);

/* Create the message loop. */
while(GetMessage(&msg, NULL, 0, 0))
{
  if(!TranslateAccelerator(hwnd, hAccel, &msg)) {
    TranslateMessage(&msg); /* allow use of keyboard */
    DispatchMessage(&msg); /* return control to Windows */
  }
}
return msg.wParam;
}

/* This function is called by Windows 95 and is passed
   messages from the message queue.
*/
```

```
LRESULT CALLBACK WindowFunc(HWND hwnd, UINT message,
                            WPARAM wParam, LPARAM lParam)
{
  int response;

  switch(message) {
    case WM_COMMAND:
      switch(LOWORD(wParam)) {
        case IDM_THREAD: /* create the threads */
          CreateThread(NULL, 0, (LPTHREAD_START_ROUTINE)MyThread1,
                       (LPVOID) hwnd, 0, &Tid1);
          CreateThread(NULL, 0, (LPTHREAD_START_ROUTINE)MyThread2,
                       (LPVOID) hwnd, 0, &Tid2);
          break;
        case IDM_EXIT:
          response = MessageBox(hwnd, "Quit the Program?",
                                "Exit", MB_YESNO);
          if(response == IDYES) PostQuitMessage(0);
          break;
        case IDM_HELP:
          MessageBox(hwnd,
                     "F1: Help\nF2: Demonstrate Threads",
                     "Help", MB_OK);
          break;
      }
      break;
    case WM_DESTROY: /* terminate the program */
      PostQuitMessage(0);
      break;
    default:
      /* Let Windows 95 process any messages not specified in
      the preceding switch statement. */
      return DefWindowProc(hwnd, message, wParam, lParam);
  }
  return 0;
}

/* A thread of execution within the process. */
DWORD MyThread1(LPVOID param)
{
  int i;
  HDC hdc;

  for(i=0; i<MAX; i++) {
    sprintf(str, "Thread 1: loop # %5d ", i);
    hdc = GetDC((HWND) param);
    TextOut(hdc, 1, 1, str, strlen(str));
```

9

```
      ReleaseDC((HWND) param, hdc);
    }
    return 0;
}

/* Another thread of execution within the process. */
DWORD MyThread2(LPVOID param)
{
  int i;
  HDC hdc;

  for(i=0; i<MAX; i++) {
    sprintf(str, "Thread 2: loop # %5d ", i);
    hdc = GetDC((HWND) param);
    TextOut(hdc, 1, 20, str, strlen(str));
    ReleaseDC((HWND) param, hdc);
  }
  return 0;
}
```

This program uses the THREAD.H file shown here:

```
#define IDM_THREAD 100
#define IDM_HELP   101
#define IDM_EXIT   102
```

The program also requires this resource file:

```
#include <windows.h>
#include "thread.h"

MYMENU MENU
{
  POPUP "&Threads" {
    MENUITEM "Demonstrate &Threads", IDM_THREAD
    MENUITEM "&Exit", IDM_EXIT
  }
  MENUITEM "&Help", IDM_HELP
}

MYMENU ACCELERATORS
{
  VK_F2, IDM_THREAD, VIRTKEY
  VK_F1, IDM_HELP, VIRTKEY
}
```

Sample output from the program is shown in Figure 9-1.

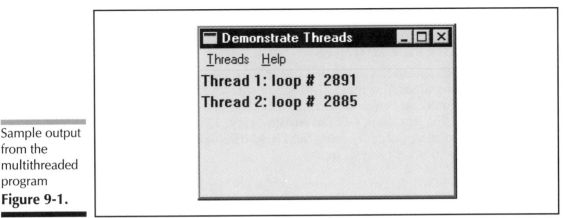

A Closer Look at the Multithreaded Program

Each time the menu option Demonstrate Threads is chosen, the following
code executes.

```
case IDM_THREAD:
    CreateThread(NULL, 0, (LPTHREAD_START_ROUTINE)MyThread1,
                 (LPVOID) hwnd, 0, &Tid1);
    CreateThread(NULL, 0, (LPTHREAD_START_ROUTINE)MyThread2,
                 (LPVOID) hwnd, 0, &Tid2);
    break;
```

As you can see, the first call to **CreateThread( )** activates **MyThread1( )**,
and the second call activates **MyThread2( )**. Notice that the handle of the
main window (**hwnd**) is passed as a parameter to each thread function. This
handle is used by the threads to obtain a device context so that they can
output information to the main window.

Once started, each thread of execution (including the main thread) runs
independently. For example, while the threads are executing, you can
activate the Help message box, exit the program, or even start another
set of threads. If you exit the program, then any child threads will be
automatically terminated.

Before continuing, you might want to experiment with this program. For
example, as it now stands, each thread terminates when its associated
function terminates. Try terminating a thread early by using **ExitThread( )**.
Also, try starting multiple instances of each thread.

Thread Priorities

Each thread has associated with it a priority setting. A thread's priority determines how much CPU time the thread receives. When a thread is first created, it is given normal priority. You can obtain a thread's priority setting by calling **GetThreadPriority( )**. You can increase or decrease a thread's priority by using **SetThreadPriority( )**. The prototypes for these functions are shown here:

> BOOL SetThreadPriority(HANDLE *hThread*, int *Priority*);

> int GetThreadPriority(HANDLE *hThread*);

For both functions, *hThread* is the handle of the thread. For **SetThreadPriority( )**, *Priority* is the new priority setting. For **GetThreadPriority( )**, the current priority setting is returned. The priority settings are listed here:

THREAD_PRIORITY_ABOVE_NORMAL	THREAD_PRIORITY_BELOW_NORMAL
THREAD_PRIORITY_HIGHEST	THREAD_PRIORITY_IDLE
THREAD_PRIORITY_LOWEST	THREAD_PRIORITY_NORMAL
THREAD_PRIORITY_TIME_CRITICAL	

To see the effect of changing a thread's priority, try substituting the following **WindowFunc( )** into the sample thread program.

```
LRESULT CALLBACK WindowFunc(HWND hwnd, UINT message,
                            WPARAM wParam, LPARAM lParam)
{
  int response;

  switch(message) {
    case WM_COMMAND:
      switch(LOWORD(wParam)) {
        case IDM_THREAD:
          hThread1 = CreateThread(NULL, 0,
                          (LPTHREAD_START_ROUTINE)MyThread1,
                          (LPVOID) hwnd, 0, &Tid1);
          hThread2 = CreateThread(NULL, 0,
                          (LPTHREAD_START_ROUTINE)MyThread2,
                          (LPVOID) hwnd, 0, &Tid2);
          break;
        case IDM_EXIT:
          response = MessageBox(hwnd, "Quit the Program?",
                          "Exit", MB_YESNO);
```

```
            if(response == IDYES) PostQuitMessage(0);
            break;
          case IDM_HELP:
            MessageBox(hwnd, "F1: Help\nF2: Demonstrate Threads",
                      "Help", MB_OK);
            break;
        }
        break;
      case WM_LBUTTONDOWN: /* set thread1 to low priority */
        SetThreadPriority(hThread1, THREAD_PRIORITY_LOWEST);
        SetThreadPriority(hThread2, THREAD_PRIORITY_HIGHEST);
        break;
      case WM_RBUTTONDOWN: /* set thread1 to high priority */
        SetThreadPriority(hThread1, THREAD_PRIORITY_HIGHEST);
        SetThreadPriority(hThread2, THREAD_PRIORITY_LOWEST);
        break;
      case WM_DESTROY: /* terminate the program */
        PostQuitMessage(0);
        break;
      default:
        /* Let Windows 95 process any messages not specified in
        the preceding switch statement. */
        return DefWindowProc(hwnd, message, wParam, lParam);
    }
    return 0;
}
```

You will also need to declare these two global handles:

```
HANDLE hThread1, hThread2;
```

After you make these changes, each time you press the left mouse button, **MyThread1( )** will be set to the lowest priority, and **MyThread2( )** will be set to the highest priority. Pressing the right mouse button reverses this situation. As you will see, the results will be quite dramatic. The high-priority thread will run much faster than the low-priority thread.

One final point: thread priorities are governed by the overall priority class of the process that spawns them. That is, a thread's actual priority is determined by combining the process's priority class with the thread's individual priority level. You can obtain the current priority class by calling **GetPriorityClass( )**, and you can set the priority class by calling **SetPriorityClass( )**. You will want to explore these two functions on your own.

9

Synchronization

When you use multiple threads or processes, it is sometimes necessary to synchronize the activities of two or more. This is most commonly necessary when two or more threads need access to a shared resource that can only be used by one thread at a time. For example, when one thread is writing to a file, a second thread must be prevented from doing so at the same time. The mechanism that prevents this is called *serialization*. Another need for synchronization arises when one thread is waiting for an event that is caused by another thread. In this case, there must be some means by which the first thread is held in a suspended state until the event has occurred. Then, the waiting thread must resume execution.

There are two general states that a task may be in. First, it may be *executing* (or ready to execute as soon as it obtains its time slice). Second, a task may be *blocked,* awaiting some resource or event. In this case, its execution is *suspended* until the needed resource is available or the event occurs.

If you are not familiar with the need for synchronization and with the serialization problem or its most common solution—the semaphore—the next section discusses it. (If this is familiar territory for you, skip ahead.)

Understanding the Serialization Problem

Windows 95 must provide special services that allow access to a shared resource to be serialized, because without help from the operating system, there is no way for one process or thread to know that it has sole access to a resource. To understand this, imagine that you are writing programs for a multitasking operating system that does not provide any serialization support. Further imagine that you have two concurrently executing processes, A and B, both of which, from time to time, require access to some resource R (such as a disk file) that must only be accessed by one task at a time. As a means of preventing one program from accessing R while the other is using it, you try the following solution. First, you establish a variable called **flag** that can be accessed by both programs. Your programs initialize **flag** to 0. Next, before using each piece of code that accesses R, you wait for the flag to be cleared, then set the flag, access R, and finally clear the flag. That is, to access R, each program executes this piece of code:

```
while(flag) ; /* wait for flag to be cleared */
flag = 1; /* set flag */         •

/* ... access resource R ... */

flag = 0; /* clear the flag */
```

The idea behind this code is that neither process will access R if **flag** is set. Conceptually, this approach is in the spirit of the correct solution. However, it actually leaves much to be desired for one simple reason: it won't always work! Let's see why.

By use of the code just given, it is possible for both processes to access R at the same time. The **while** loop is, in essence, performing repeated load and compare instructions on **flag** or, in other words, it is testing the flag's value. When the flag is cleared, the next line of code sets the flag's value. The trouble is, it is possible for these two operations to be performed in two different time slices. Between the two time slices, the value of **flag** might have been accessed by a different process, thus allowing R to be used by both processes at the same time. To understand this, imagine that process A enters the **while** loop and finds that **flag** is 0, which is the green light to access R. However, before it can set **flag** to 1, its time slice expires and process B resumes execution. If B executes its **while**, it too will find that **flag** is not set and assume that it is safe to access R. However, when A resumes, it will also begin accessing R. The crucial aspect of the problem is that the testing and setting of **flag** do not comprise one uninterruptible operation. Rather, as just illustrated, they can be separated by a time slice. No matter how you try, there is no way, using only application-level code, that you can absolutely guarantee that one and only one process will access R at one time.

The solution to the serialization problem is as elegant as it is simple. The operating system (in this case Windows 95) provides a routine that in one uninterrupted operation, tests and, if possible, sets a flag. In the language of operating systems engineers, this is called a *test and set* operation. For historical reasons, the flags used to control serialization and provide synchronization between threads (and processes) are called *semaphores*. The core Windows 95 functions that support semaphores are discussed in the next section.

Windows 95 Synchronization Objects

Windows 95 supports four types of synchronization objects. All are based, in one way or another, on the concept of the semaphore. The first type is the *classic* semaphore. A semaphore can be used to allow a limited number of processes or threads access to a resource. When you use a semaphore, the resource can be completely serialized, in which case one and only one thread or process can access it at one time, or the semaphore can be used to allow no more than a small number of processes or threads access at one time. Semaphores are implemented by use of a counter that is decremented when a task is granted the semaphore and incremented when the task releases it.

The second synchronization object is the *mutex* semaphore. A mutex semaphore is used to serialize a resource so that one and only one thread or process can access it one time. In essence, a mutex semaphore is a special-case version of a standard semaphore.

The third synchronization object is the *event object*. It can be used to block access to a resource until some other thread or process signals that it can be used. (That is, an event object signals that a specified event has occurred.)

Finally, you can prevent a section of code from being used by more than one thread at a time by making it into a *critical section* using a critical section object. Once a critical section is entered by one thread, no other thread can use it until the first thread has left the critical section. (Critical sections only apply to threads within a process.)

With the exception of critical sections, the other synchronization objects can be used to serialize threads within a process or processes themselves. In fact, semaphores are a common and simple means of interprocess communication.

This chapter describes how to create and use a semaphore. After you understand this synchronization object, the others will be easy for you to master on your own.

Using a Semaphore to Synchronize Threads

Before you can use a semaphore, you must create one by using **CreateSemaphore( )**, which has this prototype:

```
HANDLE CreateSemaphore(LPSECURITY_ATTRIBUTES lpAttr,
                       LONG InitialCount,
                       LONG MaxCount,
                       LPSTR lpszName);
```

Here, *lpAttr* is a pointer to the security attributes, or **NULL** if no security attributes are used (as is the case for Windows 95).

A semaphore can allow one or more tasks access to an object. The number of tasks allowed to simultaneously access an object is determined by the value of *MaxCount*. If this value is 1, then the semaphore acts much like a mutex semaphore, allowing one and only one thread or process access to the resource at one time.

Semaphores use a counter to keep track of how many tasks have currently been granted access. If the count is zero, then no further access can be granted until one task releases the semaphore. The initial count of the semaphore is specified in *InitialCount*. If this value is zero, then initially all objects waiting on the semaphore will be blocked until the semaphore is released elsewhere by your program. Typically, this value is set initially to 1 or higher, indicating that the semaphore can be granted to at least one task. In any event, *InitialCount* must be nonnegative and less than or equal to the value specified in *MaxCount*.

lpszName points to a string that becomes the name of the semaphore object. Semaphores are global objects that can be used by other processes. As such, when two processes each open a semaphore by using the same name, both are referring to the same semaphore. In this way, two processes can be synchronized. The name may also be **NULL**, in which case the semaphore is localized to one process.

The **CreateSemaphore( )** function returns a handle to the semaphore if successful or **NULL** on failure.

Once you have created a semaphore, you use it by calling two related functions: **WaitForSingleObject( )** and **ReleaseSemaphore( )**. The prototypes for these functions are shown here:

DWORD WaitForSingleObject(HANDLE *hObject*, DWORD *dwHowLong*);

BOOL ReleaseSemaphore(HANDLE *hSema*, LONG *Count*,
                      LPLONG *lpPrevCount*);

WaitForSingleObject( ) waits on a semaphore (or other type of object). Here, *hObject* is the handle to the semaphore created earlier. The *dwHowLong* parameter specifies, in milliseconds, how long the calling routine will wait. Once the specified time has elapsed, a time-out error will be returned. To wait indefinitely, use the value **INFINITE**. The function returns **WAIT_OBJECT_0** when successful (that is, when access is granted). It returns **WAIT_TIMEOUT** when time-out is reached. Each time **WaitForSingleObject( )** succeeds, the counter associated with the semaphore is decremented.

ReleaseSemaphore( ) releases the semaphore and allows another thread to use it. Here, *hSema* is the handle to the semaphore. *Count* determines what value will be added to the semaphore counter. Typically, this value is 1. The *lpPrevCount* parameter points to a variable that will contain the previous semaphore count. If you don't need this count, pass **NULL** for this parameter. The function returns nonzero if successful and zero on failure.

The following program demonstrates how to use a semaphore. It reworks the previous program so that the two threads will not execute concurrently. That is, it forces the threads to be serialized. Notice that the semaphore handle is a global variable that is created when the window is first created.

9

This allows it to be used by all threads (including the main thread) in the
program.

```c
/* A multithreaded program that uses a semaphore. */

#include <windows.h>
#include <string.h>
#include <stdio.h>
#include "thread.h"

#define MAX 5000

LRESULT CALLBACK WindowFunc(HWND, UINT, WPARAM, LPARAM);
DWORD MyThread1(LPVOID param);
DWORD MyThread2(LPVOID param);

char szWinName[] = "MyWin"; /* name of window class */

char str[255]; /* holds output strings */

DWORD Tid1, Tid2; /* thread IDs */

HANDLE hSema; /* handle to semaphore */

int WINAPI WinMain(HINSTANCE hThisInst, HINSTANCE hPrevInst,
                   LPSTR lpszArgs, int nWinMode)
{
  HWND hwnd;
  MSG msg;
  WNDCLASSEX wcl;
  HANDLE hAccel;

  /* Define a window class. */
  wcl.hInstance = hThisInst; /* handle to this instance */
  wcl.lpszClassName = szWinName; /* window class name */
  wcl.lpfnWndProc = WindowFunc; /* window function */
  wcl.style = 0; /* default style */

  wcl.cbSize = sizeof(WNDCLASSEX); /* set size of WNDCLASSEX */

  wcl.hIcon = LoadIcon(NULL, IDI_APPLICATION); /* large icon */
  wcl.hIconSm = LoadIcon(NULL, IDI_APPLICATION); /* small icon */

  wcl.hCursor = LoadCursor(NULL, IDC_ARROW); /* cursor style */

  /* specify name of menu resource */
  wcl.lpszMenuName = "MYMENU"; /* main menu */
```

```
    wcl.cbClsExtra = 0; /* no extra */
    wcl.cbWndExtra = 0; /* information needed */

    /* Make the window white. */
    wcl.hbrBackground = GetStockObject(WHITE_BRUSH);

    /* Register the window class. */
    if(!RegisterClassEx(&wcl)) return 0;

    /* Now that a window class has been registered, a window
       can be created. */
    hwnd = CreateWindow(
      szWinName, /* name of window class */
      "Use a Semaphore", /* title */
      WS_OVERLAPPEDWINDOW, /* window style - normal */
      CW_USEDEFAULT, /* X coordinate - let Windows decide */
      CW_USEDEFAULT, /* Y coordinate - let Windows decide */
      CW_USEDEFAULT, /* width - let Windows decide */
      CW_USEDEFAULT, /* height - let Windows decide */
      HWND_DESKTOP, /* no parent window */
      NULL, /* no menu */
      hThisInst, /* handle of this instance of the program */
      NULL /* no additional arguments */
    );

    /* load accelerators */
    hAccel = LoadAccelerators(hThisInst, "MYMENU");

    /* Display the window. */
    ShowWindow(hwnd, nWinMode);
    UpdateWindow(hwnd);

    /* Create the message loop. */
    while(GetMessage(&msg, NULL, 0, 0))
    {
      if(!TranslateAccelerator(hwnd, hAccel, &msg)) {
        TranslateMessage(&msg); /* allow use of keyboard */
        DispatchMessage(&msg); /* return control to Windows */
      }
    }
    return msg.wParam;
}

/* This function is called by Windows 95 and is passed
   messages from the message queue.
*/
LRESULT CALLBACK WindowFunc(HWND hwnd, UINT message,
                            WPARAM wParam, LPARAM lParam)
```

9

```
{
  int response;

  switch(message) {
    case WM_CREATE:
      hSema = CreateSemaphore(NULL, 1, 1, "mysem");
      break;
    case WM_COMMAND:
      switch(LOWORD(wParam)) {
        case IDM_THREAD:
          CreateThread(NULL, 0, (LPTHREAD_START_ROUTINE)MyThread1,
                       (LPVOID) hwnd, 0, &Tid1);
          CreateThread(NULL, 0, (LPTHREAD_START_ROUTINE)MyThread2,
                       (LPVOID) hwnd, 0, &Tid2);
          break;
        case IDM_EXIT:
          response = MessageBox(hwnd, "Quit the Program?",
                                "Exit", MB_YESNO);
          if(response == IDYES) PostQuitMessage(0);
          break;
        case IDM_HELP:
          MessageBox(hwnd,
                     "F1: Help\nF2: Demonstrate Threads",
                     "Help", MB_OK);
          break;
      }
      break;
    case WM_DESTROY: /* terminate the program */
      PostQuitMessage(0);
      break;
    default:
      /* Let Windows 95 process any messages not specified in
      the preceding switch statement. */
      return DefWindowProc(hwnd, message, wParam, lParam);
  }
  return 0;
}

/* A thread of execution within the process. */
DWORD MyThread1(LPVOID param)
{
  int i;
  HDC hdc;

  /* wait for access to be granted */
  if(WaitForSingleObject(hSema, 10000)==WAIT_TIMEOUT) {
    MessageBox((HWND)param, "Time Out Thread 1",
```

```
                           "Semaphore Error", MB_OK);
      return 0;
    }

  for(i=0; i<MAX; i++) {

    if(i==MAX/2) {
      /* Release at halfway point. This allows
         MyThread2 to run. */
      ReleaseSemaphore(hSema, 1, NULL);

      /* Next, once again wait for access to be granted. */
      if(WaitForSingleObject(hSema, 10000)==WAIT_TIMEOUT) {
        MessageBox((HWND)param, "Time Out Thread 1",
                   "Semaphore Error", MB_OK);
        return 0;
      }
    }

    sprintf(str, "Thread 1: loop # %5d ", i);
    hdc = GetDC((HWND) param);
    TextOut(hdc, 1, 1, str, strlen(str));
    ReleaseDC((HWND) param, hdc);
  }

  ReleaseSemaphore(hSema, 1, NULL);

  return 0;
}

/* Another thread of execution within the process. */
DWORD MyThread2(LPVOID param)
{
  int i;
  HDC hdc;

  /* wait for access to be granted */
  if(WaitForSingleObject(hSema, 10000)==WAIT_TIMEOUT) {
    MessageBox((HWND)param, "Time Out Thread 2",
               "Semaphore Error", MB_OK);
    return 0;
  }

  for(i=0; i<MAX; i++) {
    sprintf(str, "Thread 2: loop # %5d ", i);
    hdc = GetDC((HWND) param);
    TextOut(hdc, 1, 20, str, strlen(str));
    ReleaseDC((HWND) param, hdc);
  }
```

9

```
ReleaseSemaphore(hSema, 1, NULL);

return 0;
}
```

A Closer Look at the Semaphore Program

hSema holds the handle to a semaphore which is used to serialize the two threads. In the program, **MyThread1( )** is activated before **MyThread2( )**. Therefore, when **MyThread1( )** is created, it immediately acquires the semaphore and begins execution. When **MyThread2( )** is created, it cannot acquire the semaphore, so it enters a wait state. Meanwhile, when the **for** loop inside **MyThread1( )** reaches **MAX**/2, it releases the semaphore. This allows **MyThread2( )** to acquire it and begin execution. **MyThread1( )** then enters a wait state. Finally, **MyThread2( )** finishes and releases the semaphore. This allows **MyThread1( )** to resume.

Here are some experiments to try. First, since the semaphore only allows one thread access to it at any one time, try substituting a mutex semaphore. Second, try allowing multiple instances of the threads to execute by increasing the count associated with **hSema** to 2 or 3. Observe the effect.

Some Other Synchronization Functions

The Windows 95 synchronization subsystem contains over 20 functions. To begin exploring this area of Windows 95 programming, you will want to examine the following functions:

Function	Purpose
CreateEvent( )	Creates an event object
OpenEvent( )	Opens an existing event object, which can be in another process
CreateMutex( )	Creates a mutex semaphore
OpenMutex( )	Opens an existing mutex semaphore, which can be in another process
OpenSemaphore( )	Opens an existing semaphore, which can be in another process
InitializeCriticalSection( )	Initializes a critical section
EnterCriticalSection( )	Acquires access to a critical section
LeaveCriticalSection( )	Releases access to a critical section
WaitForMultipleObjects( )	Monitors more than one object

Creating a Separate Task

Although Windows 95's thread-based multitasking will have the most direct impact on how you program, it is, of course, still possible to utilize process-based multitasking where appropriate. When you use process-based multitasking, instead of starting another thread, one program starts the execution of another program. In Windows 95, this is accomplished by use of the **CreateProcess( )** API function, whose prototype is shown here.

```
BOOL CreateProcess(LPCSTR lpszName, LPCSTR lpszComLine,
                LPSECURITY_ATTRIBUTES lpProcAttr,
                LPSECURITY_ATTRIBUTES lpThreadAttr,
                BOOL InheritAttr, DWORD How,
                LPVOID lpEnv, LPSTR lpszDir,
                LPSTARTUPINFO lpStartInfo,
                LPPROCESS_INFORMATION lpPInfo);
```

The name of the program to execute, which may include a full path, is specified in the string pointed to by *lpszName*. Any command-line parameters required by the program are specified in the string pointed to by *lpszComLine*. However, if you specify *lpszName* as **NULL**, then the first token in the string pointed to by *lpszComLine* will be used as the program name. Thus, typically, *lpszName* is specified as **NULL**, and the program name and any required parameters are specified in the string pointed to by *lpszComLine*.

The *lpProcAttr* and *lpThreadAttr* parameters are used to specify any security attributes related to the process being created. These may be specified as **NULL**, in which case no security attributes are used. If *InheritAttr* is nonzero, handles used by the creating process are inherited by the new process. If this parameter is zero, then handles are not inherited.

By default, the new process is run "normally." However, the *How* parameter can be used to specify certain additional attributes that affect how the new process will be created. (For example, you will use the *How* to specify a special priority for the process or to indicate that the process will be debugged.) If *How* is zero, then the new process is created as a normal process.

The *lpEnv* parameter points to a buffer that contains the new process's environmental parameters. If this parameter is **NULL**, then the new process inherits the creating process' environment.

The current drive and directory of the new process can be specified in the string pointed to by *lpszDir*. If this parameter is **NULL**, then the current drive and directory of the creating process is used.

9

lpStartInfo is a pointer to a **STARTUPINFO** structure containing information that determines how the main window of the new process will look. **STARTUPINFO** is defined as shown here:

```
typedef struct _STARTUPINFO {
  DWORD cb; /* size of STARTUPINFO */
  LPSTR lpReserved; /* must be NULL */
  LPSTR lpDesktop; /* name of desktop -- not used by Windows 95 */
  LPSTR lpTitle; /* title of console (consoles only) */
  DWORD dwX; /* upper left corner of */
  DWORD dwY; /* new window */
  DWORD dwXSize; /* size of new window */
  DWORD dwYSize; /* size of new window */
  DWORD dwXCountChars; /* console buffer width */
  DWORD dwYCountChars; /* console buffer height */
  DWORD dwFillAttribute; /* initial text color */
  DWORD dwFlags; /* determines which fields are active */
  WORD wShowWindow; /* how window is shown */
  WORD cbReserved2; /* must be 0 */
  LPBYTE lpReserved2; /* must be NULL */
  HANDLE hStdInput; /* standard handles */
  HANDLE hStdOutput;
  HANDLE hStdError;
} STARTUPINFO;
```

Generally, the fields **dwX**, **dwY**, **dwXSize**, **dwYSize**, **dwXCountChars**, **dwYCountChars**, **dwFillAttribute**, and **wShowWindow** are ignored unless they are enabled by including the proper value as part of the **dwFlags** field. The values for **dwFlags** are listed here:

Macro	Enables
STARTF_USESHOWWINDOW	wShowWindow
STARTF_USESIZE	dwXSize and dwYSize
STARTF_USEPOSITION	dwX and dwY
STARTF_USECOUNTCHARS	dwXCountChars and dwYCountChars
STARTF_USEFILLATTRIBUTE	dwFillAttribute
STARTF_USESTDHANDLES	hStdInput, hStdOutput, and hStdError

dwFlags can also include one or more of the following values:

Value	Meaning
STARTF_FORCEONFEEDBACK	Feedback cursor is on
STARTF_FORCEOFFFEEDBACK	Feedback cursor is off
STARTF_SCREENSAVER	Process is a screen saver

Generally, you will not need to use most of the fields in **STARTUPINFO**, and you can allow most to be ignored. However, you must specify **cb**, which contains the size of the structure, and several other fields must be set to **NULL**. For example, the new process information specified in the **STARTUPINFO** structure will often be set as follows:

```
STARTUPINFO startin;
/* ... */
/* Start a new process */
startin.cb = sizeof(STARTUPINFO);
startin.lpReserved = NULL;
startin.lpDesktop = NULL;
startin.lpTitle = NULL;
startin.dwFlags = STARTF_USESHOWWINDOW;
startin.cbReserved2 = 0;
startin.lpReserved2 = NULL;
startin.wShowWindow = SW_SHOWMINIMIZED;
```

Here, the process will be started as a minimized window because **dwFlags** is set to **STARTF_USESHOWWINDOW**. This setting allows the **wShowWindow** field to be used.

The final parameter to **CreateProcess( )** is *lpPInfo,* which is a pointer to a structure of type **PROCESS_INFORMATION**, shown here:

```
typedef struct _PROCESS_INFORMATION {
  HANDLE hProcess; /* handle to new process */
  HANDLE hThread; /* handle to main thread */
  DWORD dwProcessId; /* ID of new process */
  DWORD dwThreadId; /* ID of new thread */
} PROCESS_INFORMATION;
```

Handles to the new process and the main thread of that process are passed back to the creating process in **hProcess** and **hThread**. The new process and thread IDs are returned in **dwProcessId** and **dwThreadId**. Your program can use this information or ignore it.

CreateProcess( ) returns nonzero if successful and zero otherwise. Once created, the new process is largely independent. The parent process can terminate the child, however, by using the **TerminateProcess( )** API function.

9

CHAPTER 10

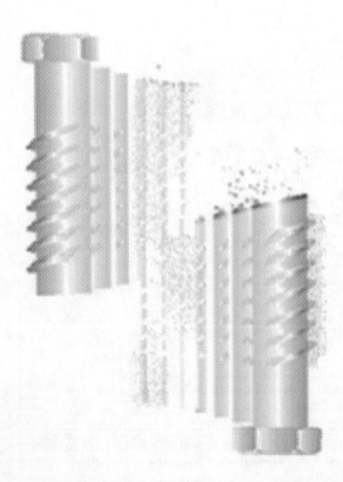

Using Graphics

The last topic that will be examined is graphics.
Windows 95 (like all previous versions of
Windows) supports a wide array of graphics-
oriented API functions. For example, earlier in
this book, you learned about bitmapped graphics.
In this chapter, you will learn about the graphics
functions that allow you to draw in a window.
Since Windows is a graphical operating system,
graphics are an important part of nearly every
major Windows application. As you will see,
graphics are easy to handle within a Windows
program because they are fully integrated into the
overall landscape of the Windows environment.

While it is not possible to examine every graphics-related function supported by Windows 95, this chapter describes the most important, including those used to draw a point, a line, a rectangle, and an ellipse. It also explains how to change the way graphics output is written to a window. Keep in mind that the discussion of graphics and related topics in this chapter only scratches the surface. The Windows 95 graphics system is quite powerful, and you will want to explore it further on your own.

To demonstrate the graphics functions and techniques, a simple version of the standard Paint accessory is developed. As you will see, because of the power of the Windows 95 graphics subsystem, surprisingly little code is required for this program.

The Graphics Coordinate System

The graphics coordinate system is the same as that used by the text-based functions. This means that, by default, the upper-left corner is location 0, 0 and that logical units are equivalent to pixels. However, the coordinate system and the mapping of logical units to pixels is under your control and can be changed. (See the Fast Track Tip at the end of this chapter.)

Windows 95 (and Windows in general) maintains a *current position* that is used and updated by certain graphics functions. When your program begins, the current location is set to 0, 0. Keep in mind that the location of the current position is completely invisible. That is, no graphics "cursor" is displayed. Instead, the current position is simply the next place in the window at which certain graphics functions will begin.

Pens and Brushes

The Windows graphics system is based upon two important objects: *pens* and *brushes*. By default, closed graphics shapes, such as rectangles and ellipses, are filled by the currently selected brush. Pens are resources that draw the lines and curves specified by the various graphics functions. The default pen is black and 1 pixel thick. However, you can alter these attributes.

Until now, we have only been working with stock objects, such as the stock white brush that has been used to paint the client area of a window. In this chapter you will learn how to create custom brushes and pens. There is one important thing to remember about custom objects: they must be deleted before your program ends. This is accomplished by using **DeleteObject( )**.

Setting a Pixel

You can set the color of any specific pixel by using the API function **SetPixel( )**, which has this prototype:

COLORREF SetPixel(HDC *hdc*, int *X*, int *Y*, COLORREF *color*);

Here, *hdc* is the handle of the device context. The coordinates of the point to set are specified by *X*, *Y*, and the color is specified in *color*. The function returns the original color of the pixel and returns –1 if an error occurs or if the location specified is outside the window.

Drawing a Line

To draw a line, use the **LineTo( )** function. This function draws a line using the currently selected pen. Its prototype is shown here:

BOOL LineTo(HDC *hdc*, int *X*, int *Y*);

The handle of the device context in which to draw the line is specified by *hdc*. The line is drawn from the current graphics position to the coordinates specified by *X*, *Y*. The current position is then changed to *X*, *Y*. The function returns nonzero if successful (that is, the line is drawn) and zero on failure.

Some programmers are surprised that **LineTo( )** uses the current position as its starting location and then sets the current position to the endpoint of the line that is drawn (instead of leaving it unchanged). However, there is a good reason for this. Many times, when displaying lines, one line will begin at the end of the previous line. When this is the case, **LineTo( )** operates extremely efficiently by avoiding the additional overhead of passing an extra set of coordinates. When this is not the case, you can set the current location to any position you like by using the **MoveToEx( )** function, described next, before calling **LineTo( )**.

Setting the Current Location

To set the current position, use the **MoveToEx( )** function, whose prototype is shown here:

BOOL MoveToEx(HDC *hdc*, int *X*, int *Y*, LPPOINT *lpCoord*);

The handle to the device context is specified in *hdc*. The coordinates of the new current position are specified by *X, Y*. The previous current position is returned in the **POINT** structure pointed to by *lpCoord*. **POINT** is defined like this:

```
typedef struct tagPOINT {
  LONG x;
  LONG y;
} POINT;
```

However, if you use **NULL** for the *lpCoord* parameter, then **MoveToEx( )** does not return the previous current position.

MoveToEx( ) returns nonzero if successful and zero on failure.

Drawing an Arc

You can draw an *elliptical arc* (a portion of an ellipse) in the current pen color by using the **Arc( )** function, which has this prototype:

BOOL Arc(HDC *hdc*, int *upX*, int *upY*, int *lowX*, int *lowY*,
　　　　int *startX*, int *startY*, int *endX*, int *endY*);

Here, *hdc* is the handle of the device context in which the arc will be drawn. The arc is defined by two objects. First, the arc is a portion of an ellipse that is bounded by the rectangle whose upper-left corner is at *upX, upY* and whose lower-right corner is at *lowX, lowY*. The portion of the ellipse that is actually drawn (that is, the arc) starts at the intersection of a line from the center of the rectangle through the point specified by *startX, startY* and ends at the intersection of a line from the center of the rectangle through the point *endX, endY*. The arc is drawn counterclockwise starting from *startX, startY*. Figure 10-1 illustrates how **Arc( )** works. **Arc( )** returns nonzero if successful and zero on failure.

Displaying Rectangles

You can display a rectangle in the current pen by using the **Rectangle( )** function, whose prototype is shown here:

BOOL Rectangle(HDC *hdc*, int *upX*, int *upY*, int *lowX*, int *lowY*);

As usual, *hdc* is the handle of the device context. The upper-left corner of the rectangle is specified by *upX, upY,* and the lower-right corner is specified by *lowX, lowY*. The function returns nonzero if successful and zero if an error occurs. The rectangle is automatically filled by use of the current brush.

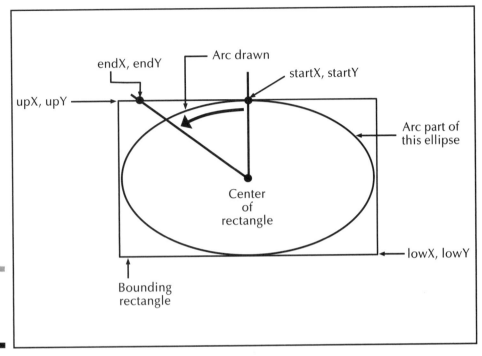

How the **Arc( )** function operates

Figure 10-1.

You can display a rounded rectangle by using the **RoundRect( )** function. A rounded rectangle has its corners rounded slightly. The prototype for **RoundRect( )** is shown here:

BOOL RoundRect(HDC *hdc*, int *upX*, int *upY*, int *lowX*, int *lowY*,
        int *curveX*, int *curveY*);

The first five parameters are the same as for **Rectangle( )**. How the corners are curved is determined by the values of *curveX* and *curveY*, which define the width and the height of the ellipse that describes the curve. The function returns nonzero if successful and zero if a failure occurs. The rounded rectangle is automatically filled by the current brush.

Drawing Ellipses and Pie Slices

To draw an ellipse or a circle in the current pen, use the **Ellipse( )** function, which has this prototype:

BOOL Ellipse(HDC *hdc*, int *upX*, int *upY*, int *lowX*, int *lowY*);

Here, *hdc* is the handle of the device content in which the ellipse will be drawn. The ellipse is defined by specifying its bounding rectangle. The upper-left corner of the rectangle is specified by *upX, upY,* and the lower-right corner is specified by *lowX, lowY.* To draw a circle, specify its bounding square.

The function returns nonzero if successful and zero if a failure occurs. The ellipse is filled by the current brush.

Related to the ellipse is the pie slice. A pie slice is an object that includes an arc and lines from each endpoint of the arc to the center. To draw a pie slice, use the **Pie( )** function, which has this prototype:

>   BOOL Pie(HDC *hdc*, int *upX*, int *upY*, int *lowX*, int *lowY*,
>   int *startX*, int *startY*, int *endX*, int *endY*);

Here, *hdc* is the handle of the device context in which the pie slice will be drawn. The arc of the slice is defined by two objects. First, the arc is a portion of an ellipse that is bounded by the rectangle whose upper-left corner is at *upX, upY* and whose lower-right corner is at *lowX, lowY.* The portion of the ellipse that is actually drawn (that is, the arc of the slice) starts at the intersection of a line from the center of the rectangle through the point specified by *startX, startY* and ends at the intersection of a line from the center of the rectangle through the point *endX, endY.*

The slice is drawn in the current pen and filled by the current brush. The **Pie( )** function returns nonzero if successful and zero if an error occurs.

Working with Pens

Graphics objects are drawn by the current pen. By default, this is a black pen that is 1 pixel wide. There are three stock pens: black, white, and null. A handle to each of these can be obtained by use of **GetStockObject( )**, discussed in Chapter 1 of this book. The macros for these stock pens are **BLACK_PEN**, **WHITE_PEN**, and **NULL_PEN**, respectively. Pen handles are of type **HPEN**.

The stock pens are quite limited, and usually you will want to define your own pens for your application. This is accomplished by the function **CreatePen( )**, whose prototype is shown here:

>   HPEN CreatePen(int *style*, int *width*, COLORREF *color*);

The *style* parameter determines what type of pen is created. It must be one of these values:

Macro	Pen Style
PS_DASH	Dashed
PS_DASHDOT	Dash-dot
PS_DASHDOTDOT	Dash-dot-dot
PS_DOT	Dotted
PS_INSIDEFRAME	Solid pen that is within a bounded region
PS_NULL	None
PS_SOLID	Solid line

The dotted and/or dashed styles can only be applied to pens that are 1 unit thick. The **PS_INSIDEFRAME** pen is a solid pen that will be completely within the dimensions of any object that is drawn, even when that pen is more than 1 unit thick. For example, if a pen with **PS_INSIDEFRAME** style and width greater than 1 is used to draw a rectangle, then the outside of the line will be within the coordinates of the rectangle. (When a wide pen of a different style is used, the line may be partially outside the dimensions of the object.)

The thickness of a pen is specified by *width*, which is in logical units. The color of the pen is specified by *color*, which is a **COLORREF** value.

Once a pen has been created, it is selected into a device context by using **SelectObject( )**. For example, the following fragment creates a red pen and then selects it for use.

```
HPEN hRedpen;

hRedpen = CreatePen(PS_SOLID, 1, RGB(255,0,0));
SelectObject(dc, hRedpen);
```

Remember, you must delete any custom pens you create by calling **DeleteObject( )** before your program terminates.

Creating Custom Brushes

Custom brushes are created in a way similar to custom pens. There are various styles of brushes. The most common custom brush is a *solid brush*. A solid brush is created by the **CreateSolidBrush( )** API function, whose prototype is shown here:

HBRUSH CreateSolidBrush(COLORREF *color*);

The color of the brush is specified in *color,* and a handle to the brush is returned.

Once a custom brush has been created, it is selected into the device context by using **SelectObject( )**. For example, the following fragment creates a green brush and then selects it for use.

```
HBRUSH hGreenbrush

hGreenbrush = CreateSolidBrush(RGB(0, 255 ,0));
SelectObject(dc, hGreenbrush);
```

Like custom pens, custom brushes must be deleted before your program terminates.

Deleting Custom Objects

You must delete custom objects before your program terminates. You do this by using the **DeleteObject( )** API function. Remember, you cannot (and must not) delete stock objects. Also, the object being deleted must not be currently selected into any device context.

Setting the Output Mode

Whenever your program outputs graphics to a window, how that output is actually copied to the window is determined by the output mode in effect at the time. By default, information is copied as-is to the window, overwriting any previous contents. However, other output modes can be used. For example, output can be ANDed, ORed, or XORed with the current contents of the window. To specify the output mode, use the **SetROP2( )** function. It has this prototype:

   int SetROP2(HDC *hdc*, int *Mode*);

Here, *hdc* is the handle of the device context being affected, and *Mode* specifies the new drawing mode. **SetROP2( )** returns the previous drawing mode or 0 on failure. *Mode* must be one of the values listed in Table 10-1.

The **R2_XORPEN** value is especially useful because it allows output to be temporarily written to the screen without losing the information that is already on the screen. The reason for this has to do with a special property of the XOR operation. Consider the following: when one value, called A, is XORed with another, called B, it produces a result which, when XORed with B a second time, produces the original value, A. Thus, if you XOR output to

Creating Other Types of Brushes

10

There are two other types of brushes that you can create: a *pattern brush* and a *hatch brush*. A pattern brush fills areas with a bitmapped image. A hatch brush uses some form of hatch-work design. These brushes are created by use of **CreatePatternBrush( )** and **CreateHatchBrush( )**, respectively. The prototypes for these functions are shown here:

HBRUSH CreatePatternBrush(HBITMAP *hBMap*);

HBRUSH CreateHatchBrush(int *Style*, COLORREF *color*);

For **CreatePatternBrush( )**, *hBMap* is the handle of the bitmap whose pattern will be used as the brush. That is, the specified bitmap will be used to fill areas and paint backgrounds. The function returns a handle to the brush or **NULL** on error.

Brushes created by **CreateHatchBrush( )** have a hatched appearance. The exact nature of the hatching is determined by the value of *Style*, which must be one of those listed here:

Style	Hatching
HS_BDIAGONAL	Angled downward
HS_CROSS	Horizontal and vertical
HS_DIAGCROSS	Angled crosshatch
HS_FDIAGONAL	Angled upward
HS_HORIZONTAL	Horizontal
HS_VERTICAL	Vertical

The color of the brush is determined by the **COLORREF** value specified in *color*. It returns a handle to the brush or **NULL** on failure.

the screen and then XOR the same output to the screen a second time, the original contents of the screen will be restored. This means that you can XOR output to the screen to display something temporarily and then simply XOR it to the screen again to restore the screen's original contents. As you will see, the graphics demonstration program that follows makes use of this fact.

Macro	Drawing Mode
R2_BLACK	Result is black.
R2_COPYPEN	Output is copied to the window, overwriting current contents.
R2_MASKPEN	Output is ANDed with the current screen color.
R2_MASKNOTPEN	Inverse of the output is ANDed with the current screen color.
R2_MASKPENNOT	Output is ANDed with the inverse of the current screen color.
R2_MERGEPEN	Output is ORed with the current screen color.
R2_MERGENOTPEN	Inverse of the output is ORed with the current screen color.
R2_MERGEPENNOT	Output is ORed with the inverse current screen color.
R2_NOP	No effect.
R2_NOT	Result is the inverse of the current screen color.
R2_NOTCOPYPEN	Inverse of the output color is copied to the window.
R2_NOTMASKPEN	Resulting color is the inverse of R2_MASKPEN.
R2_NOTMERGEPEN	Resulting color is the inverse of R2_MERGEPEN.
R2_NOTXORPEN	Resulting color is the inverse of R2_XORPEN.
R2_WHITE	Result is white.
R2_XORPEN	Output is exclusive-ORed with the current screen color.

The Windows
95 Output
Modes
Table 10-1.

One final point: The *ROP* in the name of the function stands for Raster OPerations. This function applies only to video devices. It is not applicable to printers, and so on.

A Graphics Demonstration

The following program demonstrates several of the graphics functions just discussed. It implements a simplified version of the standard Paint accessory. The program uses the virtual window technique developed in Chapter 6 to allow the window to be properly restored when a **WM_PAINT** message is received.

```
/* A Simple Paint Program. */

#include <windows.h>
```

```
#include <string.h>
#include <stdio.h>
#include "graph.h"

LRESULT CALLBACK WindowFunc(HWND, UINT, WPARAM, LPARAM);
char szWinName[] = "MyWin"; /* name of window class */

char str[255]; /* holds output strings */

int maxX, maxY; /* screen dimensions */

HDC memdc; /* handle of memory DC */
HBITMAP hbit; /* handle of compatible bitmap */
HBRUSH hCurrentbrush, hOldbrush; /* handles of brushes */
HBRUSH hRedbrush, hGreenbrush, hBluebrush, hNullbrush;

/* create pens */
HPEN hOldpen; /* handle of old pen */
HPEN hCurrentpen; /* currently selected pen */
HPEN hRedpen, hGreenpen, hBluepen, hBlackpen;

int X=0, Y=0;
int pendown = 0;
int endpoints = 0;
int StartX=0, StartY=0, EndX=0, EndY=0;
int Mode;

int WINAPI WinMain(HINSTANCE hThisInst, HINSTANCE hPrevInst,
                   LPSTR lpszArgs, int nWinMode)
{
  HWND hwnd;
  MSG msg;
  WNDCLASSEX wcl;
  HANDLE hAccel;

  /* Define a window class. */
  wcl.hInstance = hThisInst; /* handle to this instance */
  wcl.lpszClassName = szWinName; /* window class name */
  wcl.lpfnWndProc = WindowFunc; /* window function */
  wcl.style = 0; /* default style */

  wcl.cbSize = sizeof(WNDCLASSEX); /* set size of WNDCLASSEX */

  wcl.hIcon = LoadIcon(NULL, IDI_APPLICATION); /* large icon */
  wcl.hIconSm = LoadIcon(NULL, IDI_APPLICATION); /* small icon */

  wcl.hCursor = LoadCursor(NULL, IDC_ARROW); /* cursor style */
```

```
   /* specify name of menu resource */
   wcl.lpszMenuName = "MYMENU"; /* main menu */

   wcl.cbClsExtra = 0; /* no extra */
   wcl.cbWndExtra = 0; /* information needed */

   /* Make the window white. */
   wcl.hbrBackground = GetStockObject(WHITE_BRUSH);

   /* Register the window class. */
   if(!RegisterClassEx(&wcl)) return 0;

   /* Now that a window class has been registered, a window
      can be created. */
   hwnd = CreateWindow(
     szWinName, /* name of window class */
     "A Simple Paint Program", /* title */
     WS_OVERLAPPEDWINDOW, /* window style - normal */
     CW_USEDEFAULT, /* X coordinate - let Windows decide */
     CW_USEDEFAULT, /* Y coordinate - let Windows decide */
     CW_USEDEFAULT, /* width - let Windows decide */
     CW_USEDEFAULT, /* height - let Windows decide */
     HWND_DESKTOP, /* no parent window */
     NULL, /* no menu */
     hThisInst, /* handle of this instance of the program */
     NULL /* no additional arguments */
   );

   /* load accelerators */
   hAccel = LoadAccelerators(hThisInst, "MYMENU");

   /* Display the window. */
   ShowWindow(hwnd, nWinMode);
   UpdateWindow(hwnd);

   /* Create the message loop. */
   while(GetMessage(&msg, NULL, 0, 0))
   {
     if(!TranslateAccelerator(hwnd, hAccel, &msg)) {
       TranslateMessage(&msg); /* allow use of keyboard */
       DispatchMessage(&msg); /* return control to Windows */
     }
   }
   return msg.wParam;
}

/* This function is called by Windows 95 and is passed
   messages from the message queue.
*/
```

```
LRESULT CALLBACK WindowFunc(HWND hwnd, UINT message,
                            WPARAM wParam, LPARAM lParam)
{
  HDC hdc;
  PAINTSTRUCT paintstruct;

  switch(message) {
    case WM_CREATE:
      /* get screen coordinates */
      maxX = GetSystemMetrics(SM_CXSCREEN);
      maxY = GetSystemMetrics(SM_CYSCREEN);

      /* make a compatible memory image device */
      hdc = GetDC(hwnd);
      memdc = CreateCompatibleDC(hdc);
      hbit = CreateCompatibleBitmap(hdc, maxX, maxY);
      SelectObject(memdc, hbit);
      hCurrentbrush = GetStockObject(WHITE_BRUSH);
      SelectObject(memdc, hCurrentbrush);
      PatBlt(memdc, 0, 0, maxX, maxY, PATCOPY);

      /* create pens */
      hRedpen = CreatePen(PS_SOLID, 1, RGB(255,0,0));
      hGreenpen = CreatePen(PS_SOLID, 1, RGB(0,255,0));
      hBluepen = CreatePen(PS_SOLID, 1, RGB(0,0,255));

      /* create brushes */
      hRedbrush = CreateSolidBrush(RGB(255,0,0));
      hGreenbrush = CreateSolidBrush(RGB(0,255,0));
      hBluebrush = CreateSolidBrush(RGB(0,0,255));
      hNullbrush = GetStockObject(HOLLOW_BRUSH);

      /* save default pen */
      hBlackpen = hOldpen = SelectObject(memdc, hRedpen);
      hCurrentpen = hOldpen;
      SelectObject(memdc, hOldpen);

      ReleaseDC(hwnd, hdc);
      break;
    case WM_RBUTTONDOWN: /* start defining a region */
      endpoints = 1;
      X = StartX = LOWORD(lParam);
      Y = StartY = HIWORD(lParam);
      break;
    case WM_RBUTTONUP: /* stop defining a region */
      endpoints = 0;
      EndX = LOWORD(lParam);
      EndY = HIWORD(lParam);
```

```
      break;
case WM_LBUTTONDOWN: /* start drawing */
  pendown = 1;
  X = LOWORD(lParam);
  Y = HIWORD(lParam);
  break;
case WM_LBUTTONUP: /* stop drawing */
  pendown = 0;
  break;
case WM_MOUSEMOVE:
  if(pendown) { /* draw */
    hdc = GetDC(hwnd);
    SelectObject(memdc, hCurrentpen);
    SelectObject(hdc, hCurrentpen);
    MoveToEx(memdc, X, Y, NULL);
    MoveToEx(hdc, X, Y, NULL);
    X = LOWORD(lParam);
    Y = HIWORD(lParam);
    LineTo(memdc, X, Y);
    LineTo(hdc, X, Y);
    MoveToEx(memdc, X, Y, NULL);
    MoveToEx(hdc, X, Y, NULL);
    ReleaseDC(hwnd, hdc);
  }
  if(endpoints) { /* display region boundaries */
    hdc = GetDC(hwnd);

    /* select "shadow" pen */
    hOldpen = SelectObject(hdc, hRedpen);

    /* change display mode to XOR */
    Mode = SetROP2(hdc, R2_XORPEN);

    /* display, but don't fill */
    hOldbrush =
        SelectObject(hdc, GetStockObject(HOLLOW_BRUSH));

    /* erase old shadow rectangle */
    Rectangle(hdc, StartX, StartY, X, Y);

    X = LOWORD(lParam);
    Y = HIWORD(lParam);

    /* display new shadow rectangle */
    Rectangle(hdc, StartX, StartY, X, Y);

    /* restore default brush */
    SelectObject(hdc, hOldbrush);
```

```
      SelectObject(hdc, hOldpen);
      SetROP2(hdc, Mode);
      ReleaseDC(hwnd, hdc);
    }
    break;
  case WM_COMMAND:
    switch(LOWORD(wParam)) {
      case IDD_LINE:
        /* select current pen */
        SelectObject(memdc, hCurrentpen);

        /* draw the line */
        MoveToEx(memdc, StartX, StartY, NULL);
        LineTo(memdc, EndX, EndY);

        InvalidateRect(hwnd, NULL, 1);
        break;
      case IDD_RECTANGLE:
        /* select fill brush and pen */
        SelectObject(memdc, hCurrentbrush);
        SelectObject(memdc, hCurrentpen);

        /* draw rectangle */
        Rectangle(memdc, StartX, StartY, EndX, EndY);

        InvalidateRect(hwnd, NULL, 1);
        break;
      case IDD_ELLIPSE:
        /* select fill brush and pen */
        SelectObject(memdc, hCurrentbrush);
        SelectObject(memdc, hCurrentpen);

        /* draw ellipse */
        Ellipse(memdc, StartX, StartY, EndX, EndY);

        InvalidateRect(hwnd, NULL, 1);
        break;
      case IDD_RED:
        hCurrentpen = hRedpen;
        break;
      case IDD_BLUE:
        hCurrentpen = hBluepen;
        break;
      case IDD_GREEN:
        hCurrentpen = hGreenpen;
        break;
      case IDD_BLACK:
        hCurrentpen = hBlackpen;
```

```
        break;
      case IDD_REDFILL:
        hCurrentbrush = hRedbrush;
        break;
      case IDD_BLUEFILL:
        hCurrentbrush = hBluebrush;
        break;
      case IDD_GREENFILL:
        hCurrentbrush = hGreenbrush;
        break;
      case IDD_WHITEFILL:
        hCurrentbrush = hOldbrush;
        break;
      case IDD_NULLFILL:
        hCurrentbrush = hNullbrush;
        break;
      case IDD_RESET:
        /* reset current position to 0,0 */
        MoveToEx(memdc, 0, 0, NULL);

        /* erase by repainting background */
        SelectObject(memdc, hOldbrush);
        PatBlt(memdc, 0, 0, maxX, maxY, PATCOPY);

        InvalidateRect(hwnd, NULL, 1);
        break;
      case IDD_HELP:
        MessageBox(hwnd, "F2: Line\nF3: Rectangle\n"
                   "F4: Ellipse\nF5: Reset",
                   "Paint Hot Keys", MB_OK);
        break;
    }
    break;
  case WM_PAINT: /* process a repaint request */
    hdc = BeginPaint(hwnd, &paintstruct); /* get DC */

    /* now, copy memory image onto screen */
    BitBlt(hdc, 0, 0, maxX, maxY, memdc, 0, 0, SRCCOPY);

    EndPaint(hwnd, &paintstruct); /* release DC */
    break;
  case WM_DESTROY: /* terminate the program */
    DeleteObject(hRedpen); /* delete pens */
    DeleteObject(hGreenpen);
    DeleteObject(hBluepen);
    DeleteObject(hBlackpen);

    DeleteObject(hRedbrush); /* delete brushes */
```

```
        DeleteObject(hGreenbrush);
        DeleteObject(hBluebrush);

        DeleteDC(memdc);
        PostQuitMessage(0);
        break;
      default:
       /* Let Windows 95 process any messages not specified in
          the preceding switch statement. */
       return DefWindowProc(hwnd, message, wParam, lParam);
    }
    return 0;
}
```

This program requires the following resource file:

```
#include <windows.h>
#include "graph.h"

MYMENU MENU
{
  POPUP "&Shapes"
  {
    MENUITEM "&Line", IDD_LINE
    MENUITEM "&Rectangle", IDD_RECTANGLE
    MENUITEM "&Ellipse", IDD_ELLIPSE
  }
  POPUP "&Options"
  {
    POPUP "&Pen Color"
    {
      MENUITEM "&Red", IDD_RED
      MENUITEM "&Blue", IDD_BLUE
      MENUITEM "&Green", IDD_GREEN
      MENUITEM "Bl&ack", IDD_BLACK
    }
    POPUP "&Fill Color"
    {
      MENUITEM "&Red", IDD_REDFILL
      MENUITEM "&Blue", IDD_BLUEFILL
      MENUITEM "&Green", IDD_GREENFILL
      MENUITEM "&White", IDD_WHITEFILL
      MENUITEM "&Null", IDD_NULLFILL
    }
    MENUITEM "&Reset", IDD_RESET
  }
    MENUITEM "&Help", IDD_HELP
}
```

```
MYMENU ACCELERATORS
{
  VK_F1, IDD_HELP, VIRTKEY
  VK_F2, IDD_LINE, VIRTKEY
  VK_F3, IDD_RECTANGLE, VIRTKEY
  VK_F4, IDD_ELLIPSE, VIRTKEY
  VK_F5, IDD_RESET, VIRTKEY
}
```

The program also requires the header file GRAPH.H, shown here:

```
#define IDD_LINE       100
#define IDD_RECTANGLE  101
#define IDD_ELLIPSE    102
#define IDD_RED        103
#define IDD_GREEN      104
#define IDD_BLUE       105
#define IDD_BLACK      106
#define IDD_REDFILL    107
#define IDD_GREENFILL  108
#define IDD_BLUEFILL   109
#define IDD_WHITEFILL  110
#define IDD_NULLFILL   111
#define IDD_RESET      112
#define IDD_HELP       113
```

Sample output from the program is shown in Figure 10-2.

The paint program works like this. Freestyle lines can be drawn with the mouse. To draw, press and hold the left button. The right button is used to define a region. To do this, move the mouse pointer to the first corner, press and hold the right mouse button, and then move the mouse pointer to the opposite corner. Release the right button when you reach the desired location. When you define a region, a "shadow" rectangle will appear that outlines the region as you define it. Once a region has been defined, you can then draw a line, a rectangle, or an ellipse within that region. These options are selected from the Shapes menu. Using the Options menu, you can select a new pen color, a new brush color, or erase and reset the window. Most of the code in the Paint program should be easy to understand. However, let's take a look at a few of the more interesting sections.

10

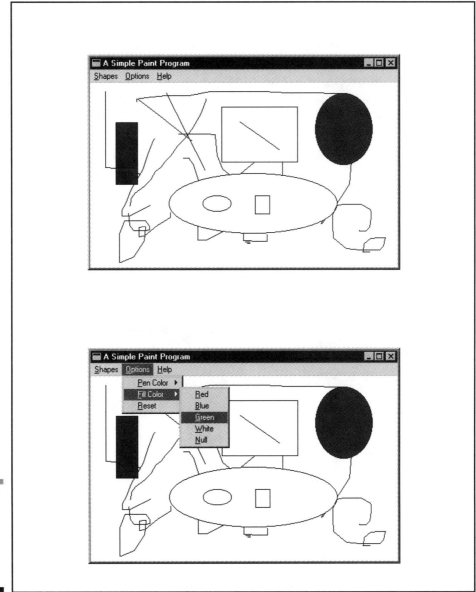

Sample output
from the
graphics
demonstration
program
Figure 10-2.

Drawing Irregular Polygons

In addition to the basic graphical elements, such as lines, ellipses, and rectangles, Windows 95 allows you to define and draw irregular objects. One such object is the *polygon*. Relative to Windows 95, a polygon consists of three or more sides that enclose an area. To draw a polygon, use the **Polygon( )** function, which has this prototype:

BOOL Polygon(HDC *hdc*, CONST POINT **vertices*, int *num*);

Here, *hdc* identifies the device context. An array containing the coordinates of the endpoints of the polygon is pointed to by *vertices,* and the number of vertices is passed in *num*. The function returns nonzero if successful and zero on failure. The polygon is drawn by the currently selected pen and is filled by the currently selected brush. The **Polygon( )** function automatically draws a line from the last point to the first point in the *vertices* array, thus ensuring that the figure is enclosed. **Polygon( )** does not use or modify the current position.

To try **Polygon( )**, add the following global declaration to the example paint program.

```
POINT polygon[5] = {
  10, 10,
  10, 40,
  40, 70,
  40, 90,
  10, 10};
```

Next, add the following line to the **IDD_LINE** case.

```
Polygon(memdc, polygon, 5);
```

Now, each time you select the Line option, the five-sided polygon will also be displayed.

Here are some other API functions that draw complex objects: **Polyline( )**, **PolylineTo( )**, **PolyPolyline( )**, **PolyPolygon( )**, **PolyBezier( )**, and **PolyBezierTo( )**.

A Closer Look at the Paint Program

10

When the program first begins execution, the following objects are created: the virtual window bitmap, all pens needed by the program, and all brushes needed by the program. The pens and brushes are destroyed when the program terminates.

The variable **pendown** is set to 1 when the left mouse button is pressed. Otherwise, it is 0. The variable **endpoints** is set to 1 when a region is being defined (by pressing the right mouse button). Otherwise it is zero.

Perhaps the most involved part of the program is contained within the **WM_MOUSEMOVE** case, shown here. Let's go through it carefully.

```
case WM_MOUSEMOVE:
  if(pendown) { /* draw */
    hdc = GetDC(hwnd);
    SelectObject(memdc, hCurrentpen);
    SelectObject(hdc, hCurrentpen);
    MoveToEx(memdc, X, Y, NULL);
    MoveToEx(hdc, X, Y, NULL);
    X = LOWORD(lParam);
    Y = HIWORD(lParam);
    LineTo(memdc, X, Y);
    LineTo(hdc, X, Y);
    MoveToEx(memdc, X, Y, NULL);
    MoveToEx(hdc, X, Y, NULL);
    ReleaseDC(hwnd, hdc);
  }
  if(endpoints) { /* display region boundaries */
    hdc = GetDC(hwnd);

    /* select "shadow" pen */
    hOldpen = SelectObject(hdc, hRedpen);

    /* change display mode to XOR */
    Mode = SetROP2(hdc, R2_XORPEN);

    /* display, but don't fill */
    hOldbrush =
        SelectObject(hdc, GetStockObject(HOLLOW_BRUSH));

    /* erase old shadow rectangle */
    Rectangle(hdc, StartX, StartY, X, Y);
```

```
      X = LOWORD(lParam);
      Y = HIWORD(lParam);

      /* display new shadow rectangle */
      Rectangle(hdc, StartX, StartY, X, Y);

      /* restore default brush */
      SelectObject(hdc, hOldbrush);
      SelectObject(hdc, hOldpen);
      SetROP2(hdc, Mode);
      ReleaseDC(hwnd, hdc);
    }
    break;
```

A **WM_MOUSEMOVE** message is sent each time the mouse is moved. The X coordinate of the mouse is passed in the low-order word of **lParam**, and the Y coordinate is passed in the high-order word of **lParam**.

If **pendown** is true, then the user is drawing a line. In this situation, each time the mouse is moved, the current pen is selected into both the window device context (**hdc**) and the virtual window device context (**memdc**). Next, a line is drawn (in both contexts) connecting the previous location of the mouse with the new location. This ensures that a smooth, unbroken line is displayed as you move the mouse. (As an experiment, try using **SetPixel( )**, rather than **LineTo( )** and observe the results. As you will see, a **WM_MOUSEMOVE** message is not generated for every pixel in the mouse's path, causing a disjointed line.) After each line is drawn, the current location is updated to the current mouse position.

If **endpoints** is true, then the mouse is being used to define a rectangular region. The first endpoint is set when the **WM_RBUTTONDOWN** message is received. The second endpoint is set when the **WM_RBUTTONUP** message is received. These messages also contain the X, Y coordinates of the mouse in **LOWORD(lParam)** and **HIWORD(lParam)**, respectively. Inside the **WM_MOUSEMOVE** case, as the mouse is moved, a "shadow" rectangle is displayed that shows the current extent of the region. This rectangle is XORed onto the window. The reason for this is that the outcome of two XORs is the original value. Therefore, by using the **R2_XORPEN** drawing mode, one call to **Rectangle( )** displays the shadow rectangle; a second call erases it. This makes it easy to display the shadow rectangle without disrupting the current contents of the window.

Things to Try

On your own, try implementing the following enhancements to the paint program. First, allow the user to select between standard rectangles and rounded rectangles. Second, allow the user to draw an arc. Third, add an option that lets the user erase a portion of the window. Fourth, allow the user to select different line thicknesses. Finally, add an "Undo" option that undoes the previous drawing command.

What Next?

Now that you have reached the end of this book, you might be wondering where you should proceed in your study of Windows 95. As you know, Windows 95 is a very large and complex operating system. While the material in this book discusses the most important and commonly used Windows 95 features, it is only a beginning. As mentioned at the start, the Windows 95 API (Win32) contains several hundred API functions. The most important thing you can do to become an expert at Windows 95 programming is to become familiar with its API. Remember, it is through the API that you access and use the various attributes and abilities present in Windows 95. A thorough understanding of the API is essential to becoming an accomplished Windows programmer.

One other point: When you program for Windows 95, sometimes unusual and nonintuitive techniques are required. The best way to learn effective Windows programming is to

♦ Study other programmers' code

♦ Write many of your own programs, experimenting with different techniques

After a few weeks of effort, you will find the creation of Windows 95 programs to be second nature. Even though Windows 95 is large, it is logically organized. In time, its overall structure will become clear.

FAST TRACK TIP

Setting the Mapping Mode

As you know, the Windows text and graphics functions operate on *logical* units. These logical units are then translated by Windows into *physical* units (that is, pixels) when an object is displayed. How the translation from logical units to physical units is made is determined by the current *mapping mode*. By default, logical units are the same as pixels. However, you can change the ratio of logical units to physical units by changing the mapping mode. To set the current mapping mode, use **SetMapMode( )**. It has this prototype:

        int SetMapMode(HDC *hdc,* int *mode*);

The handle to the device context is specified by *hdc. Mode* specifies the new mapping mode, and it can be any one of the following constants:

Mapping Mode	Meaning
MM_ANISOTROPIC	Maps logical units to programmer-defined units with arbitrarily scaled axes.
MM_HIENGLISH	Maps each logical unit to 0.001 inch.
MM_HIMETRIC	Maps each logical unit to 0.01 millimeter.
MM_ISOTROPIC	Maps logical units to programmer-defined units with equally scaled axes. (This establishes a one-to-one aspect ratio.)
MM_LOMETRIC	Maps each logical unit to 0.1 millimeter.
MM_LOENGLISH	Maps each logical unit to 0.01 inch.
MM_TEXT	Maps each logical unit to one device pixel.
MM_TWIPS	Maps each logical unit to 1/20th of a printer's point.

SetMapMode( ) returns the previous mapping mode, or zero if an error occurs. The default mapping mode is **MM_TEXT**.

There are several reasons why you might want to change the current mapping mode. First, if you want your program's output to be displayed in physical units, then you can select one of the real-world modes, such as **MM_LOMETRIC**. Second, you might want to define units for your program that best fit the nature of what you are displaying. Third, you might want to change the scale of what is displayed. (That is, you might want to enlarge or shrink the size of what is output.) Finally, you may want to establish a one-to-one aspect ratio between the X and Y axes. When this is done, each X unit represents the same physical distance as each Y unit.

If you select either the **MM_ISOTROPIC** or **MM_ANISOTROPIC** mapping modes, then you must define the size of the window in terms of logical units. (Since **MM_ISOTROPIC** and **MM_ANISOTROPIC** operate on programmer-defined units, the limits are technically undefined until you define them.) To define the X and Y extents of a window, use the **SetWindowExtEx( )** function, shown here:

BOOL SetWindowExtEx(HDC *hdc*, int *Xextent*, int *Yextent*, LPSIZE *size*);

The handle of the device context is specified in *hdc*. *Xextent* and *Yextent* specify the new horizontal and vertical extents measured in logical units. The previous window extents are copied into the **SIZE** structure pointed to by *size*. However, if *size* is **NULL**, then the previous extents are ignored. The function returns nonzero if successful, and zero on failure. **SetWindowExtEx( )** only has an effect when the mapping mode is **MM_ANISOTROPIC** or **MM_ISOTROPIC**.

Keep in mind that when you change the logical dimensions of a window, you are not changing the physical size of the window on the screen. You are simply defining the size of the window in terms of logical units that you choose. (Or, more precisely, you are defining the relationship between the logical units used by the window and the physical units (pixels) used by the device.) For example, the same window could be given logical dimensions of 100×100 or 50×75. The only difference is the ratio of logical units to pixels when an image is displayed.

APPENDIX A

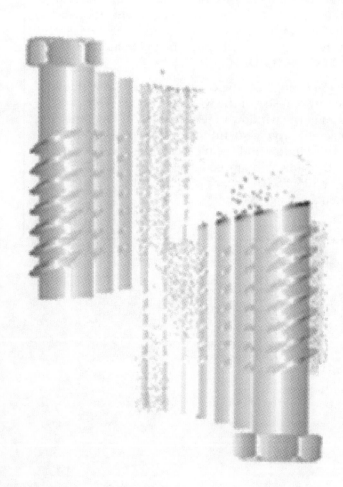

Windows 3.1 Conversion Tips

If you will be converting Windows 3.1 programs to Windows 95, then you will want to keep in mind the tips listed in this appendix.

♦ In older Windows 3.1 programs, the calling convention used for **WinMain( )** was **FAR PASCAL**. This should be changed to **WINAPI** when existing applications are ported to Windows 95.

♦ **UINT** is a 32-bit unsigned integer when Windows 95 programs are compiled. It is a 16-bit unsigned integer if you compile your code for Windows 3.1.

♦ The **hPrevInst** parameter to **WinMain( )** will always be **NULL** in a Windows 95 program. The reason for this is a fundamental change between Windows 3.1 and Windows 95. In Windows 3.1, multiple instances of a program shared window classes and various other bits of data. Therefore, it was important for an application to know if another version of itself was running in the system. However, in Windows 95 each process is isolated from the next, and there is no automatic sharing of window classes and the like. The only reason that **hPrevInst** exists in Windows 95 is for the sake of compatibility.

♦ In Windows 3.1, each window class must be registered only once. Therefore, if a second instance of a program is activated while another instance of the program is already running, then the second instance must not also define and register the window class. To avoid this possibility, the value of **hPrevInst** is tested. If it is nonzero, then the window class has already been registered by a previous instance. If not, then the window class is defined and registered. However, this test is not relevant to Windows 95.

♦ Windows 3.1 associates only one icon with an application: the large icon. A handle to this icon is stored in **hIcon**. When a Windows 3.1 application is run under Windows 95, the large icon is simply shrunk when the small icon is needed. However, you will want to define both icons when writing new programs or porting older programs. Also, Windows 3.1 does not support **RegisterClassEx( )** or **WNDCLASSEX**. Instead, Windows 3.1 uses **RegisterClass( )** and **WNDCLASS**.

♦ The **message** field of **MSG** is 16 bits long in Windows 3.1, but it is widened to 32 bits for Windows 95. Also, the **wparam** field, which is 16 bits in Windows 3.1, has been widened to 32 bits in Windows 95.

♦ In Windows 3.1, **X** and **Y** in the **POINT** structure are declared as integers. However, in Windows 95 (Win32), they are widened to **LONG**.

♦ In Windows 3.1, the **wParam** parameter to your program's window function is a 16-bit value. However, in Windows 95, it is a 32-bit value. This change causes a few messages to be different between the two versions of Windows.

♦ In Windows 3.1, a dialog function must be exported in the .DEF file associated with your program. However, this is not required by Windows 95. (In fact, DEF files are no longer used by Windows 95.)

♦ In Windows 3.1, the *lpDFunc* parameter to **DialogBox( )** (which identifies the dialog box function) must be a pointer to a *procedure-instance*, which is a short piece of code that links the dialog function with the data segment that the program is currently using. A procedure-instance is obtained with the **MakeProcInstance( )** API function. However, this does not apply to Windows 95. In Windows 95, the *lpDFunc* parameter is a pointer to the dialog function itself, and **MakeProcInstance( )** is no longer needed. You should remove calls to **MakeProcInstance( )** when converting older 3.1 code.

♦ In addition to the standard **DIALOG** resource command, Windows 95 adds an extended version called **DIALOGEX**. **DIALOGEX** contains some additional functionality that you might find valuable. Perhaps the most notable extension is that you can define a help ID value for the dialog box itself.

♦ In Windows 3.1, when a scroll bar message, such as **WM_HSCROLL**, is received, the organization of **lParam** and **wParam** differ from their equivalents in Windows 95. Specifically, the handle of the scroll bar is in the high-order word of **lParam**. The position of the slider box is in the low-order word of **lParam**. The nature of the scroll bar action is in **wParam**. Because of these differences, you must be rewrite all scroll bar code when porting from 3.1.

♦ In Windows 3.1, the functions **SetScrollInfo( )** and **GetScroll-Info( )** are not supported. Instead, Windows 3.1 uses functions such as **SetScrollPos( )**, **SetScrollRange( )**, **GetScrollPos( )**, and **GetScrollRange( )**. You must be aware of these changes when converting.

♦ Windows 3.1 does not support the **AUTOCHECKBOX** resource command. When converting from Windows 3.1, you will want to watch for check boxes that can be converted to automatic check boxes.

♦ Windows 3.1 does not support the **AUTORADIOBUTTON** resource command. Watch for opportunities to use **AUTORADIOBUTTON** when converting from Windows 3.1.

♦ In Windows 95, **GetTextExtentPoint32( )** replaces the older **GetTextExtentPoint( )** function.

♦ None of the common controls are supported by Windows 3.1. You will want to watch for opportunities to apply them when converting older programs to Windows 95. Without question, the use of the common controls will give your applications the modern look that users will come to expect from a Windows 95 program. However, you will need to be careful adding up-down controls and trackbars when porting a Windows 3.1 program. These controls generate standard **WM_HSCROLL** or **WM_VSCROLL** messages. It is not uncommon

A

for older programs to simply assume that these messages came from a standard scroll bar. When adding an up-down control or trackbar, you will frequently need to add a test to the portion of the program that processes scroll bar messages to confirm that it was actually the scroll bar (and not another type of control) that generated the message.

♦   To start a new process when using Windows 3.1, you must use the **WinExec( )** function. Windows 95 still includes this function for compatibility, but describes it as obsolete. When porting code, you should convert **WinExec( )** calls to **CreateProcess( )**.

♦   In Windows 3.1, the function that moves the current location is called **MoveTo( )**. This function is not supported by Win32.

♦   In Windows 95, the **SetWindowExtEx( )** replaces the older **SetWindowExt( )** function.

Index

D

E

F

S

MY TOUGHEST CRITICS RIDE TRICYCLES, PLAY PATTY-CAKE, AND REFUSE TO EAT THEIR PEAS.

The NEW CLASSICS

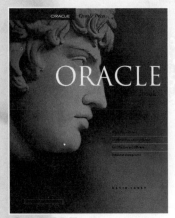

ORACLE DBA HANDBOOK

by Kevin Loney

Every DBA can learn to manage a networked Oracle database efficiently and effectively with this comprehensive guide.

Price: $34.95 U.S.A.
Available Now
ISBN: 0-07-881182-1
Pages: 704, paperback

TUNING ORACLE

by Michael J. Corey,
Michael Abbey and
Daniel J. Dechichio, Jr.

Learn to customize Oracle for optimal performance and productivity with this focused guide.

Price: $29.95 U.S.A.
Available Now
ISBN: 0-07-881181-3
Pages: 336, paperback

ORACLE WORKGROUP SERVER HANDBOOK

by Thomas B. Cox

Take full advantage of the power and flexibility of the new Oracle Workgroup Server and Oracle7 for Windows with this comprehensive handbook.

Covers Oracle7 for Windows

Price: $27.95 U.S.A.
Available Now
ISBN: 0-07-881186-4
Pages: 320, paperback

ORACLE: A BEGINNER'S GUIDE

by Michael Abbey
and Michael J. Corey

For easy-to-understand, comprehensive information about Oracle RDBMS products, this is the one book every user needs.

Price: $29.95 U.S.A.
Available Now
ISBN: 0-07-882122-3
Pages: 560, paperback

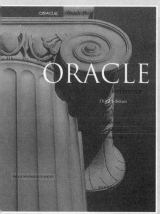

ORACLE: THE COMPLETE REFERENCE

Third Edition

by George Koch
and Kevin Loney

Get true encyclopedic coverage of Oracle with this book. Authoritative and absolutely up-to-the-minute.

Price: $34.95 U.S.A.
Available Now
ISBN: 0-07-882097-9
Pages: 1104, paperback

ORACLE BACKUP AND RECOVERY HANDBOOK

by Rama Velpuri

Keep your database running smoothly and prepare for the possibility of system failure with this comprehensive resource and guide.

Price: $29.95 U.S.A.
Available Now
ISBN: 0-07-882106-1
Pages: 400, paperback

ORACLE POWER OBJECTS DEVELOPER'S GUIDE

by Richard Finkelstein,
Kasu Sista, and Rick Greenwald

Integrate the flexibility and power of Oracle Power Objects into your applications development with this results-oriented handbook.

Price: $39.95 U.S.A.
Includes One CD-ROM
Available September, 1995
ISBN: 0-07-882163-0
Pages: 656, paperback

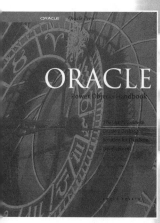

ORACLE POWER OBJECTS HANDBOOK

by Bruce Kolste
and David Petersen

This is the only book available on Oracle's new single/multi-user database product.

Price: $29.95 U.S.A.
Available August, 1995
ISBN: 0-07-882089-8
Pages: 512, paperback

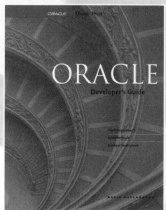

ORACLE DEVELOPER'S GUIDE

by David McClanahan

Learn to develop a database that is fast, powerful, and secure with this comprehensive guide.

Price: $29.95 U.S.A.
Available November, 1995
ISBN: 0-07-882087-1
Pages: 608, paperback

EXTRATERRESTRIAL CONNECTIONS

THESE DAYS, ANY CONNECTION IS POSSIBLE...
WITH THE INNOVATIVE BOOKS FROM LAN TIMES AND OSBORNE/McGRAW-HILL

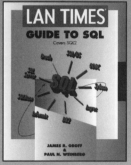

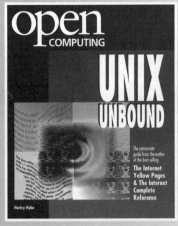

ORDER BOOKS DIRECTLY FROM OSBORNE/McGRAW-HILL

For a complete catalog of Osborne's books, call 510-549-6600 or write to us at 2600 Tenth Street, Berkeley, CA 94710

Call Toll-Free: 1-800-822-8158
24 hours a day, 7 days a week in U.S. and Canada

Mail this order form to:
McGraw-Hill, Inc.
Customer Service Dept.
P.O. Box 547
Blacklick, OH 43004

Fax this order form to:
1-614-759-3644

EMAIL
7007.1531@COMPUSERVE.COM
COMPUSERVE GO MH

Ship to:

Name _____

Company _____

Address _____

City / State / Zip _____

Daytime Telephone: _____
(We'll contact you if there's a question about your order.)

ISBN #	BOOK TITLE	Quantity	Price	Total
0-07-88				
0-07-88				
0-07-88				
0-07-88				
0-07-88				
0-07088				
0-07-88				
0-07-88				
0-07-88				
0-07-88				
0-07-88				
0-07-88				
0-07-88				
0-07-88				

Shipping & Handling Charge from Chart Below		
Subtotal		
Please Add Applicable State & Local Sales Tax		
TOTAL		

Shipping & Handling Charges

Order Amount	U.S.	Outside U.S.
Less than $15	$3.50	$5.50
$15.00 - $24.99	$4.00	$6.00
$25.00 - $49.99	$5.00	$7.00
$50.00 - $74.99	$6.00	$8.00
$75.00 - and up	$7.00	$9.00

Occasionally we allow other selected companies to use our mailing list. If you would prefer that we not include you in these extra mailings, please check here: ☐

METHOD OF PAYMENT

☐ Check or money order enclosed (payable to Osborne/McGraw-Hill)

☐ AMERICAN EXPRESS ☐ DISCOVER ☐ MasterCard ☐ VISA

Account No. |_|_|_|_|_|_|_|_|_|_|_|_|_|_|_|_|

Expiration Date _____

Signature _____

In a hurry? Call 1-800-822-8158 anytime, day or night, or visit your local bookstore.

Thank you for your order   Code BC640SL